# MACAU
## Through the Looking Glass
## A Photographic Exploration

### Hae Won Shin

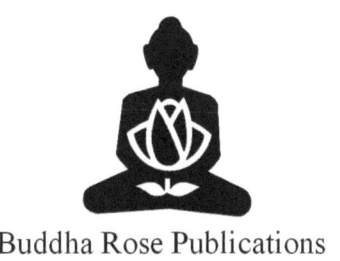

Buddha Rose Publications

Macau Through the Looking Glass
Copyright © 2019 By Hae Won Shin
www.scottshaw.com
All Rights Reserved

No part of this book may be reproduced
in any manner without the expressed
permission of the author or the publishing
company.

First Edition 2019

ISBN 10: 1-949251-15-2
ISBN 13: 978-1-949251-15-9

Printed in the United States of America
10 9 8 7 6 5 4 3 2 1

*MACAU*
**Through the Looking Glass**

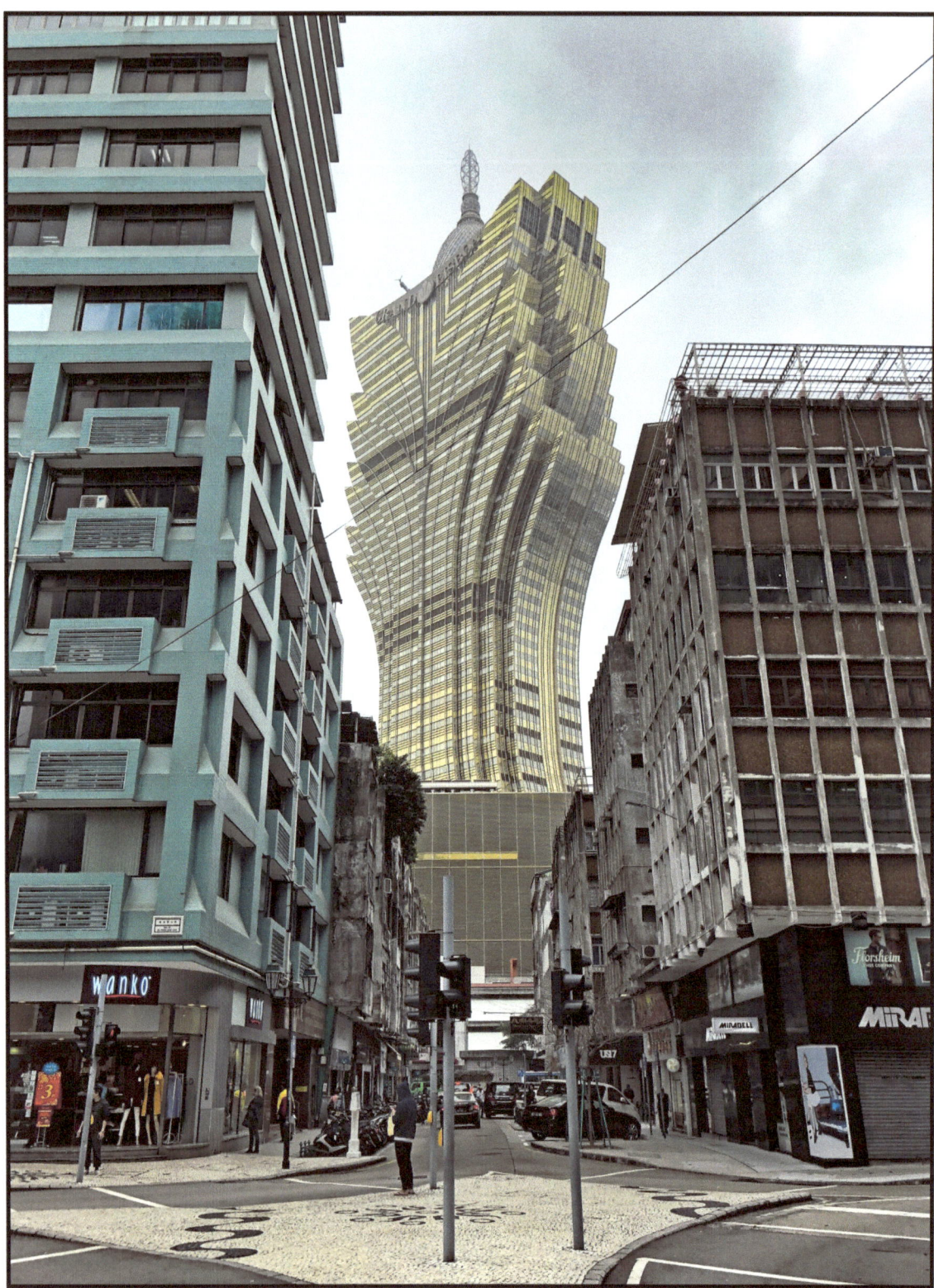

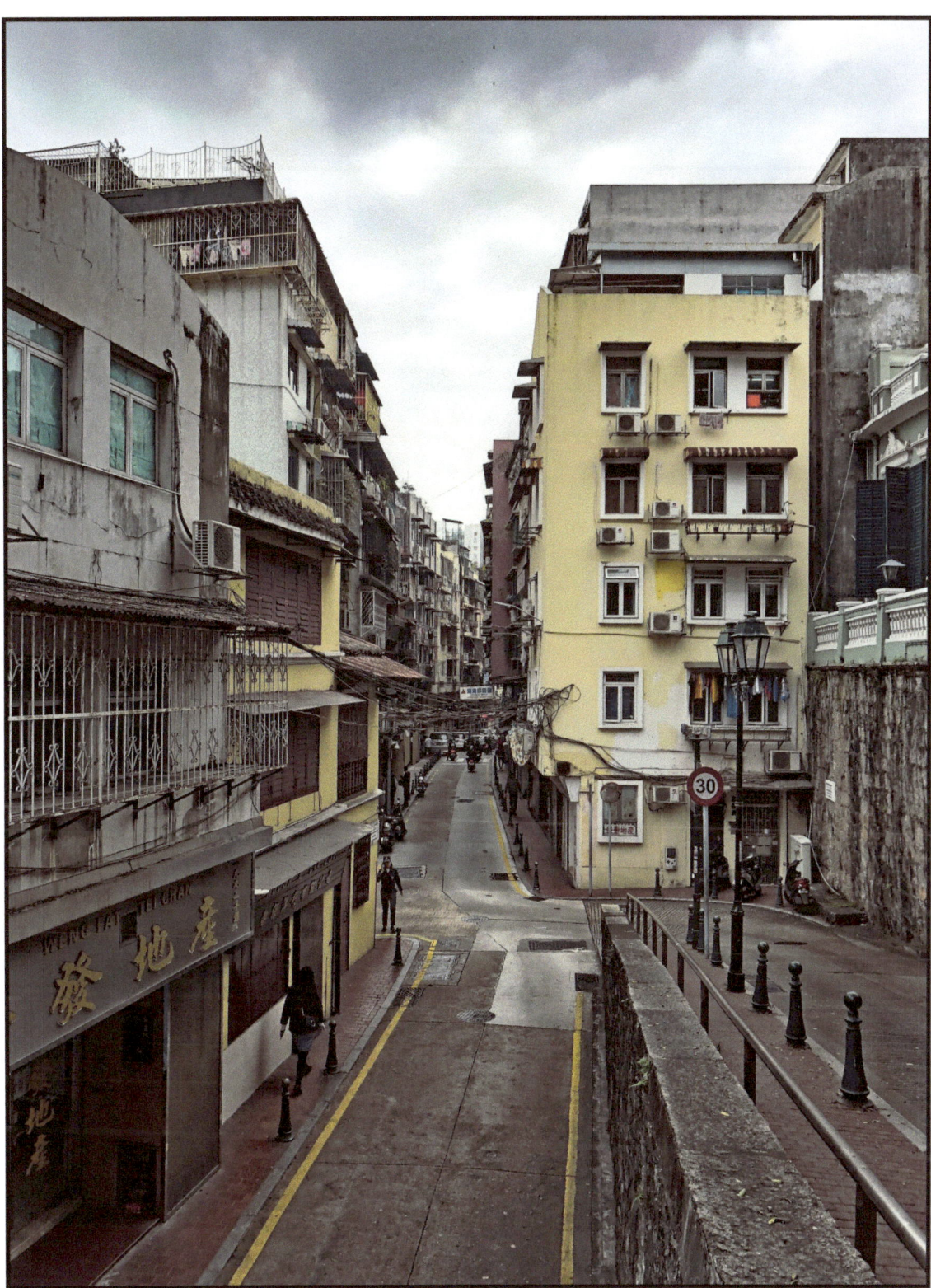

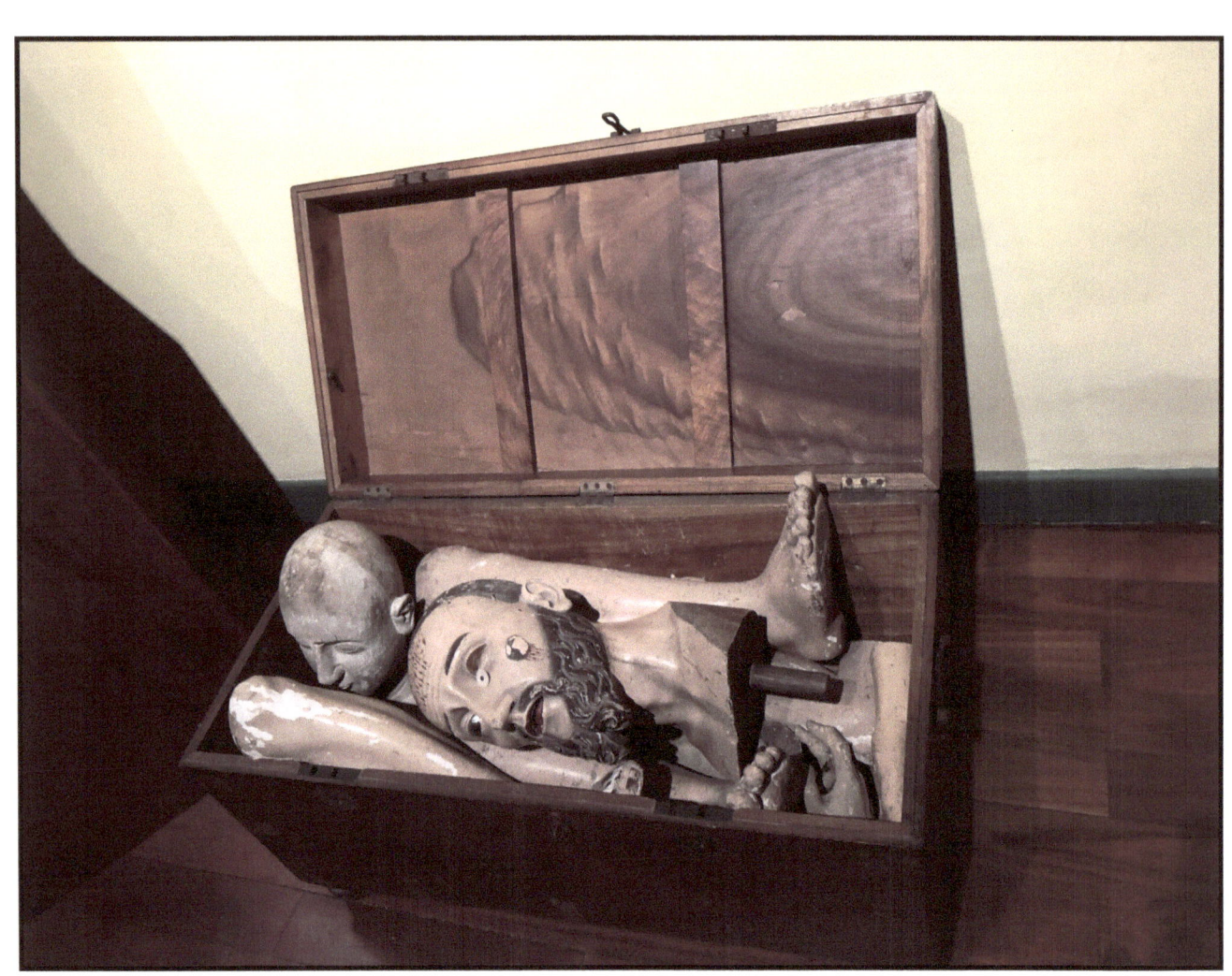

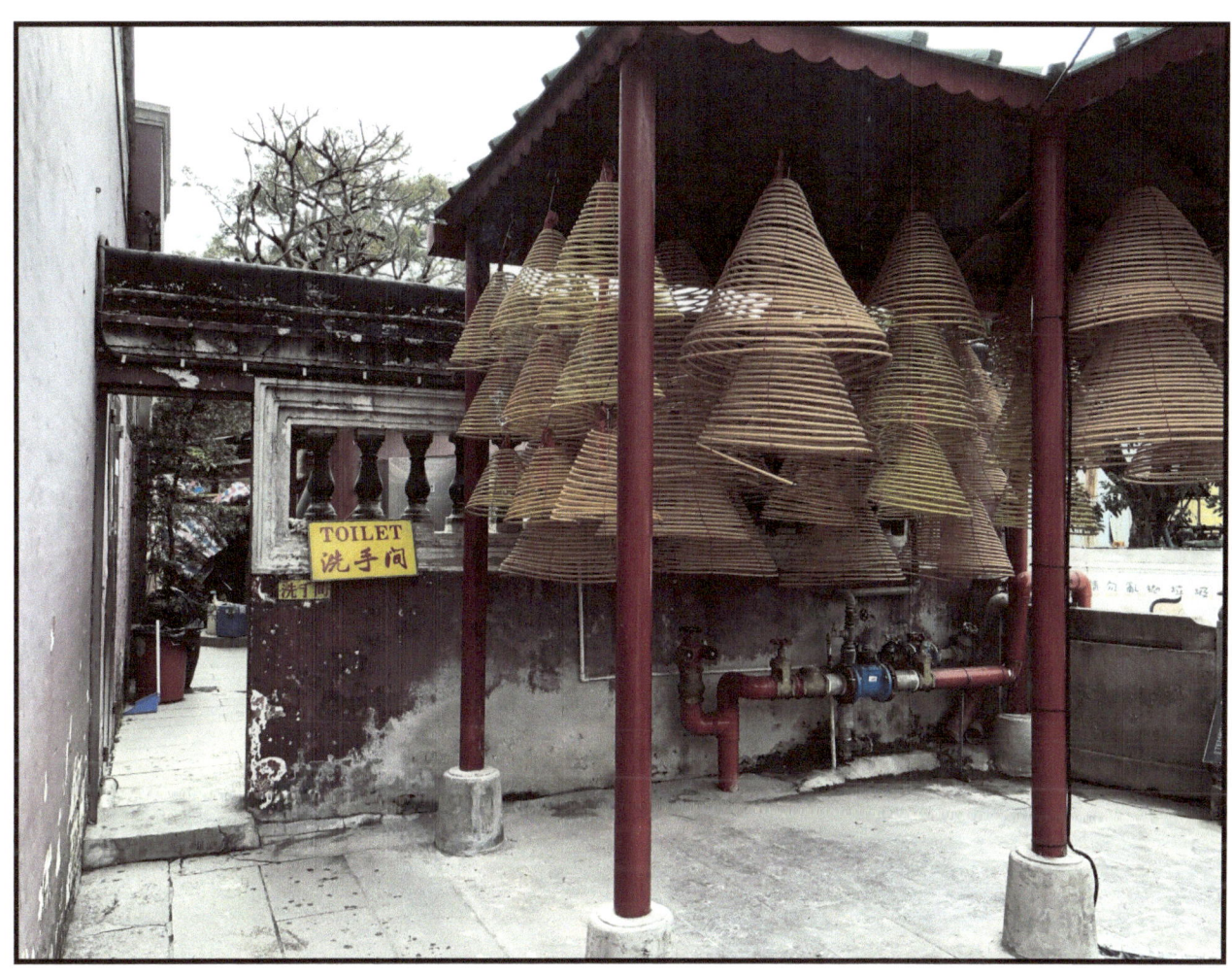

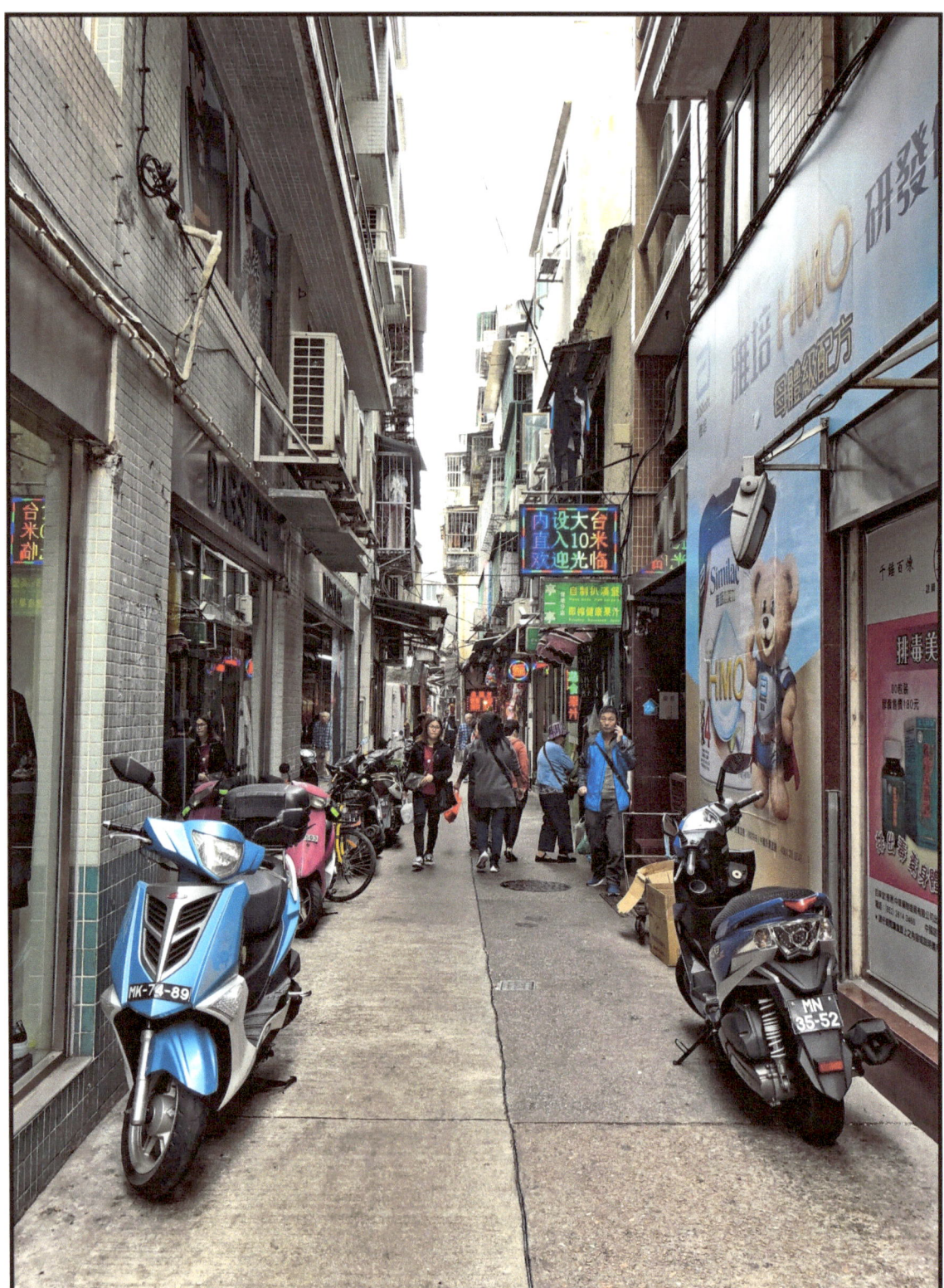

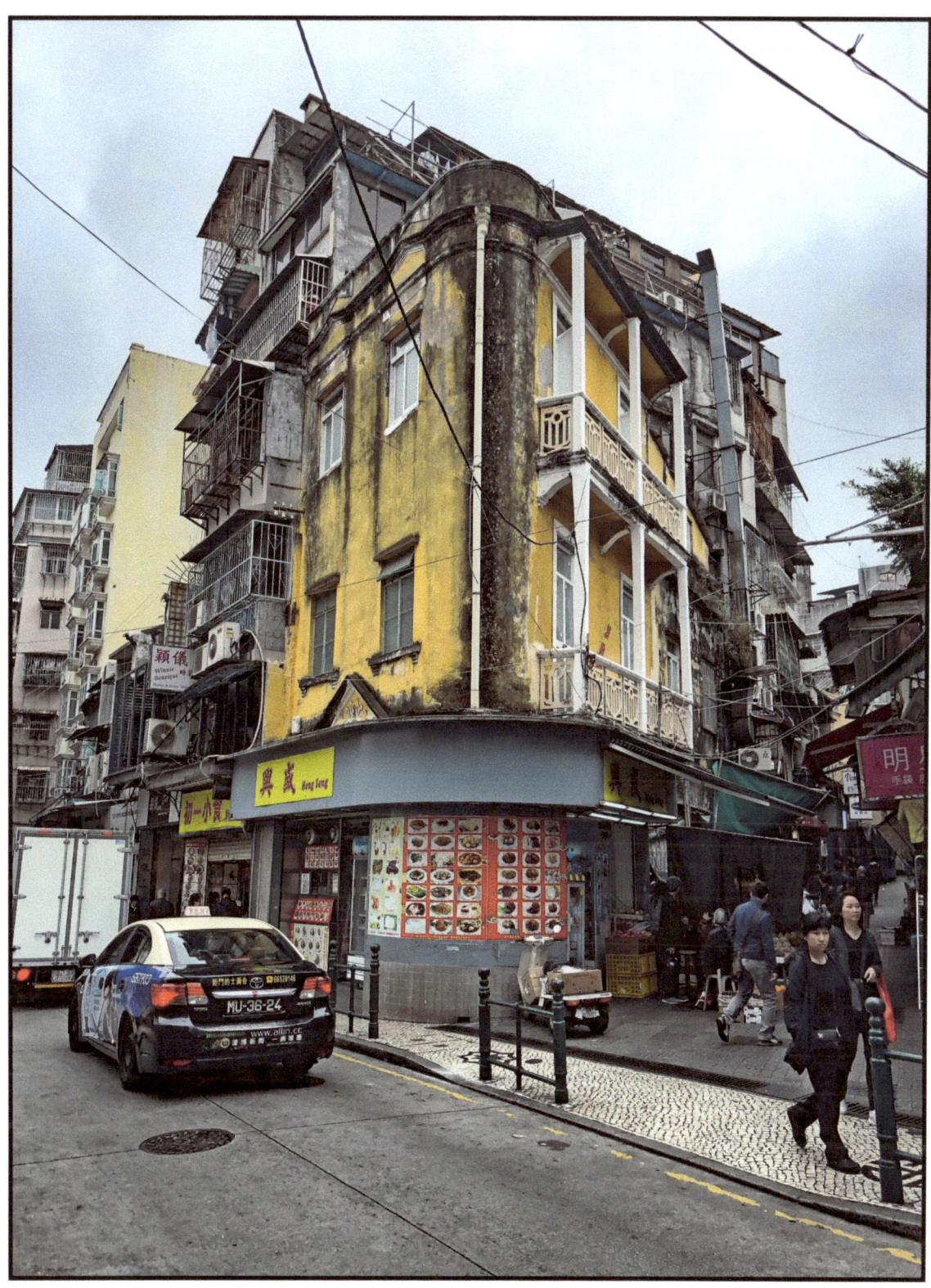

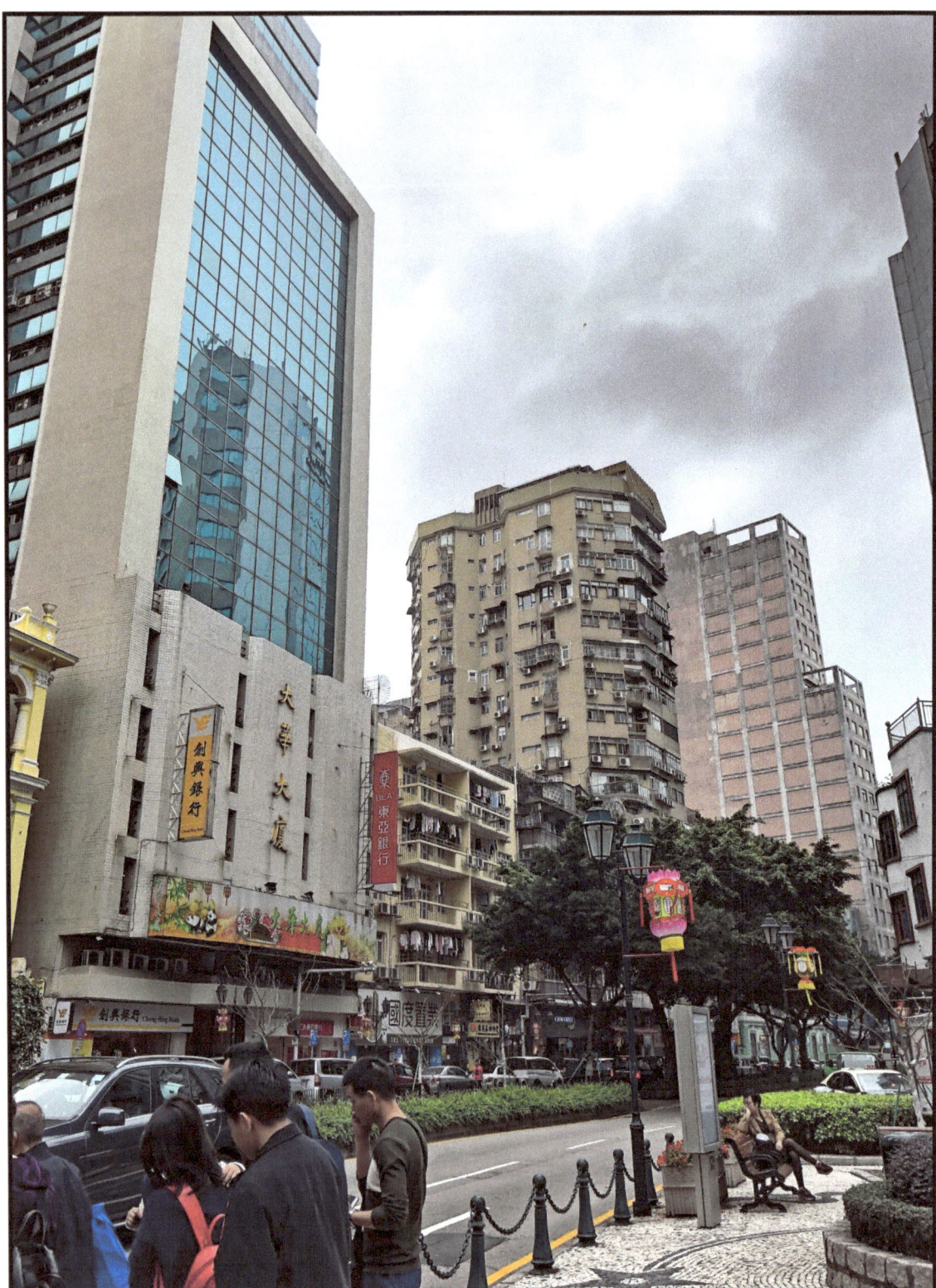

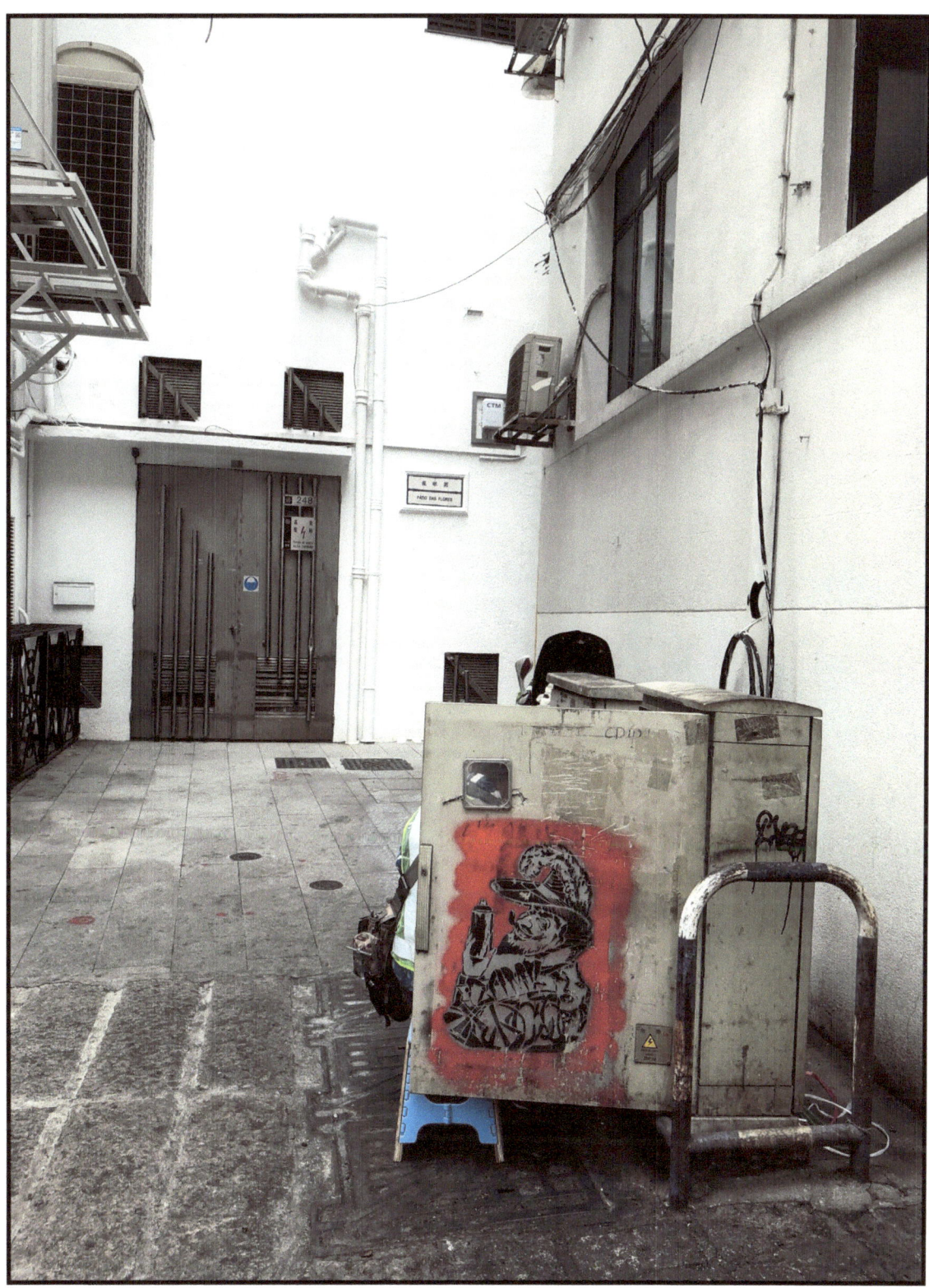

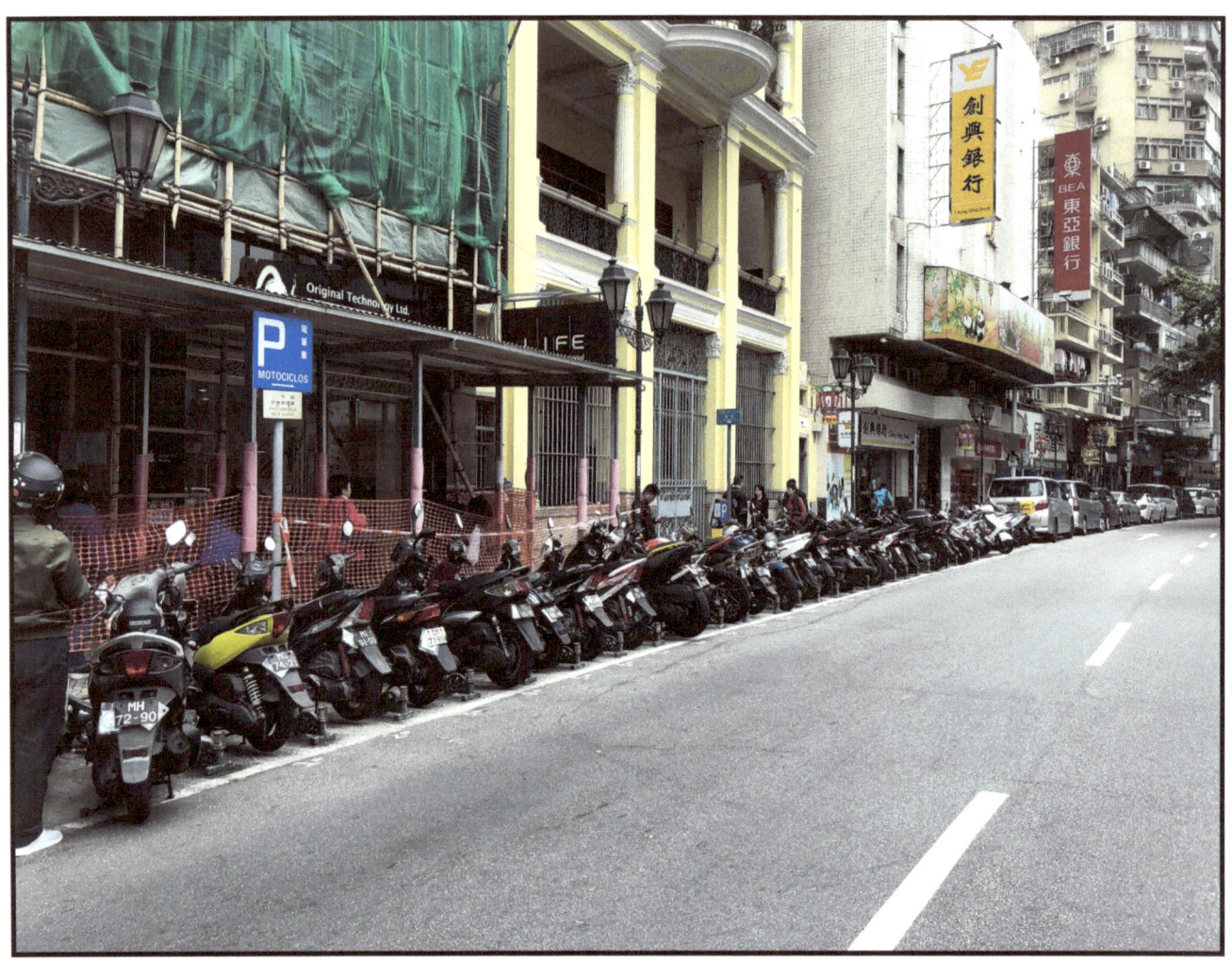

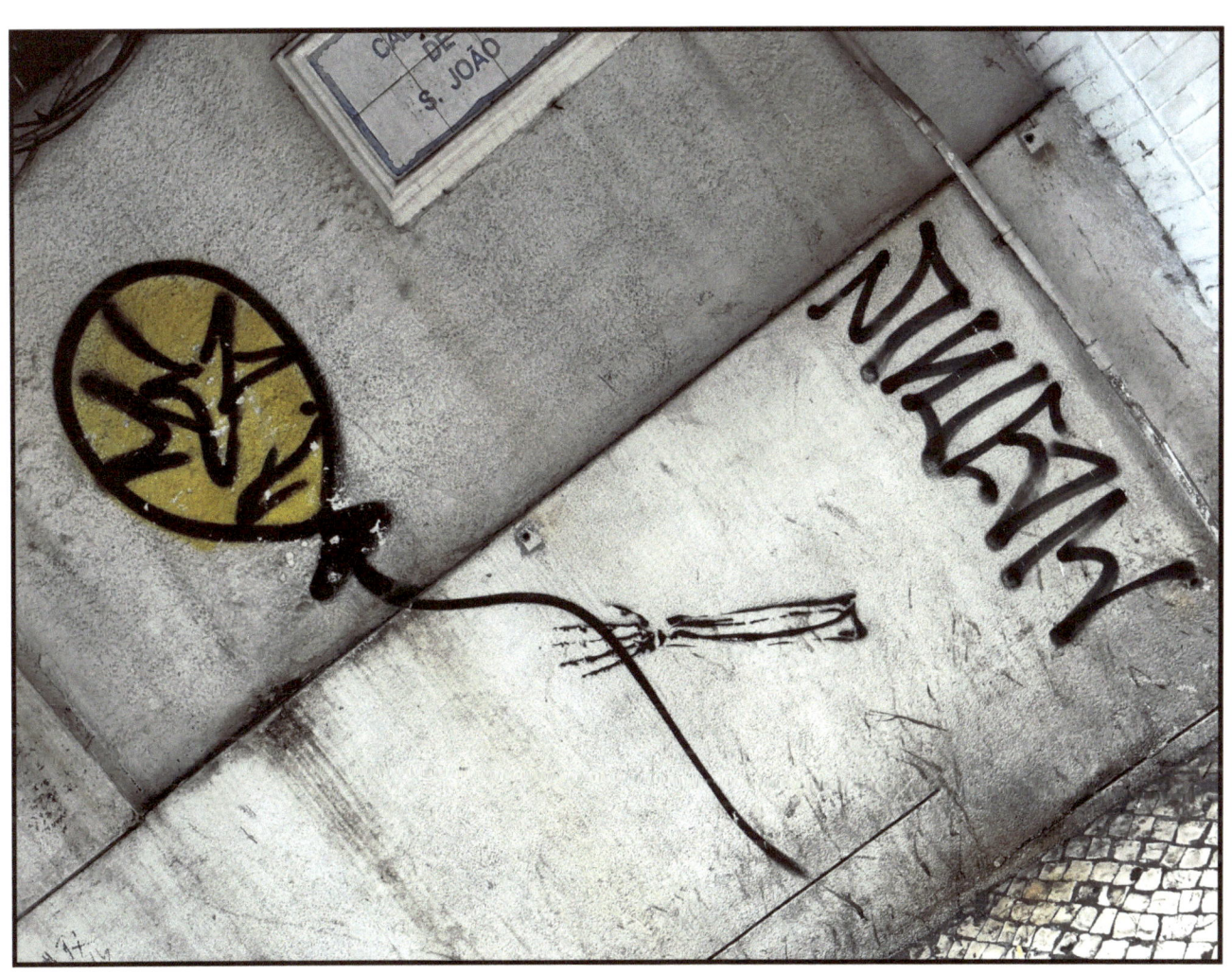

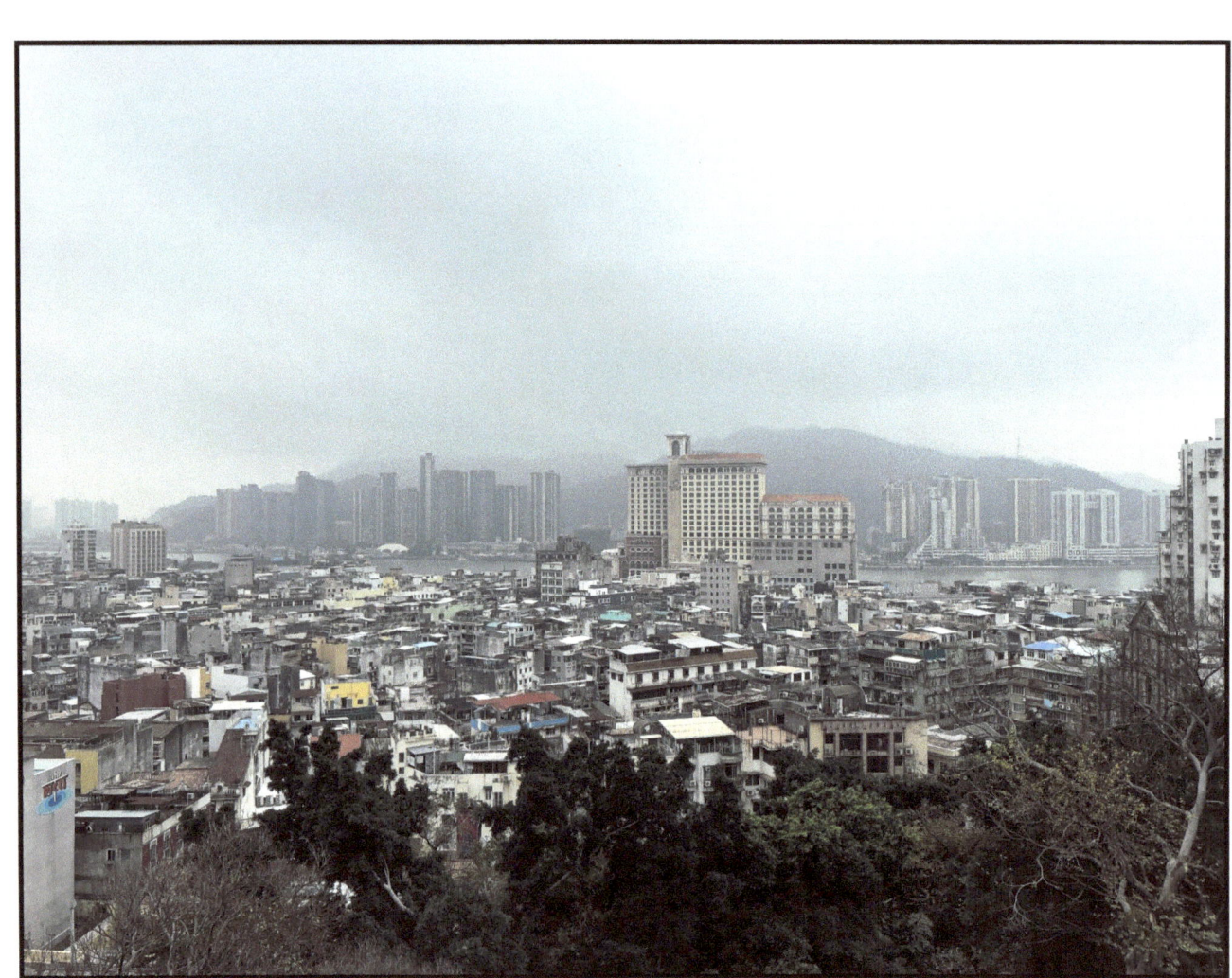

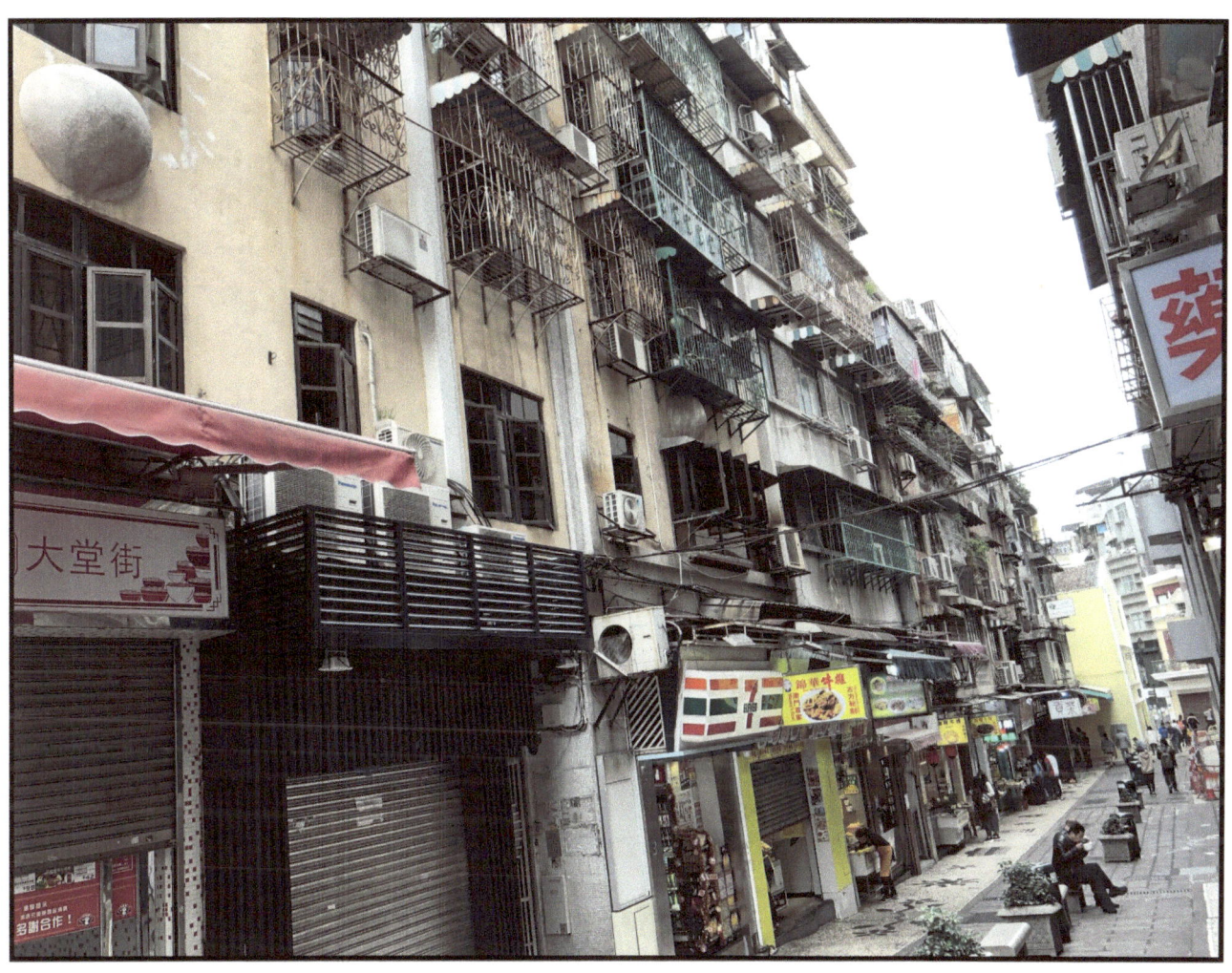

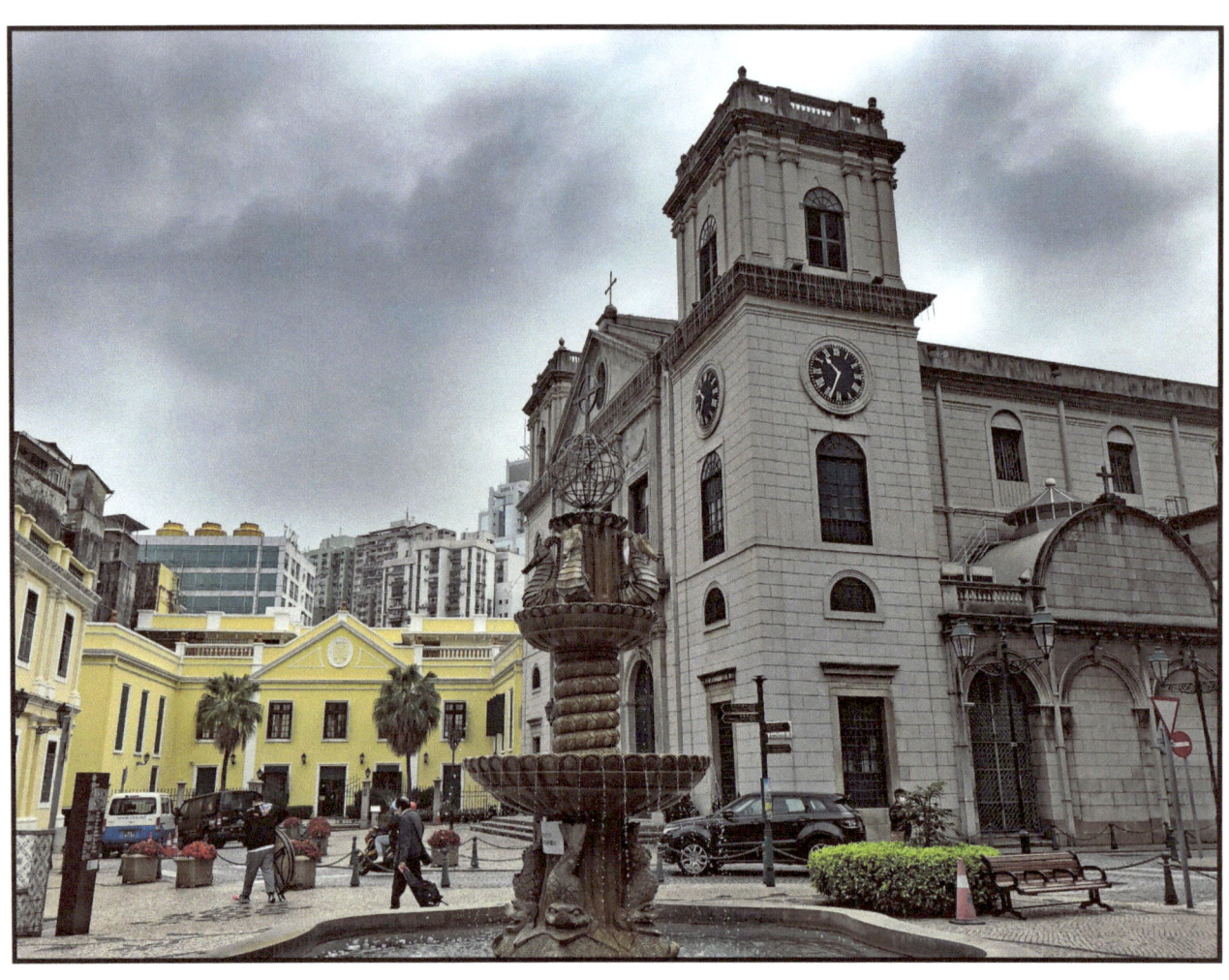

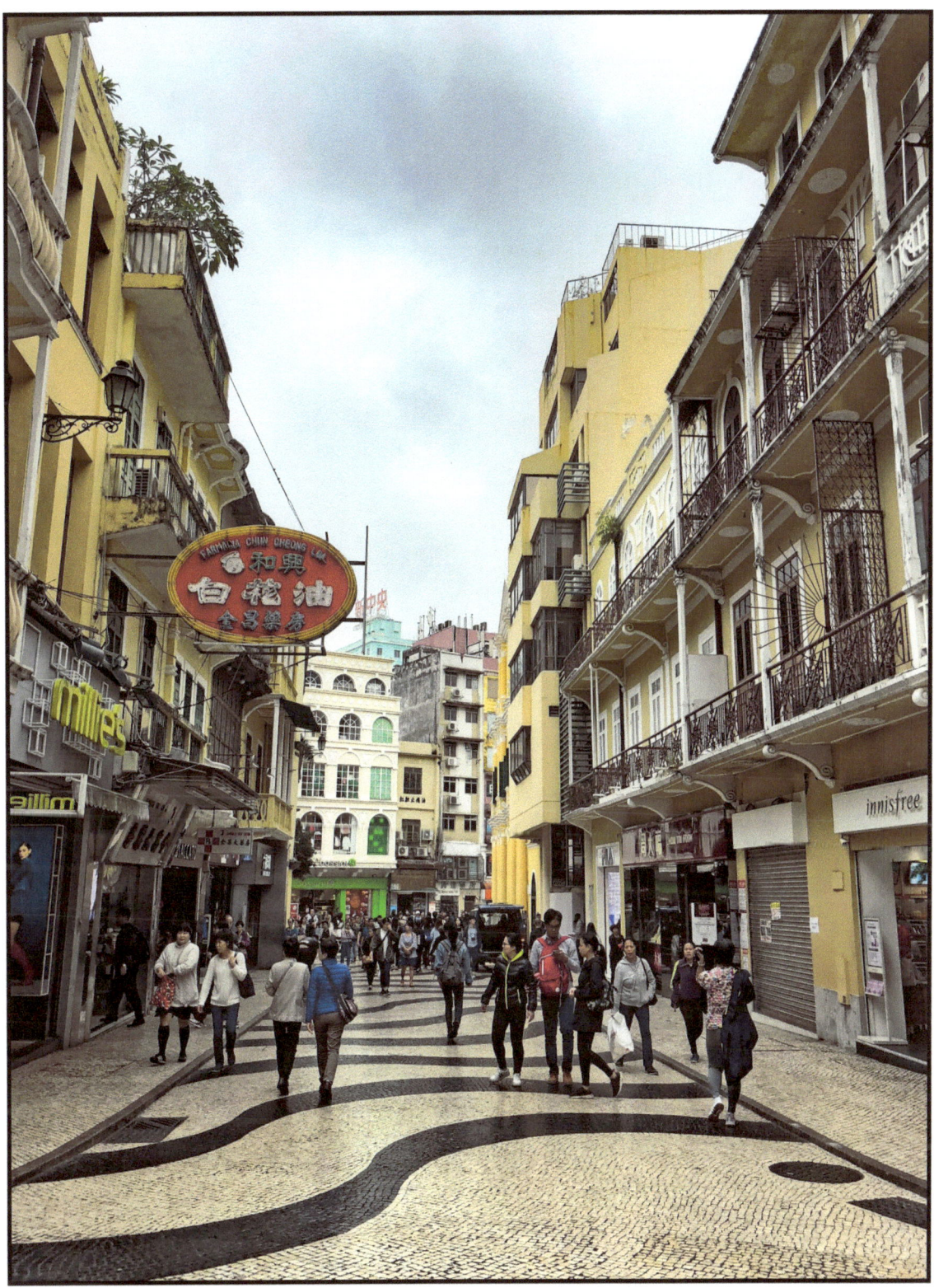

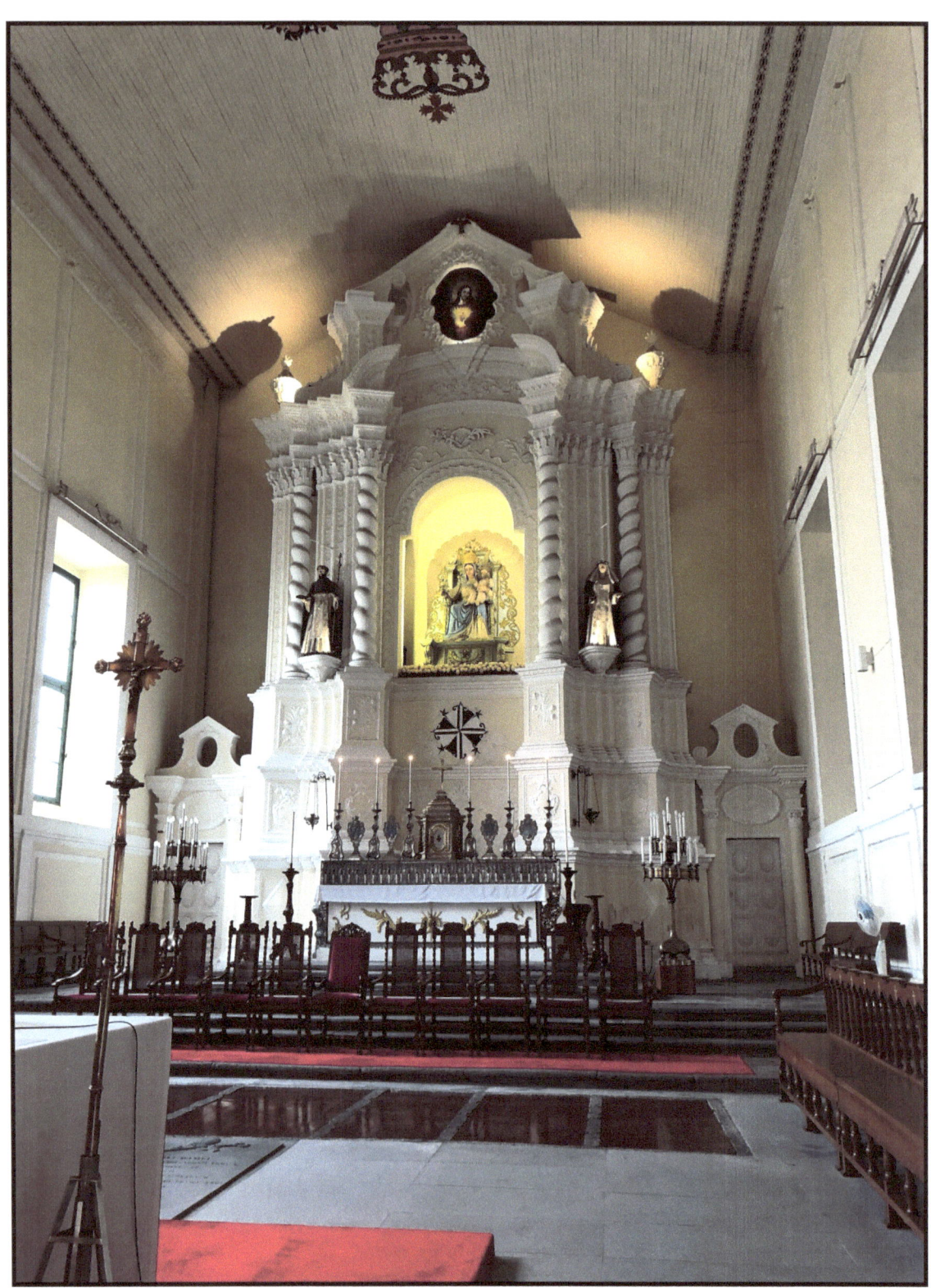

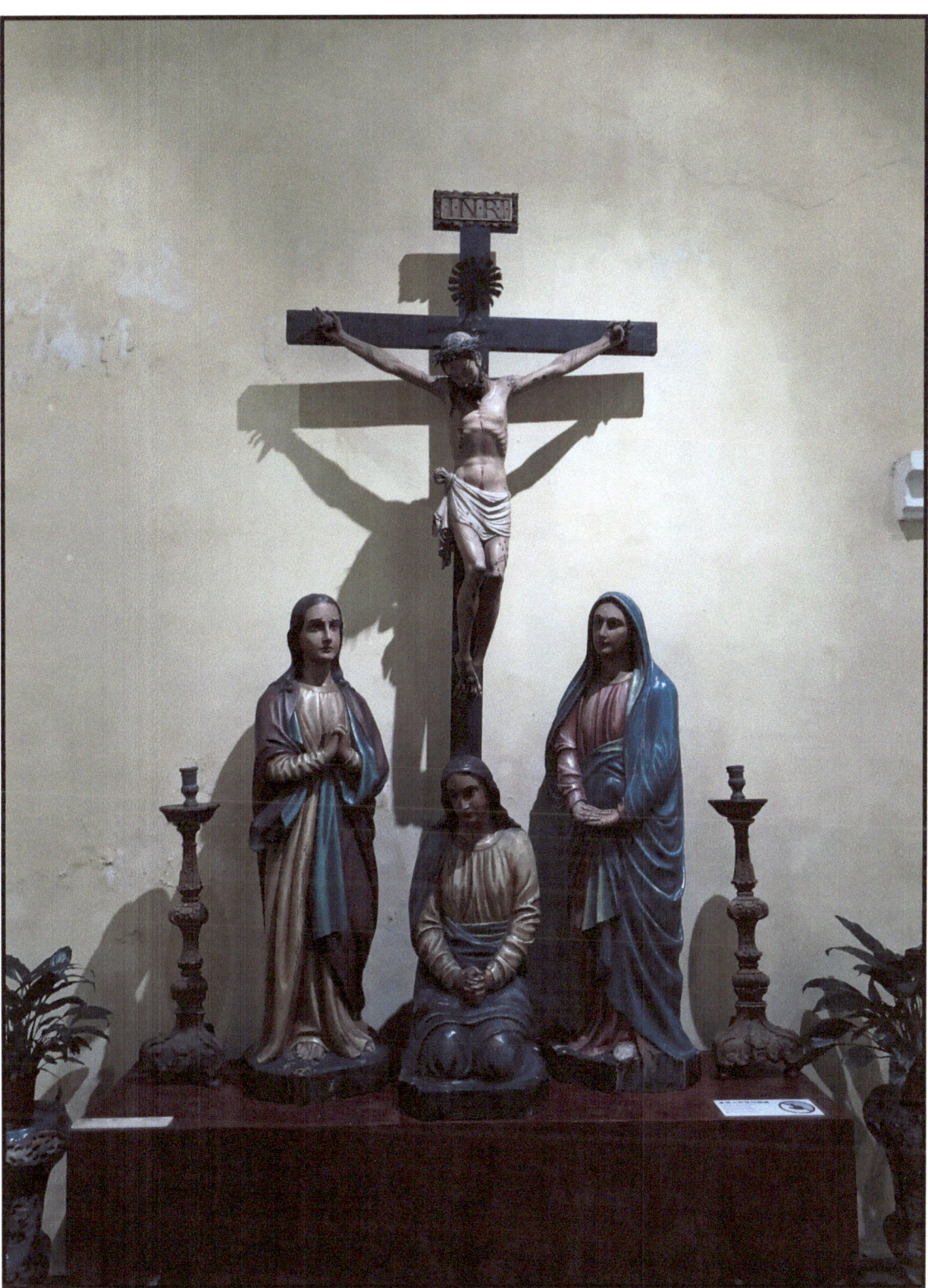

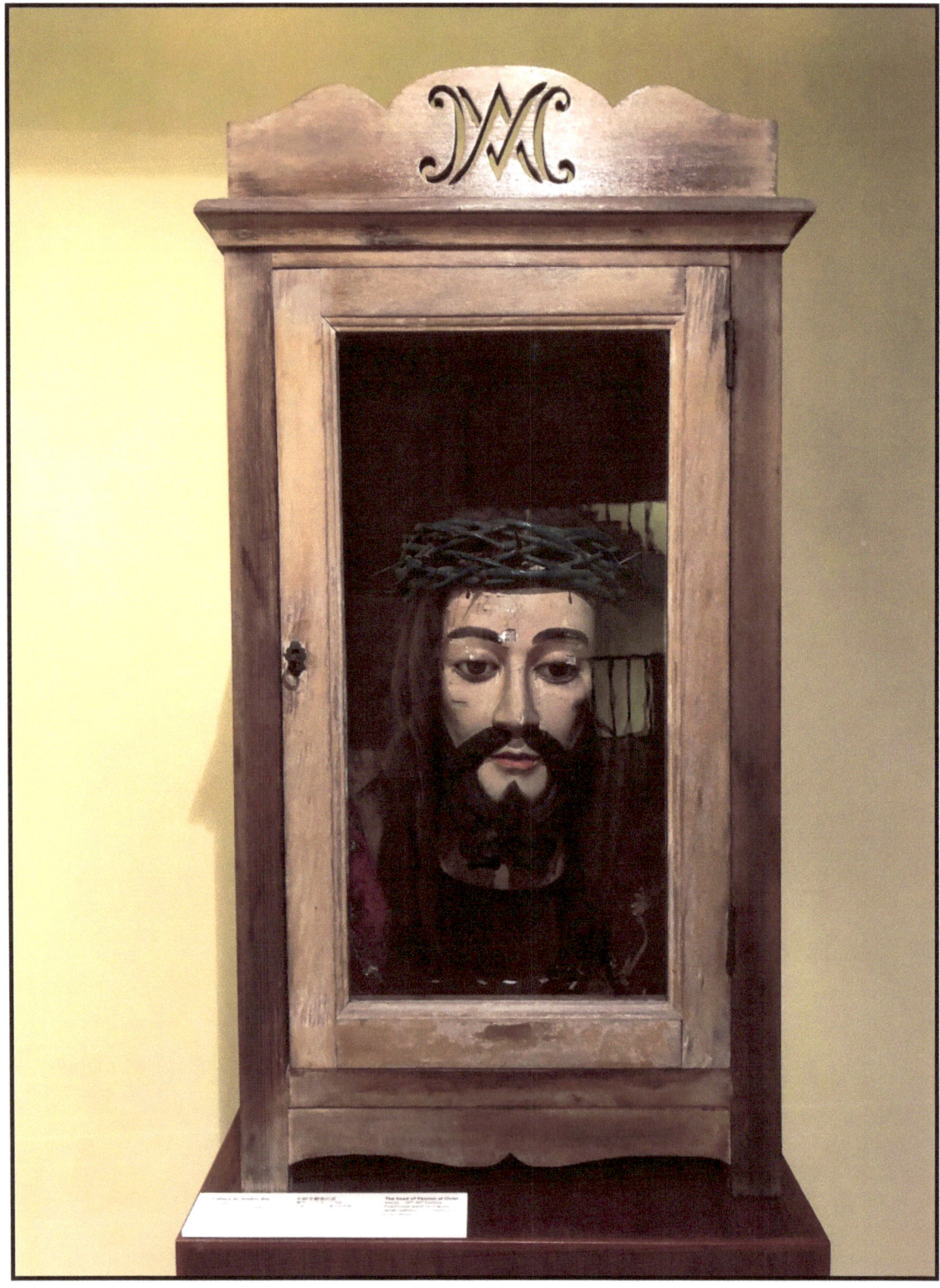

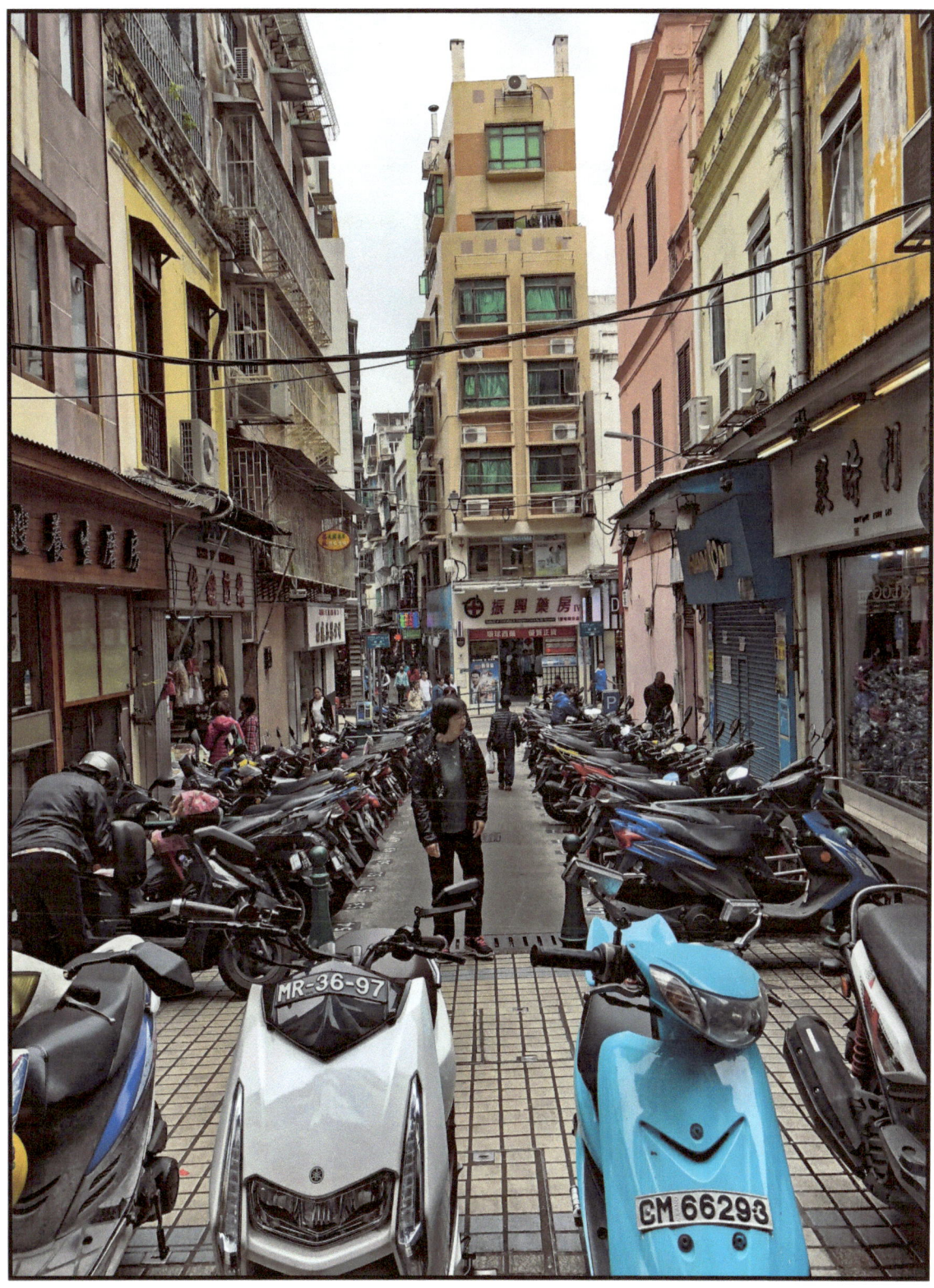

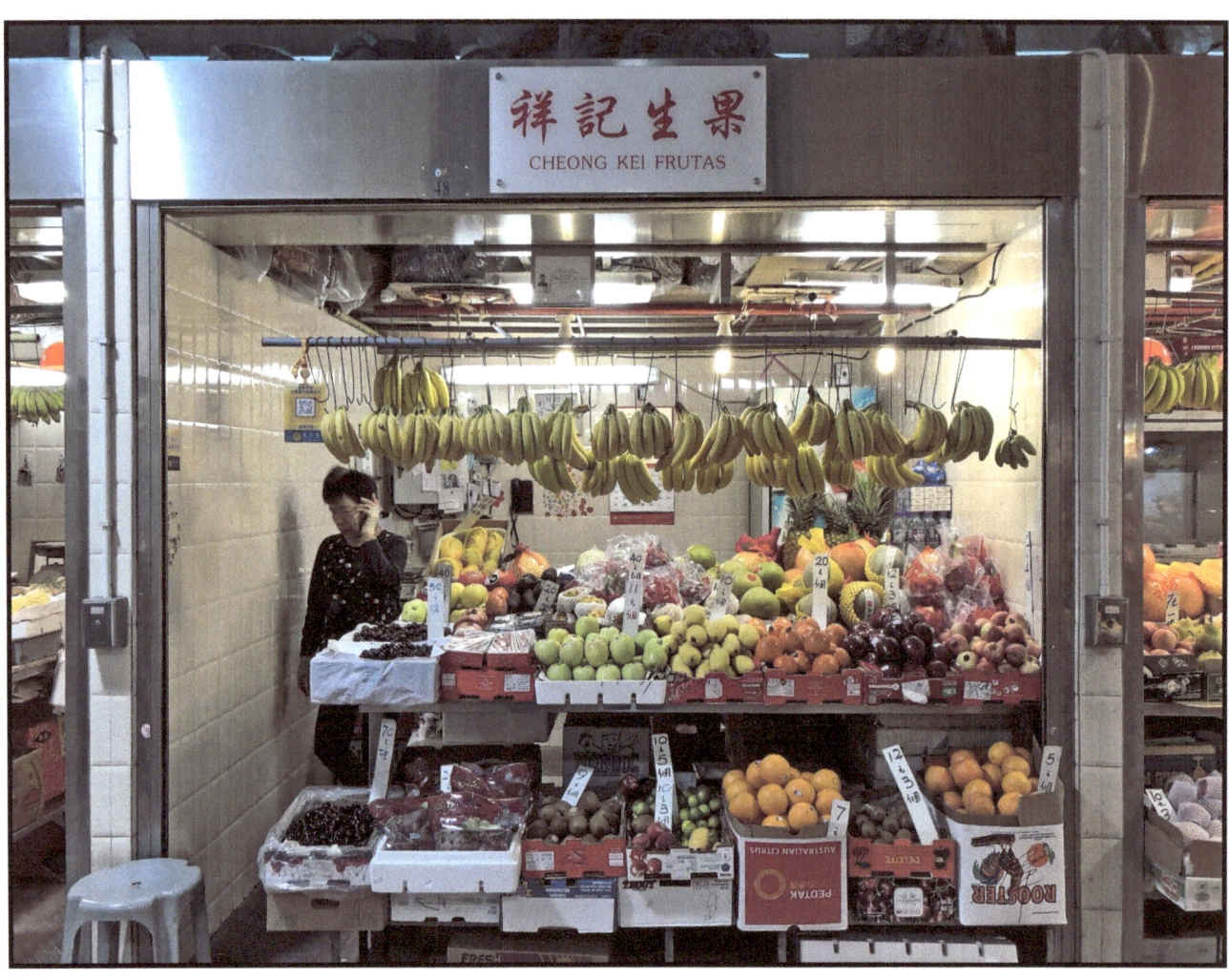

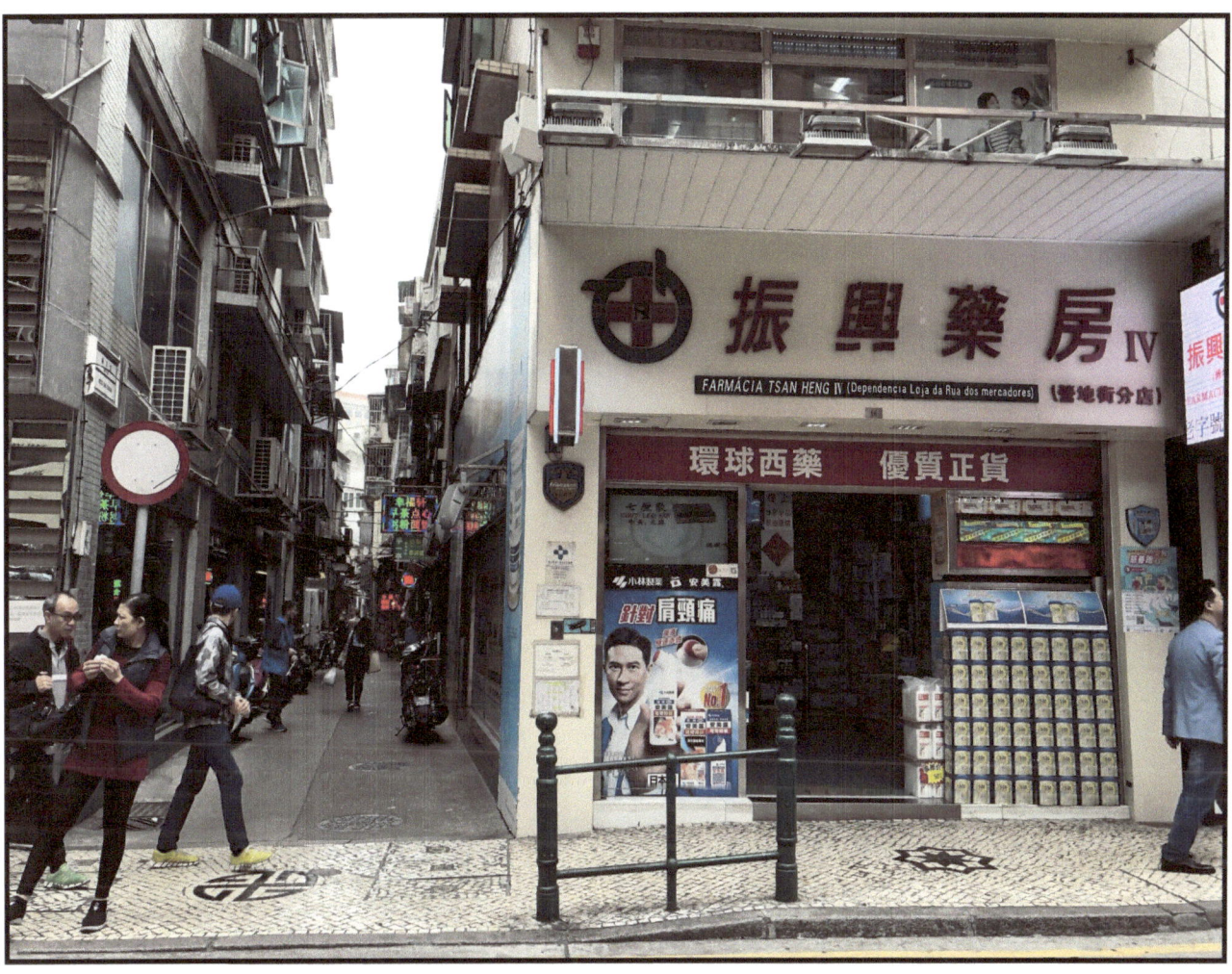

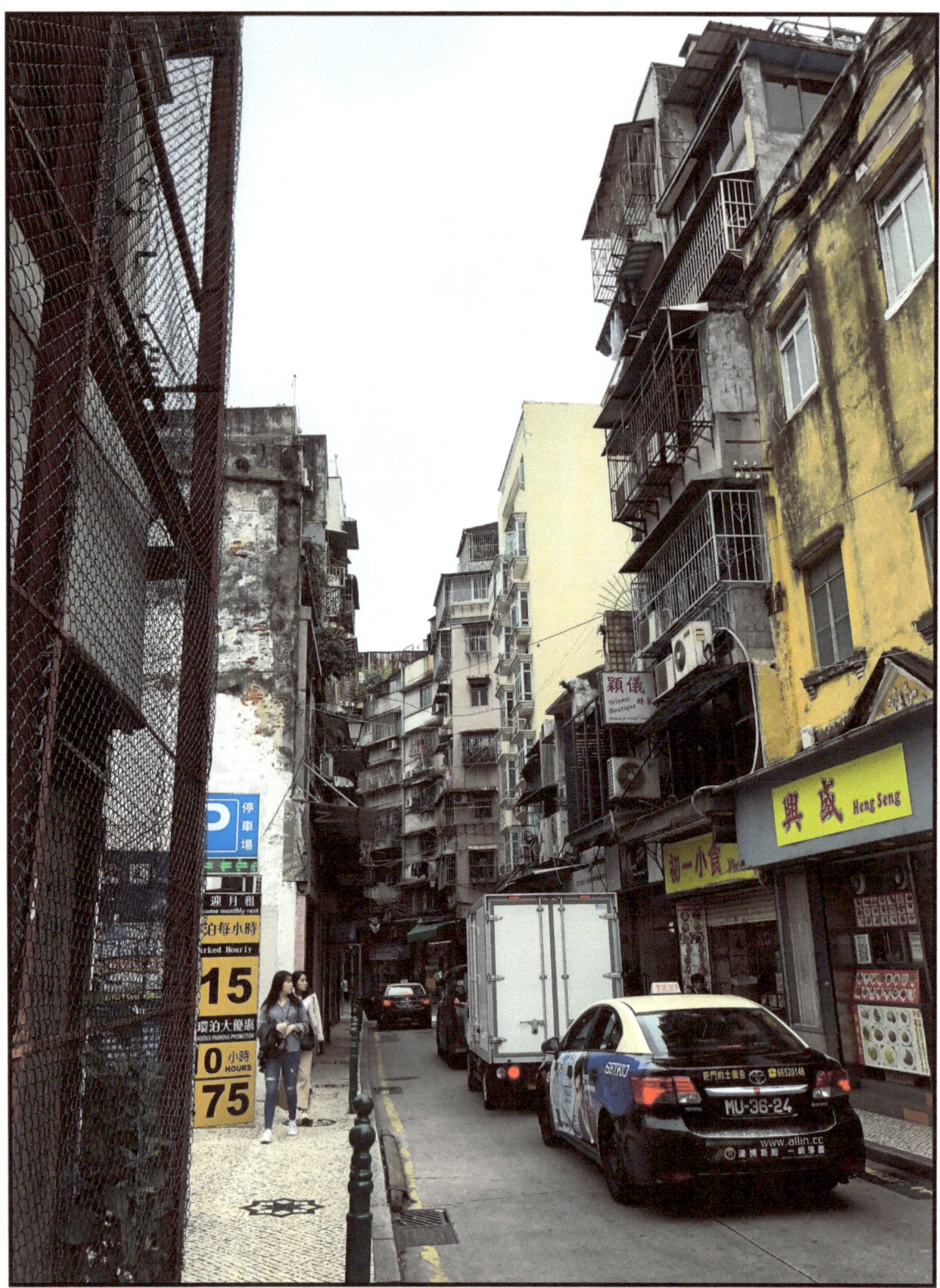

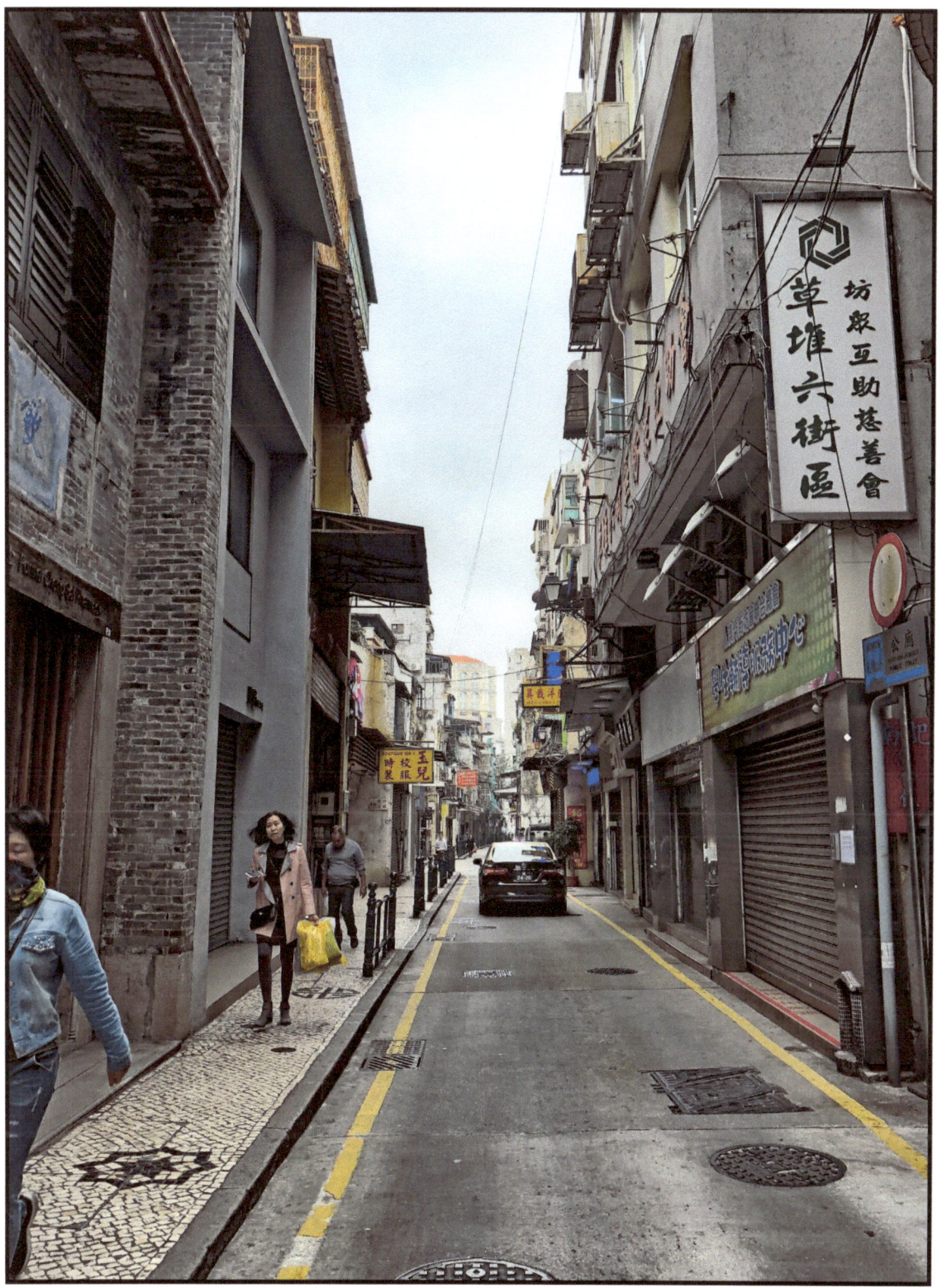

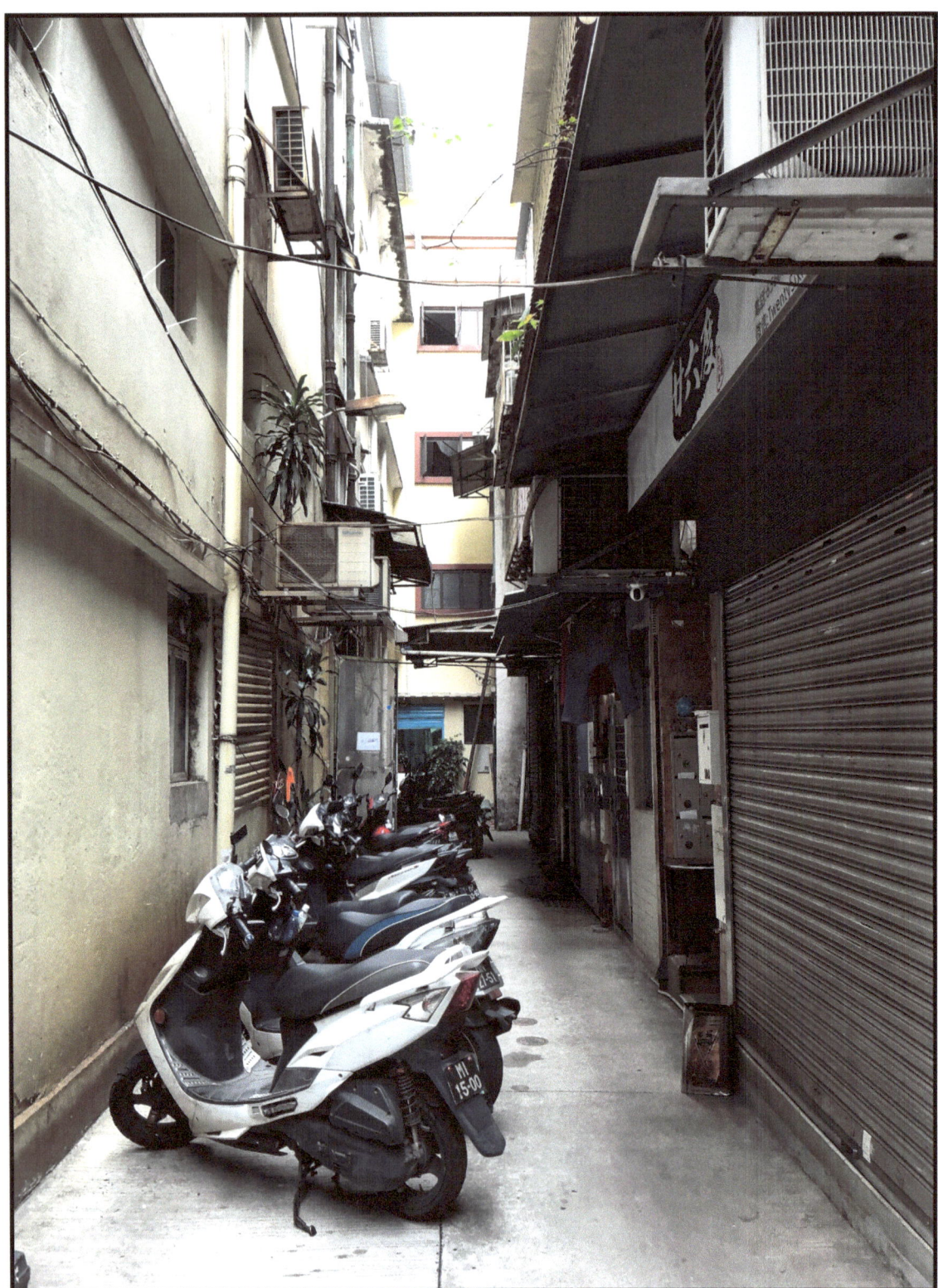

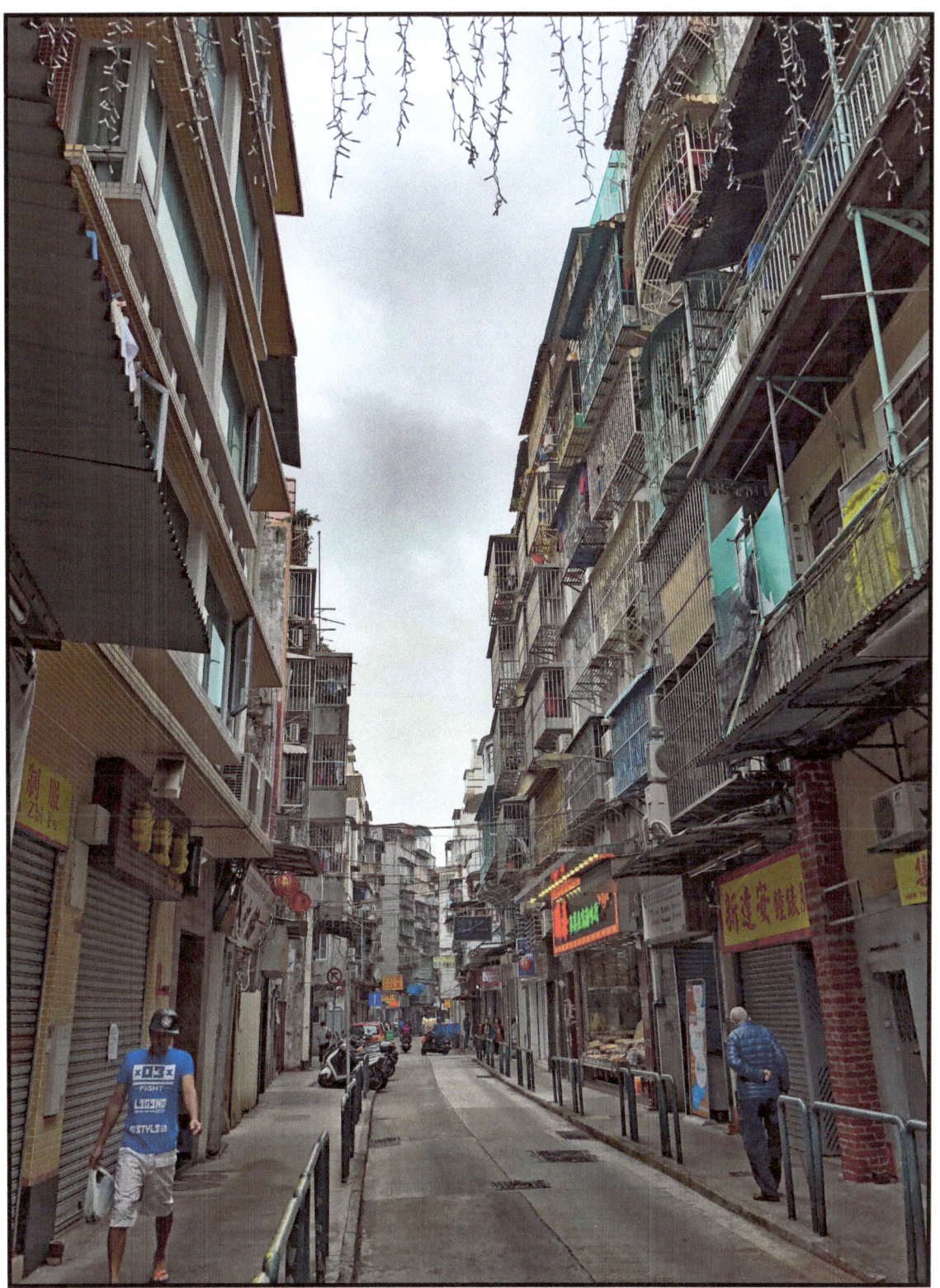

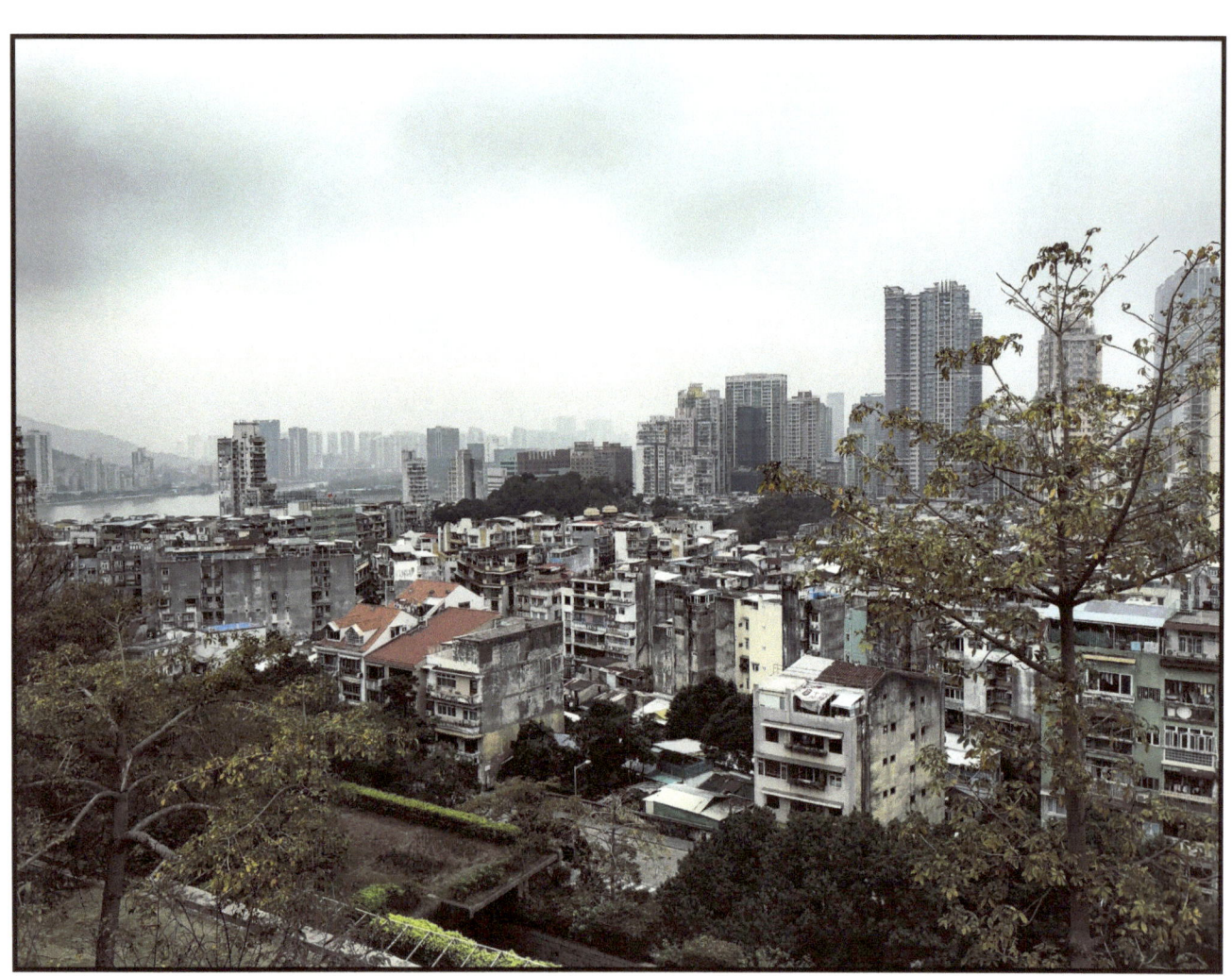

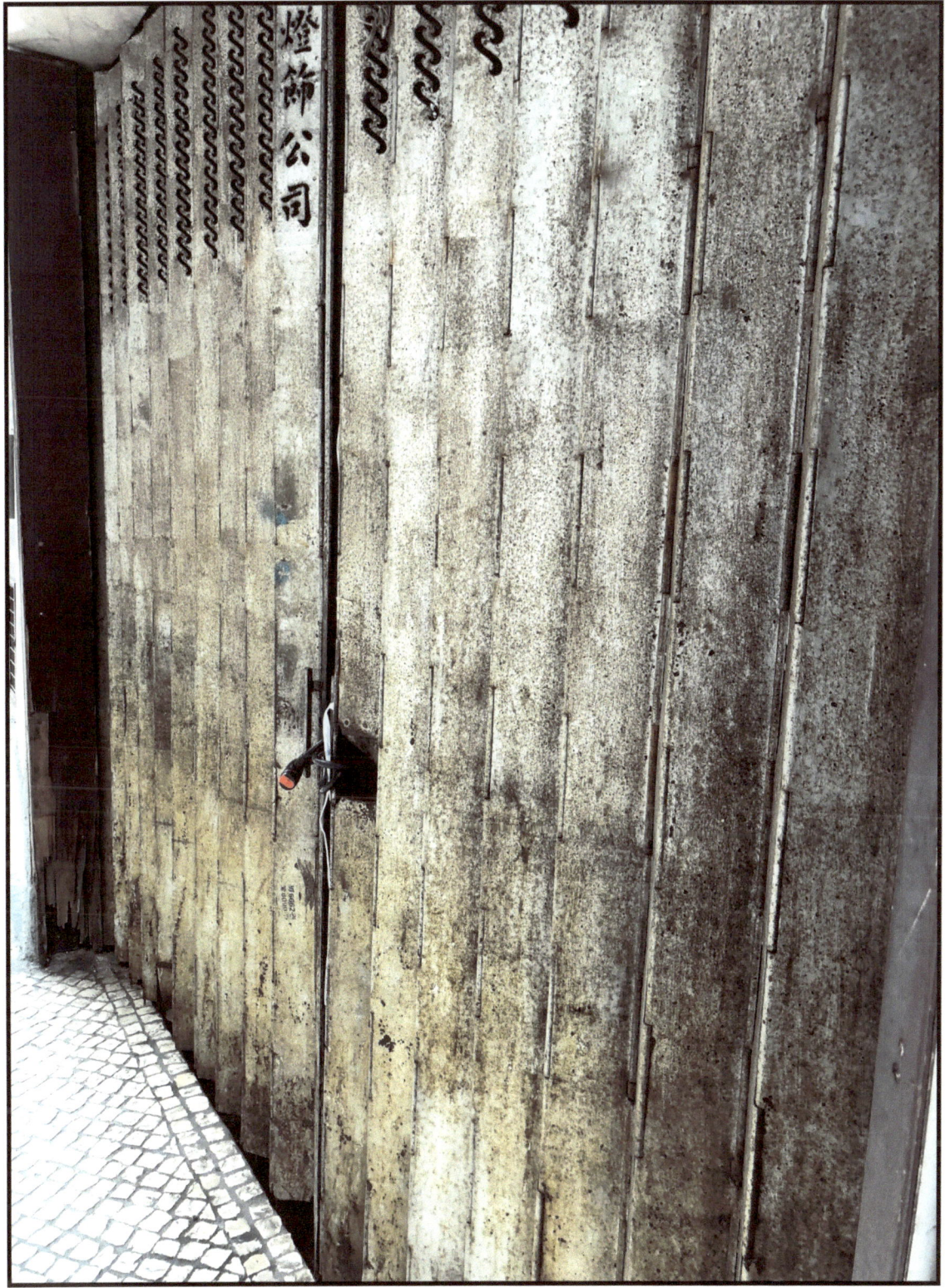

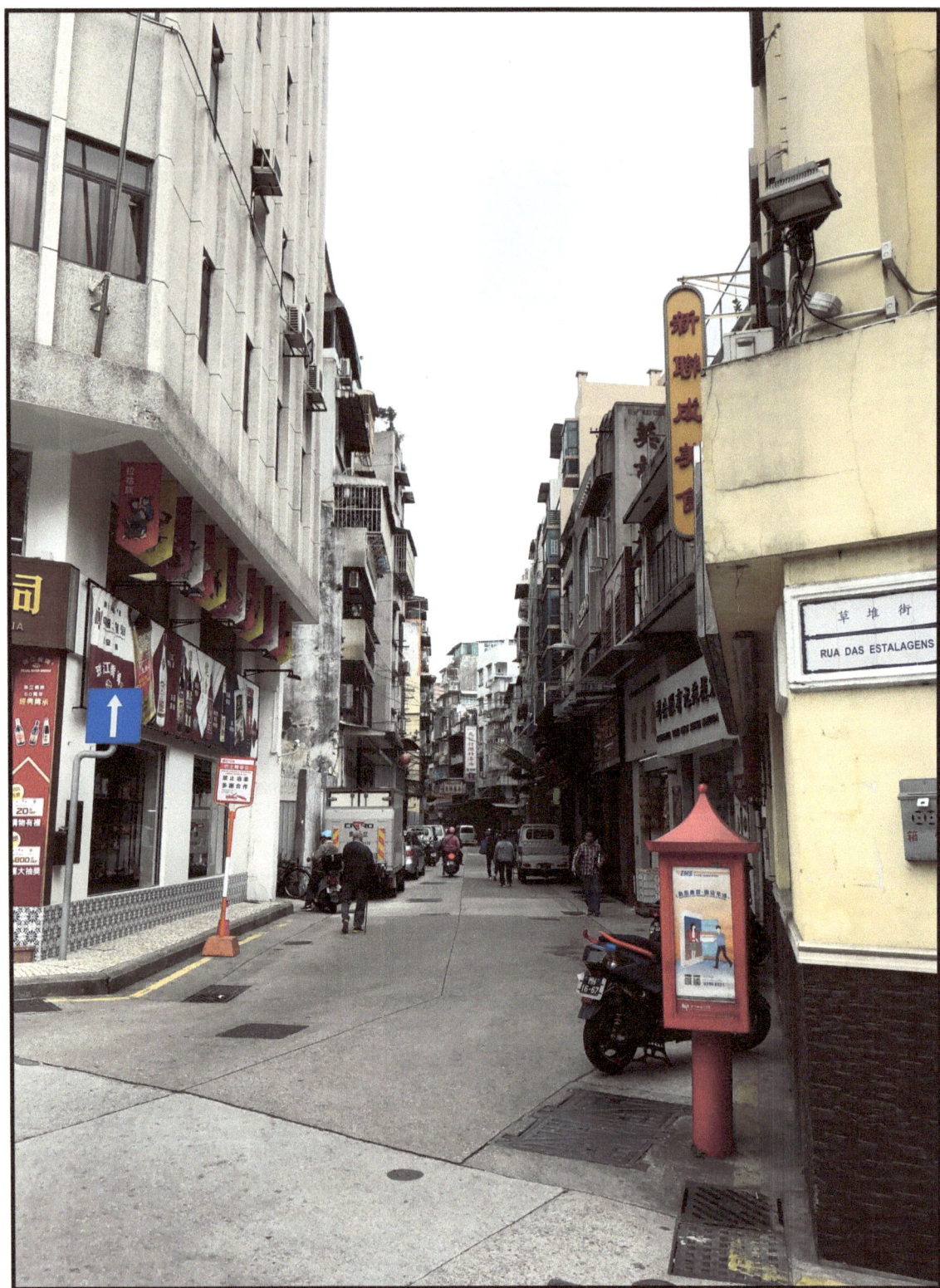

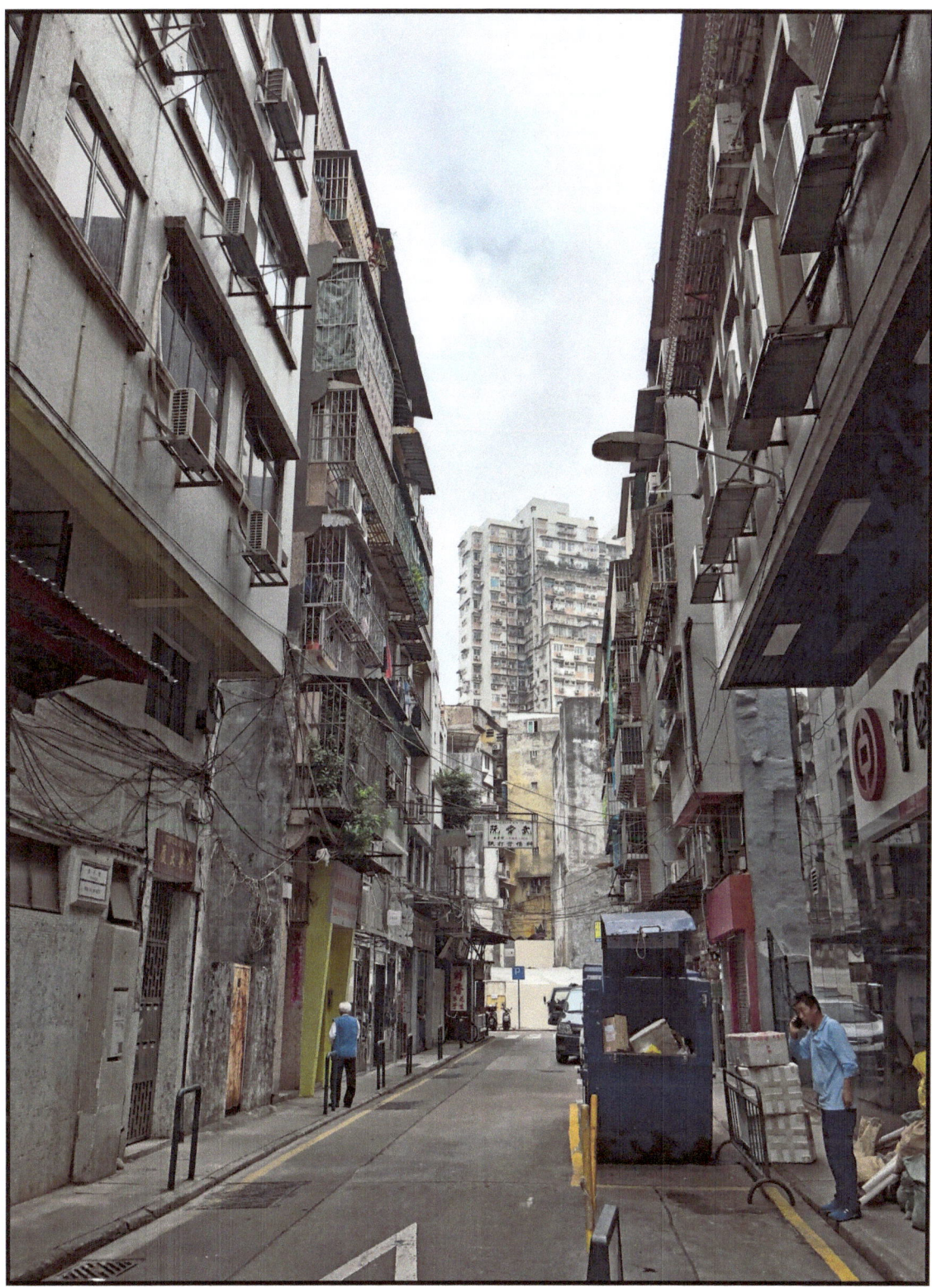

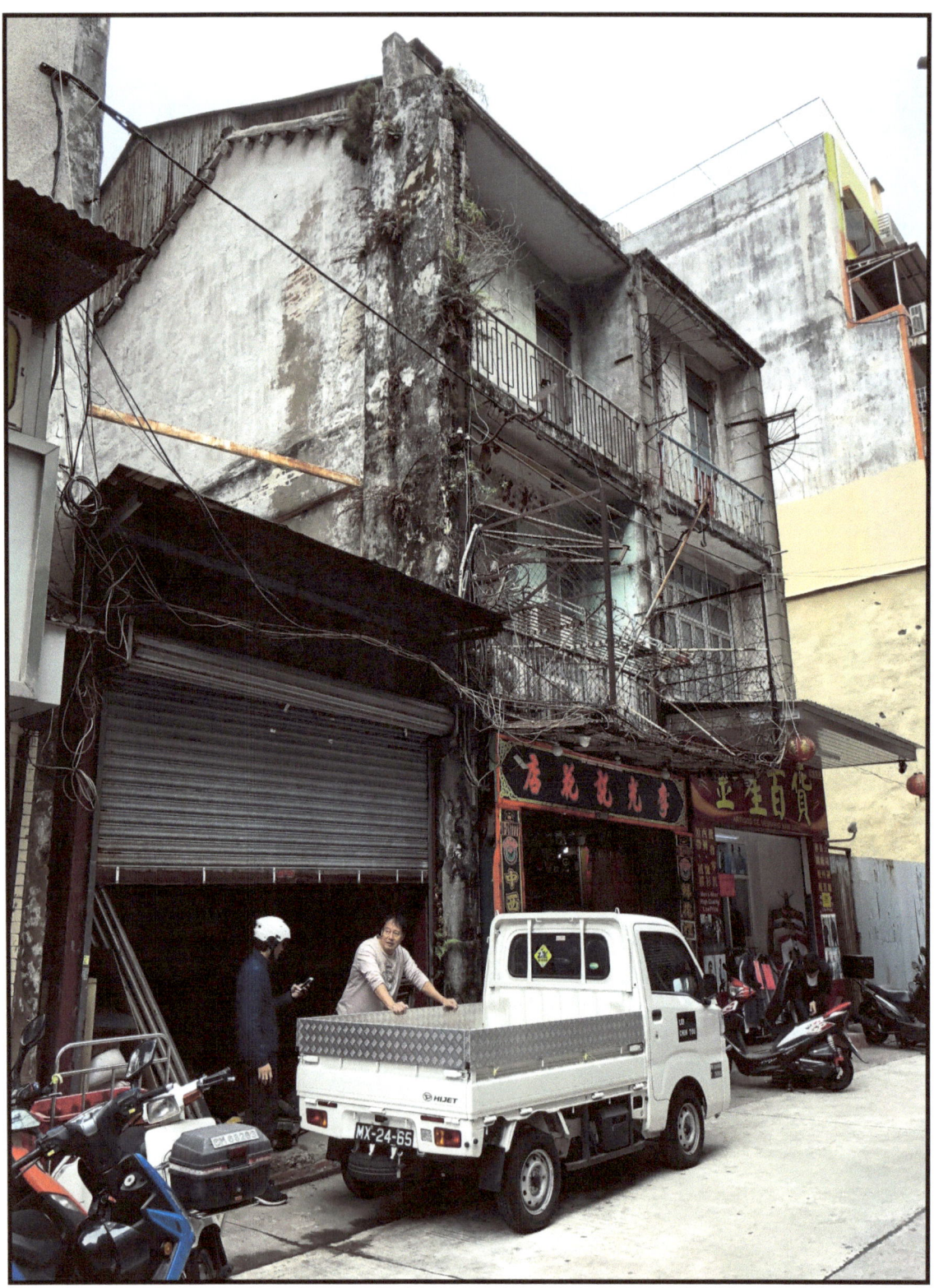

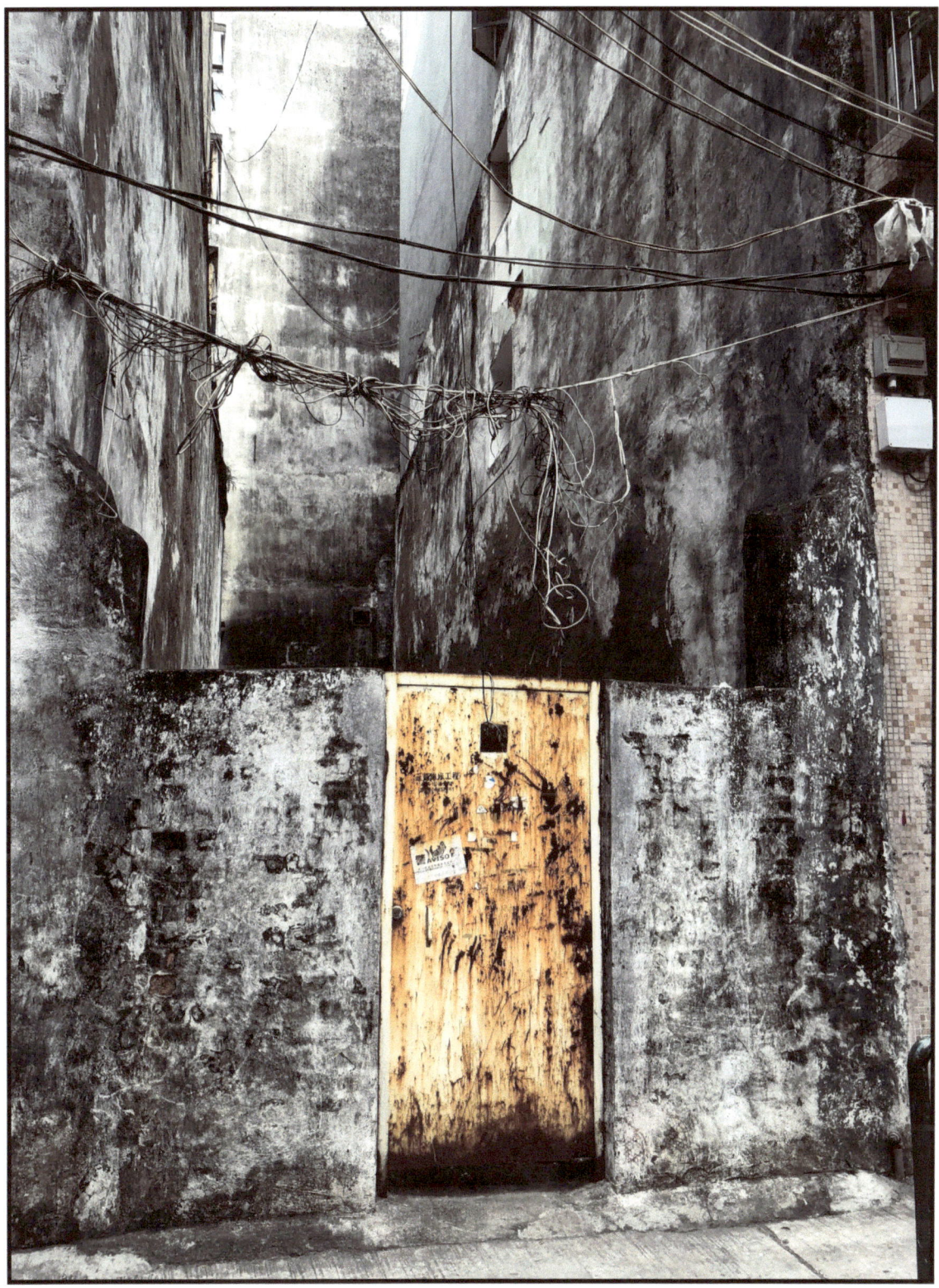

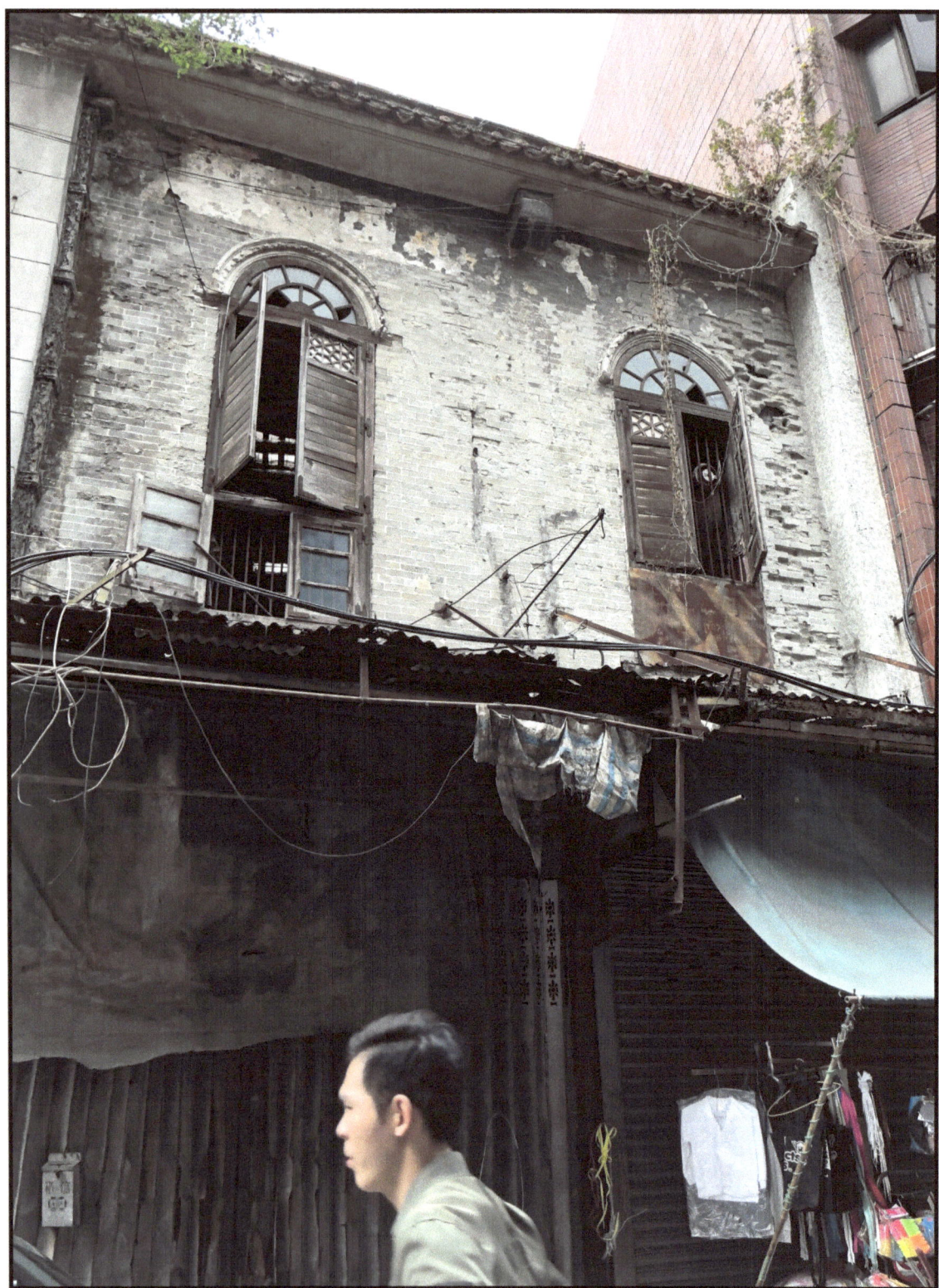

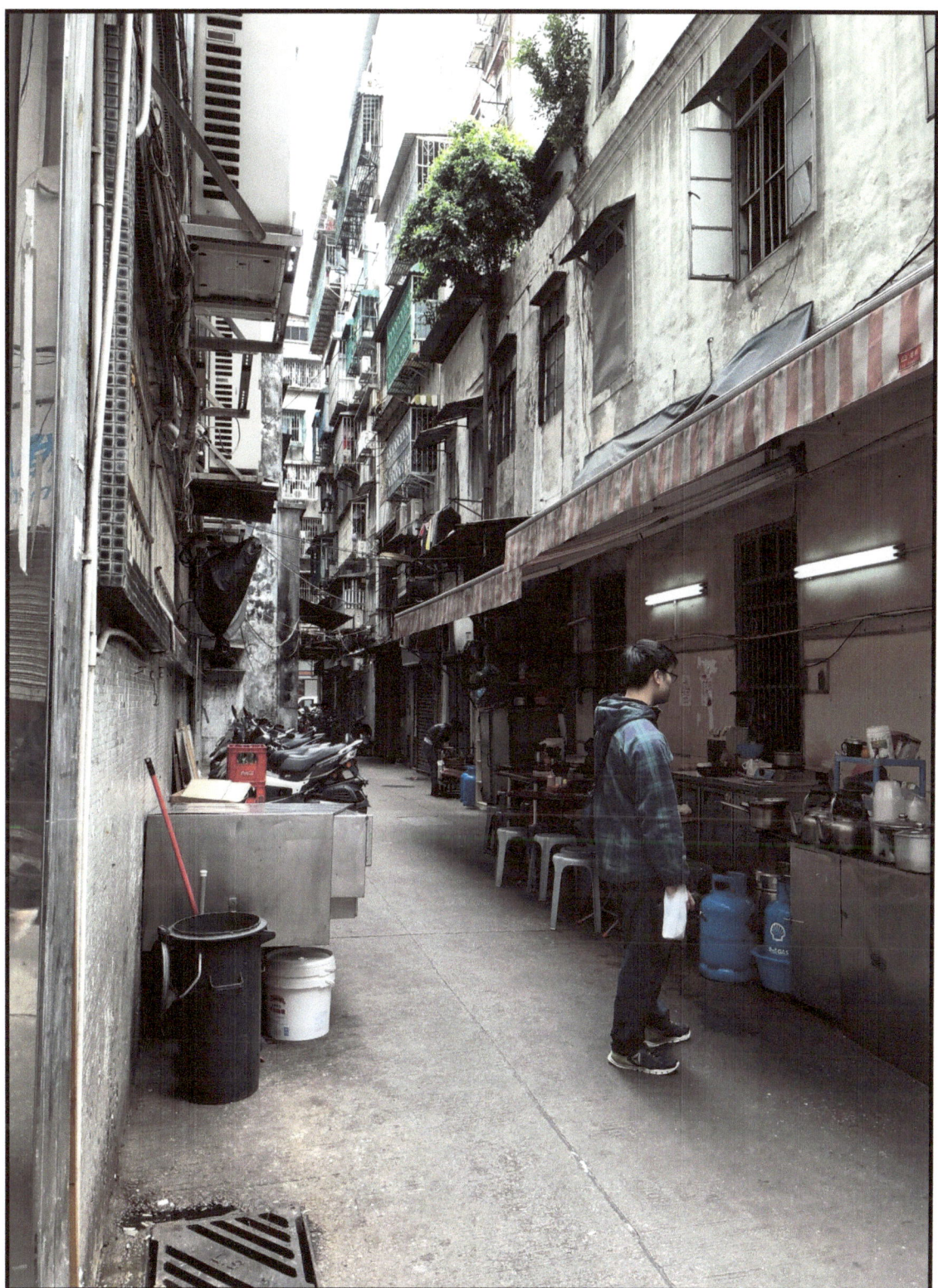

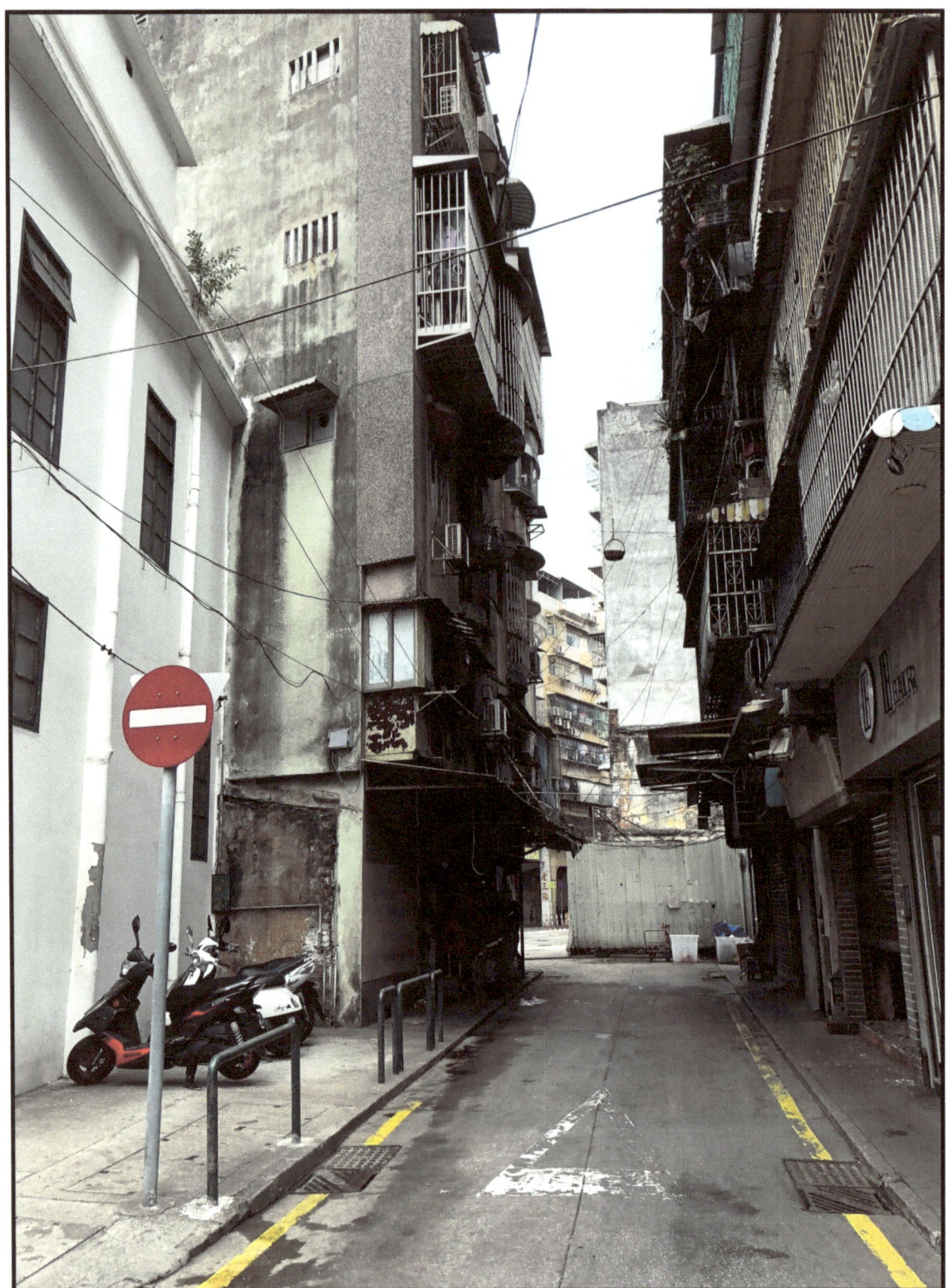

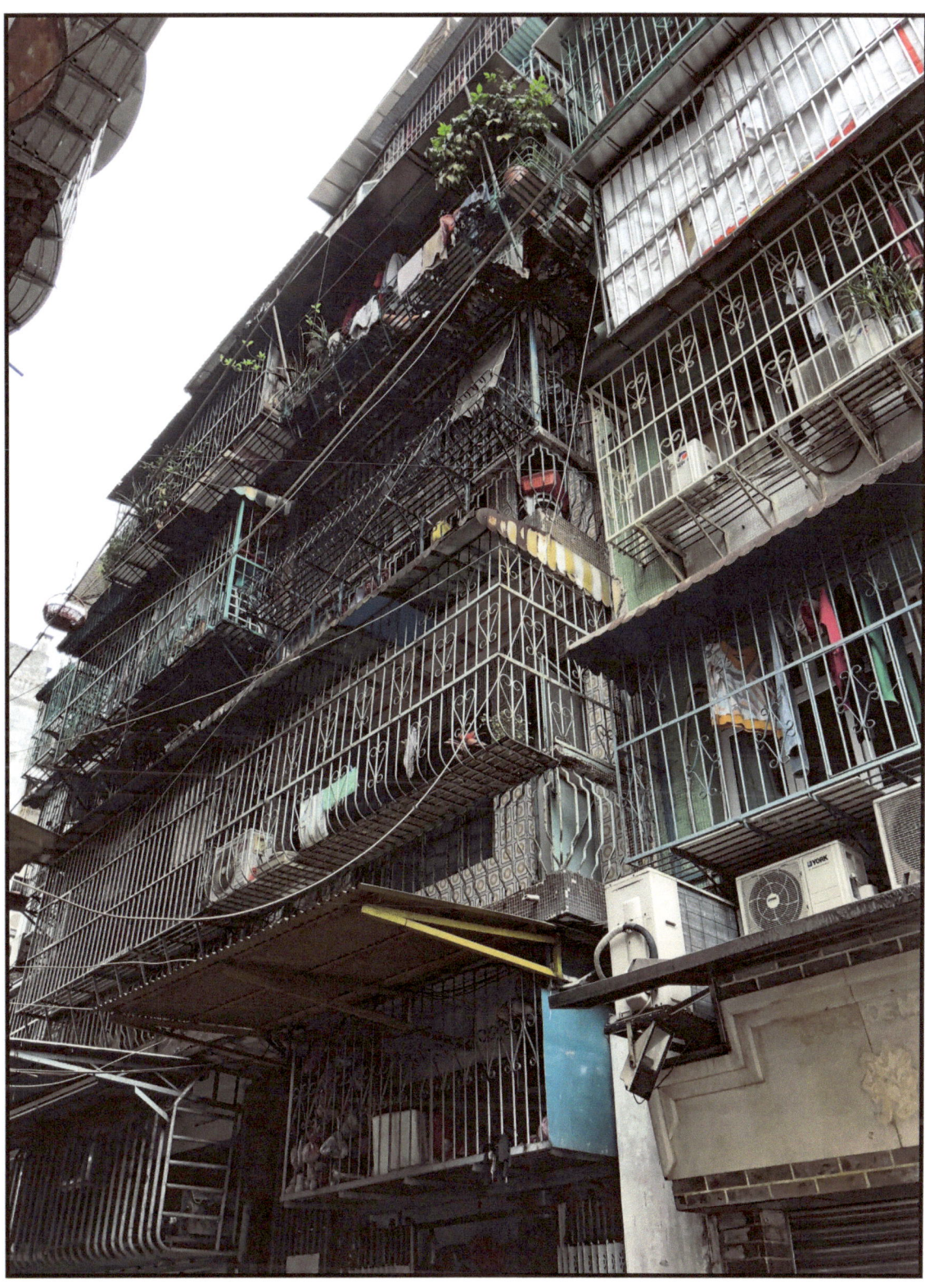

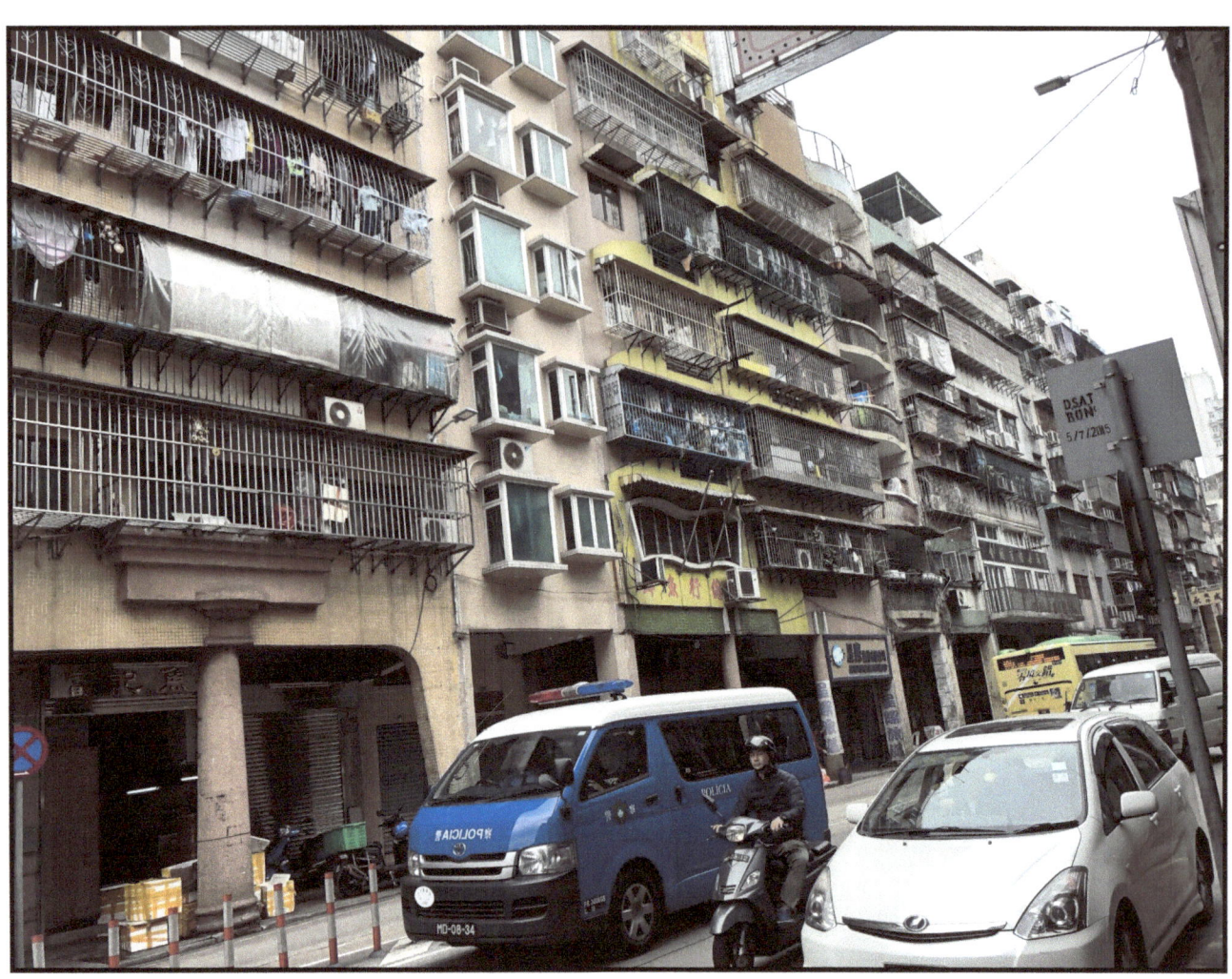

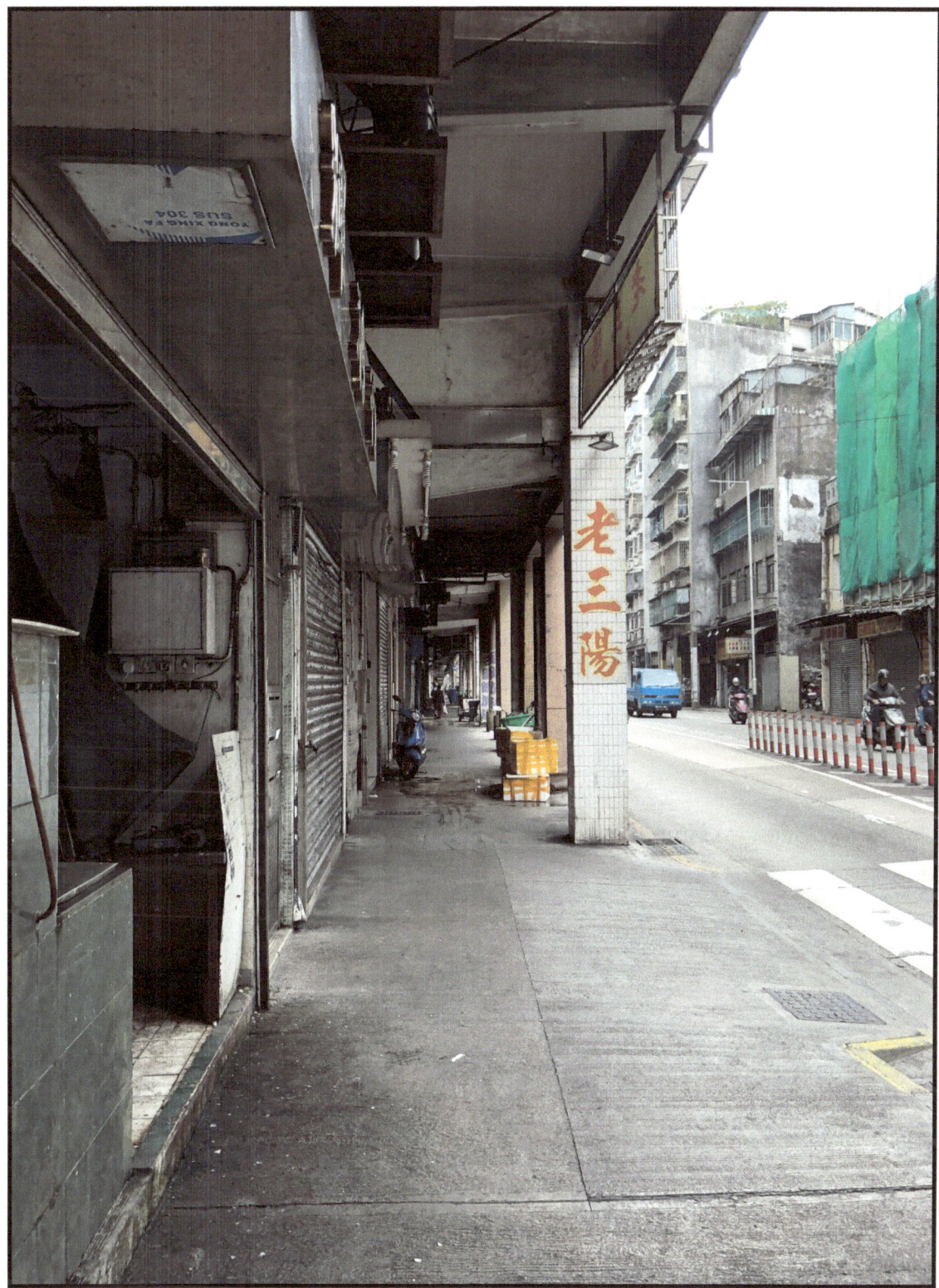

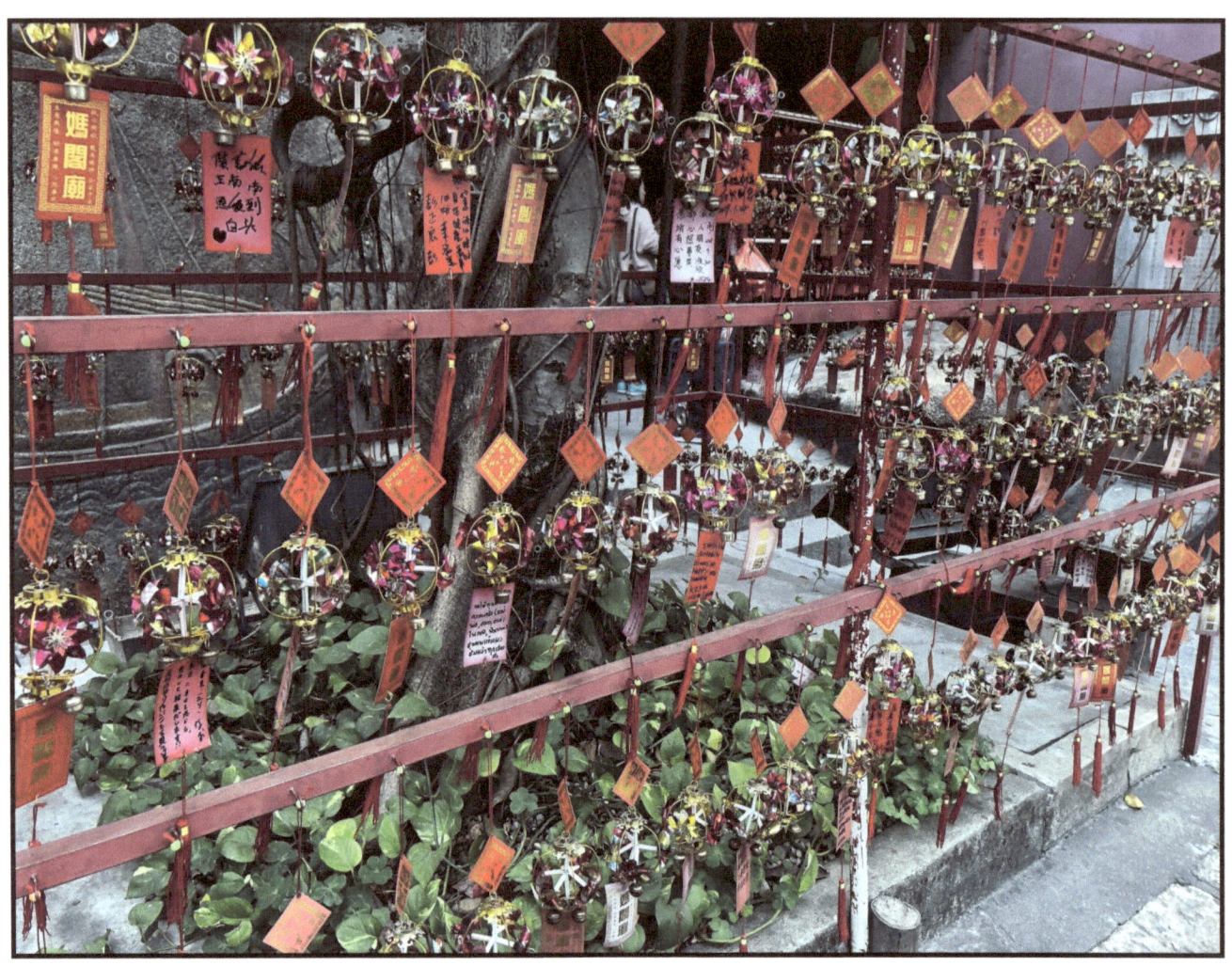

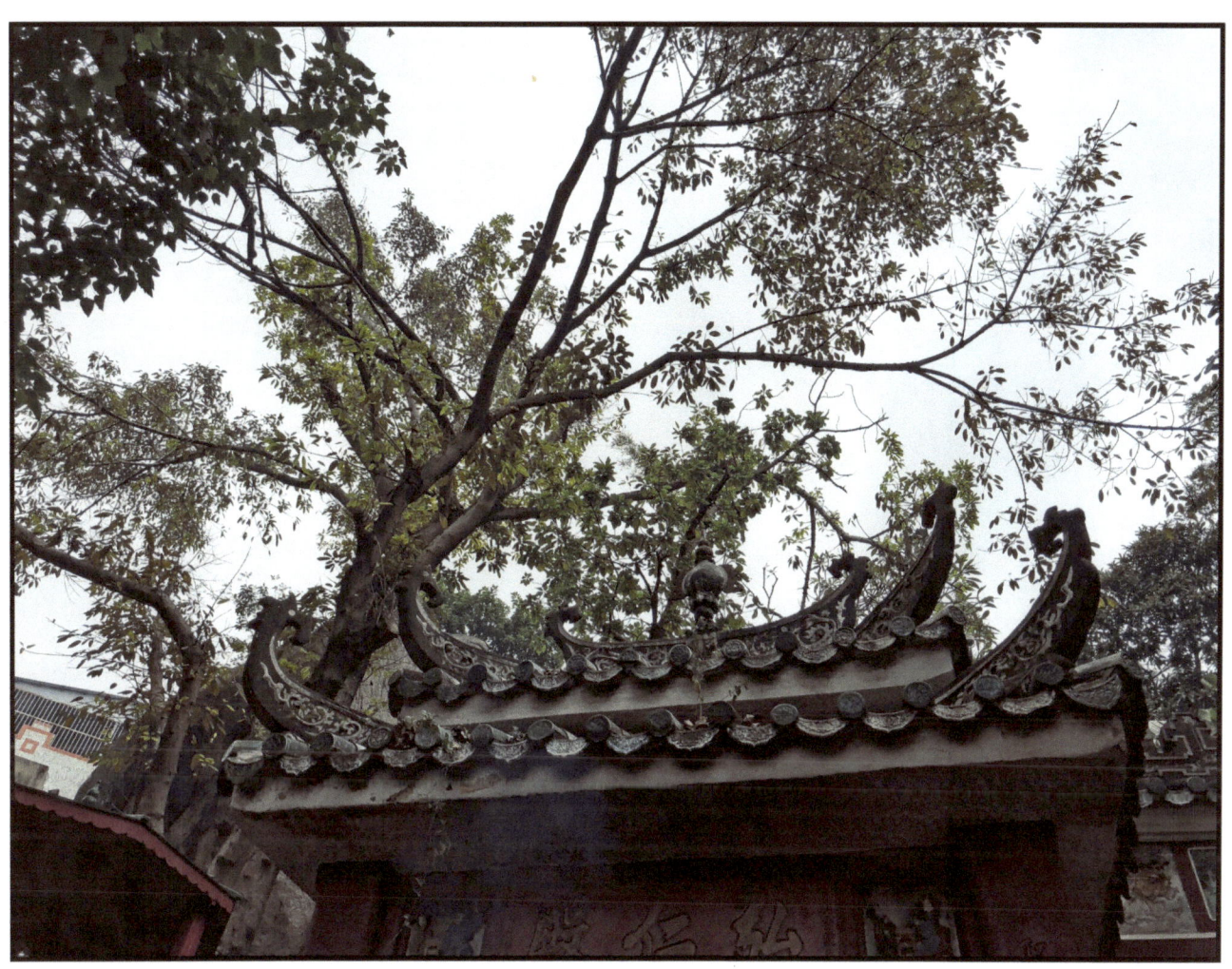

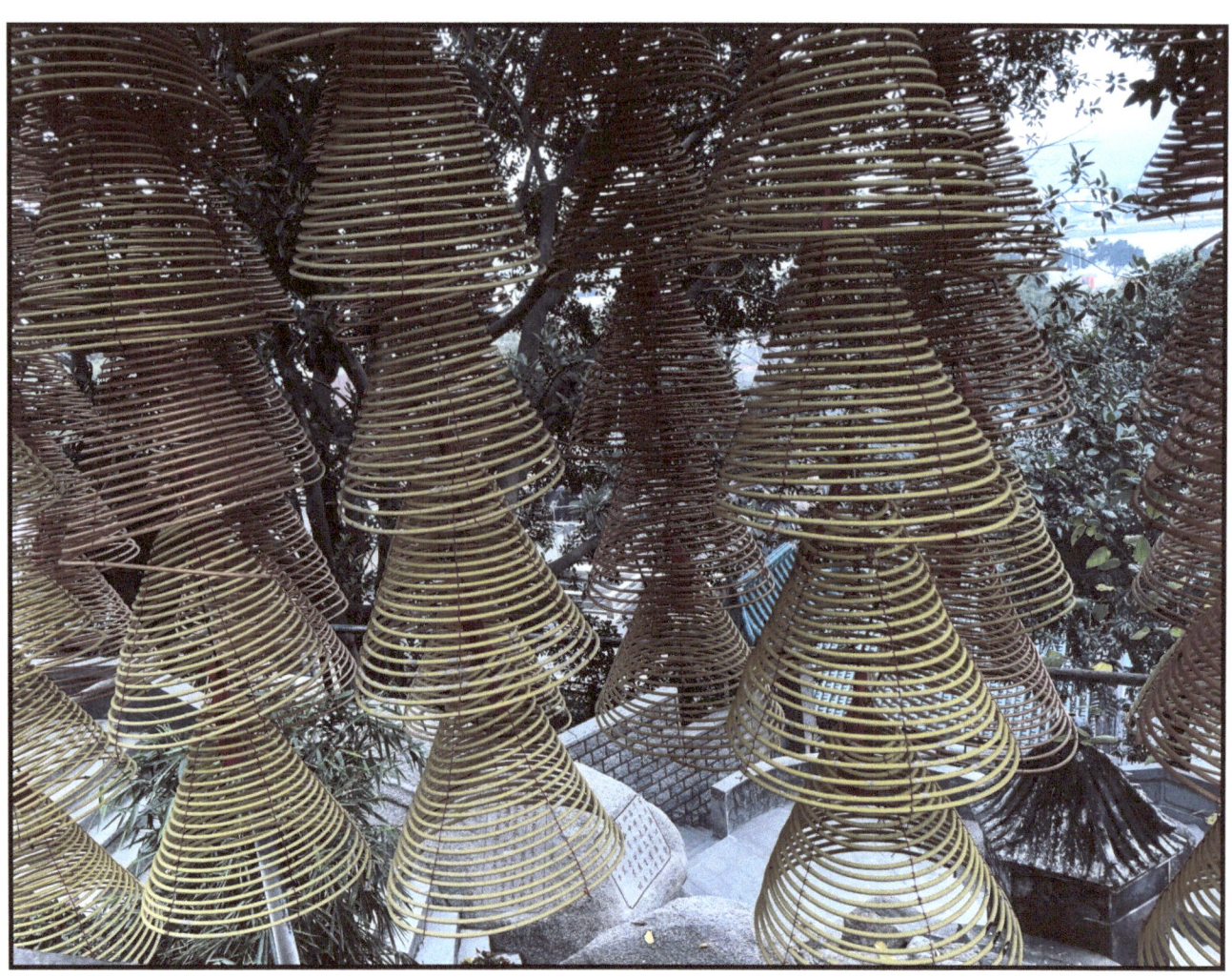

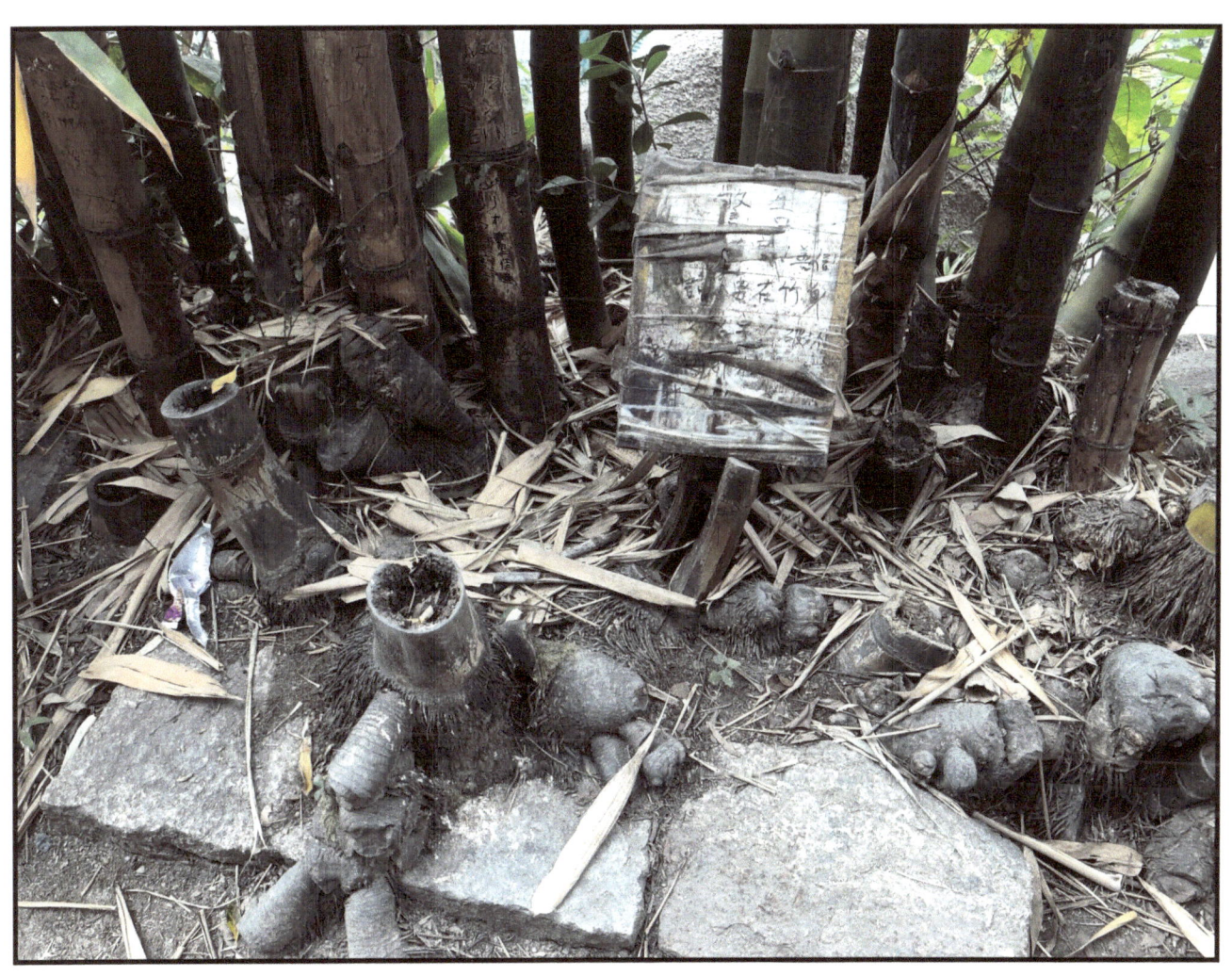

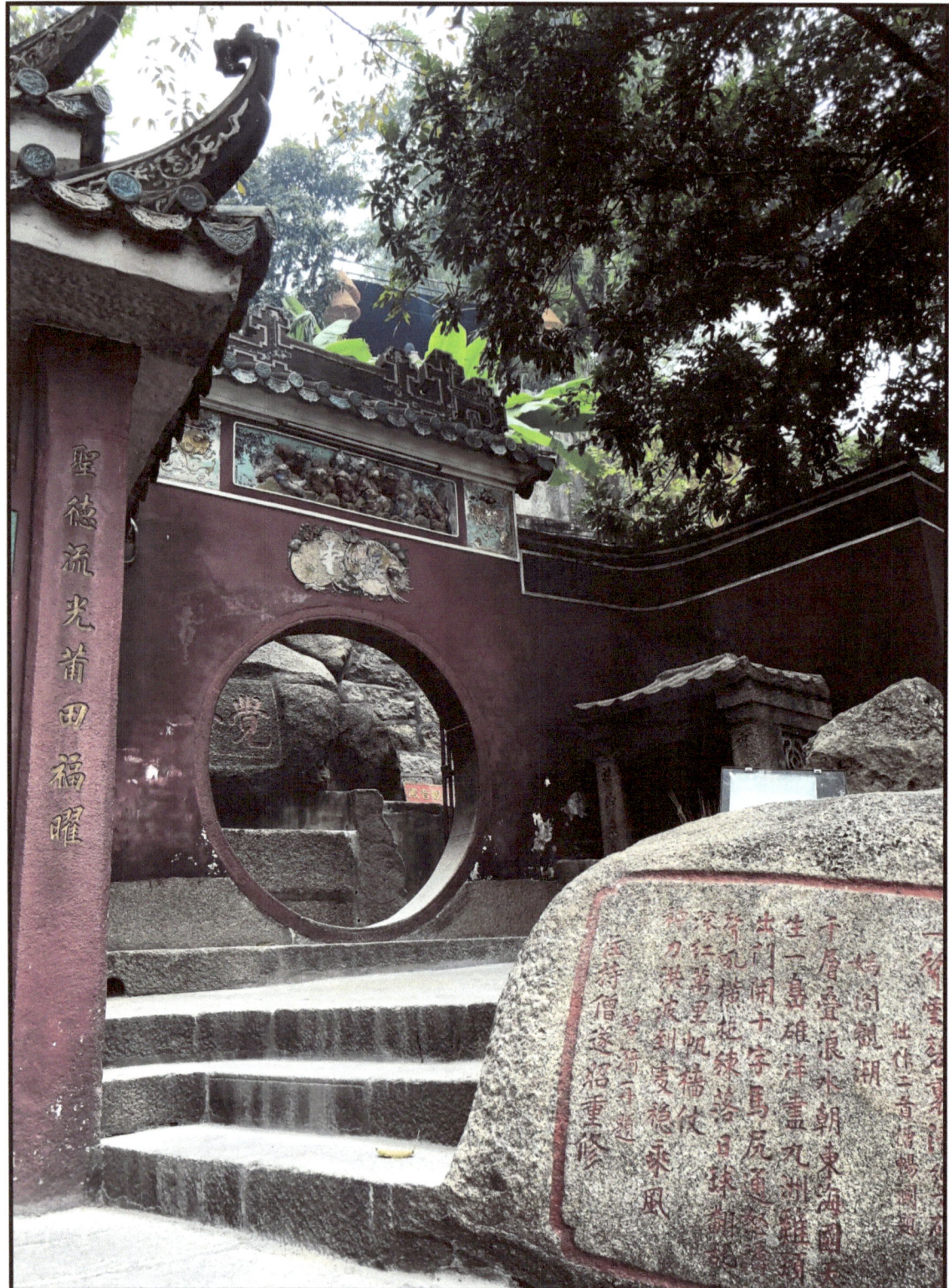

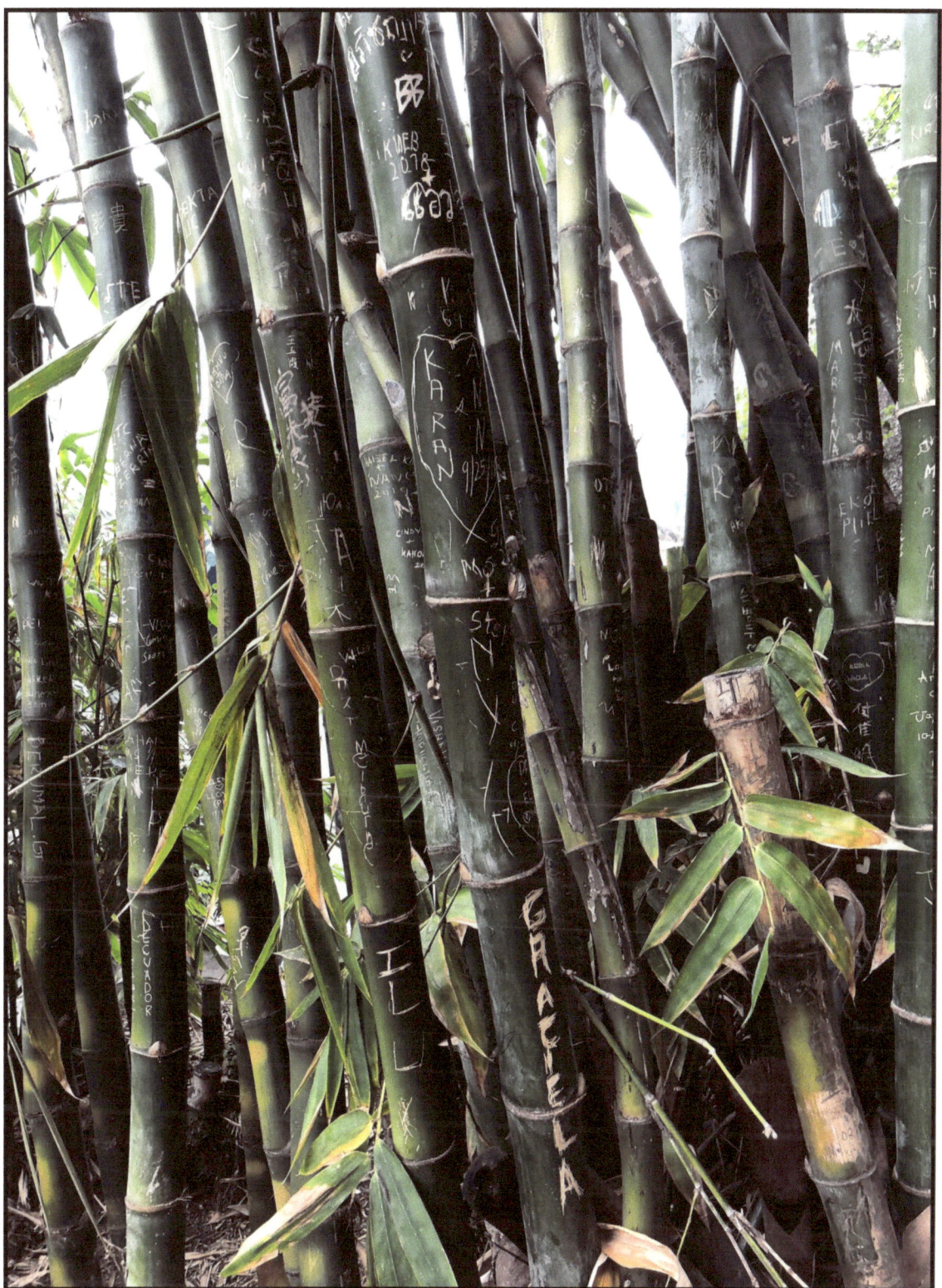

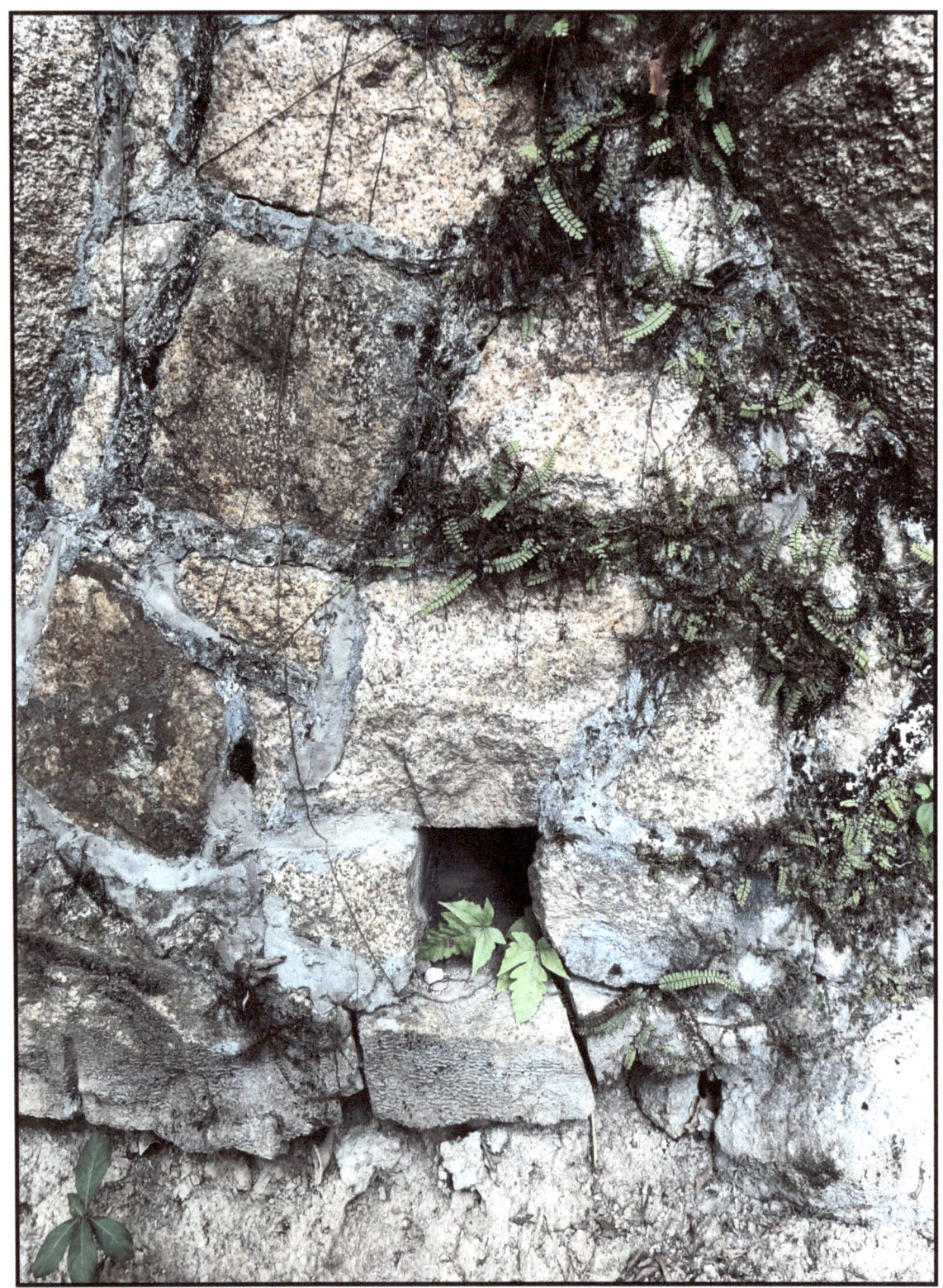

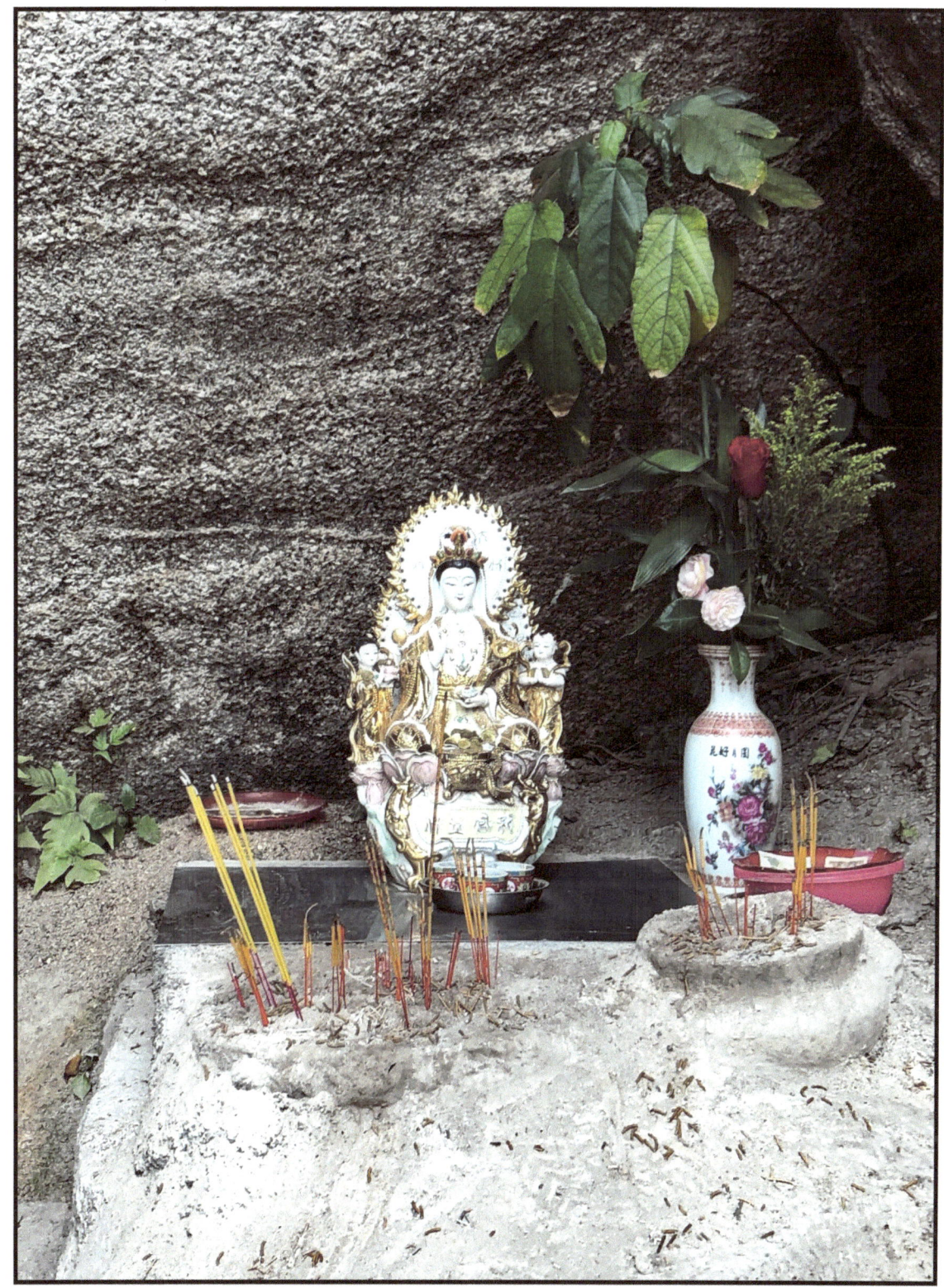

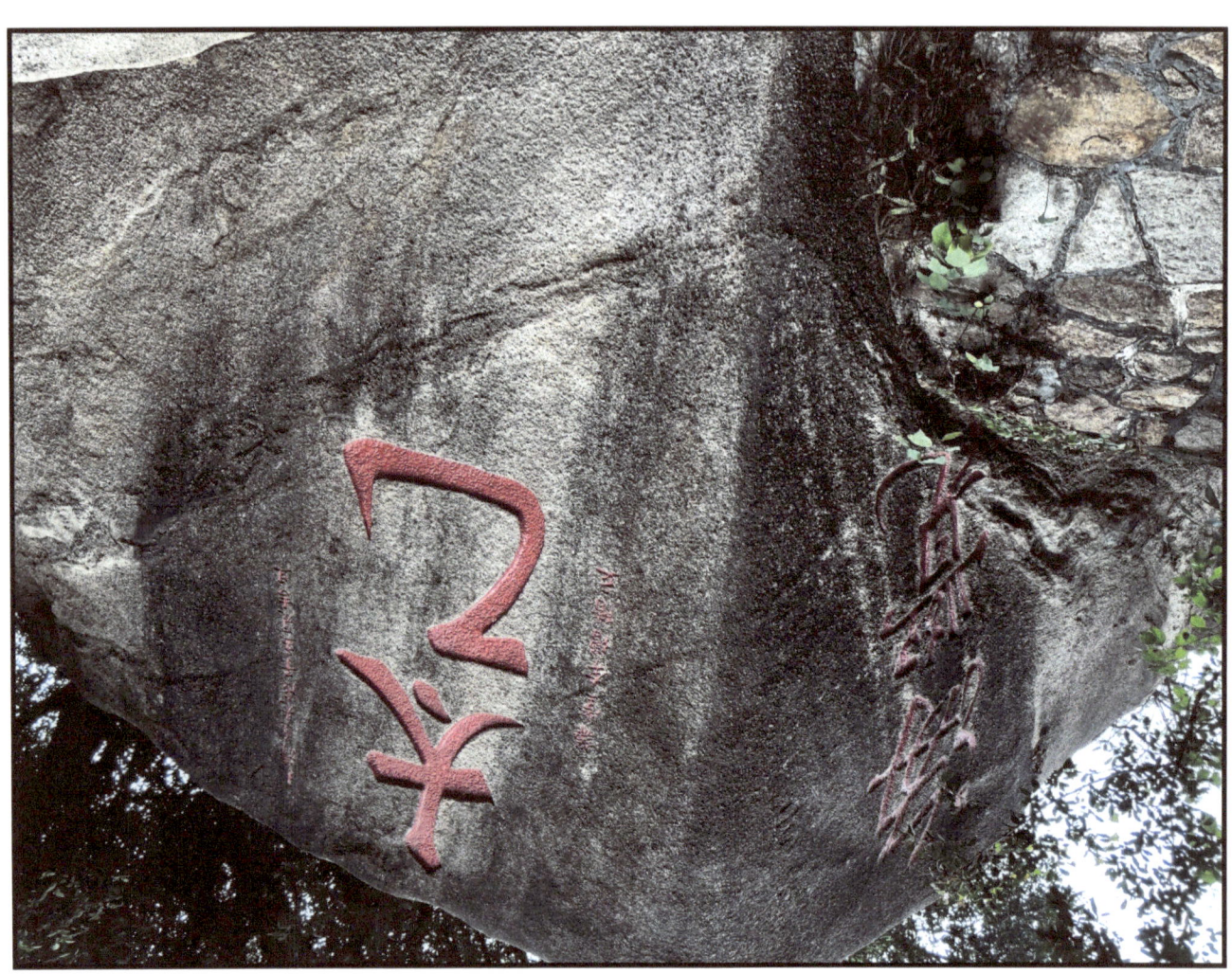

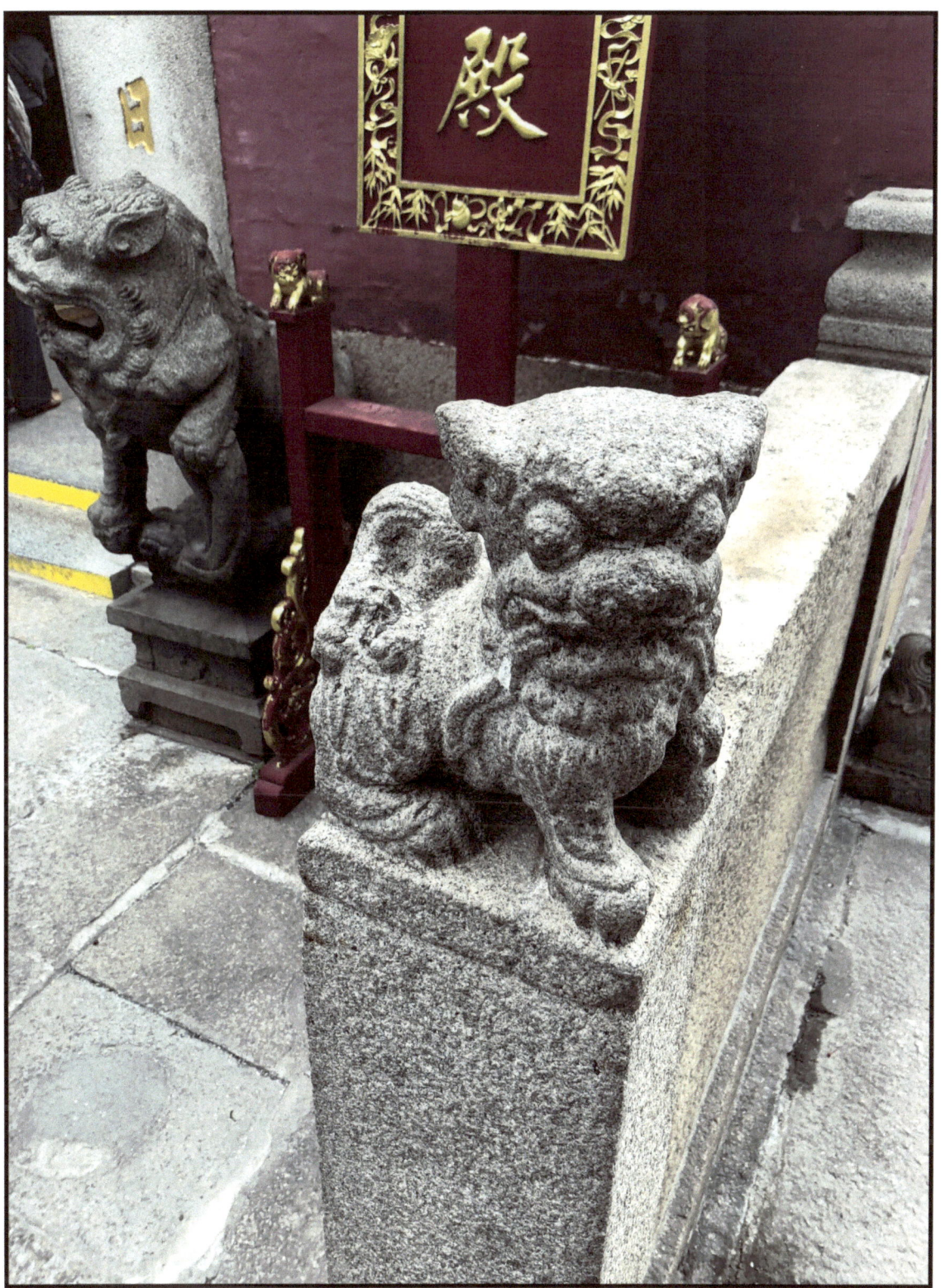

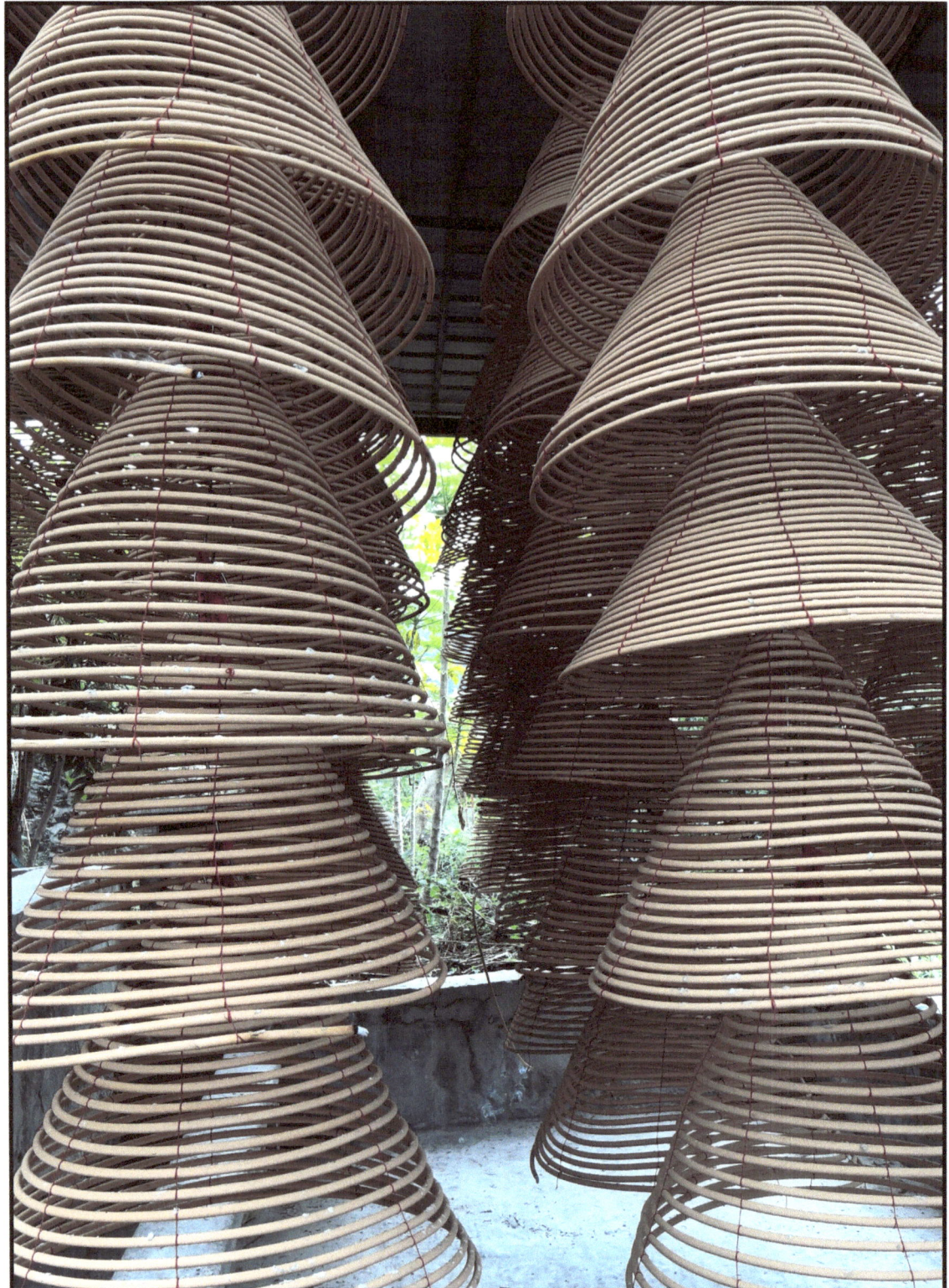

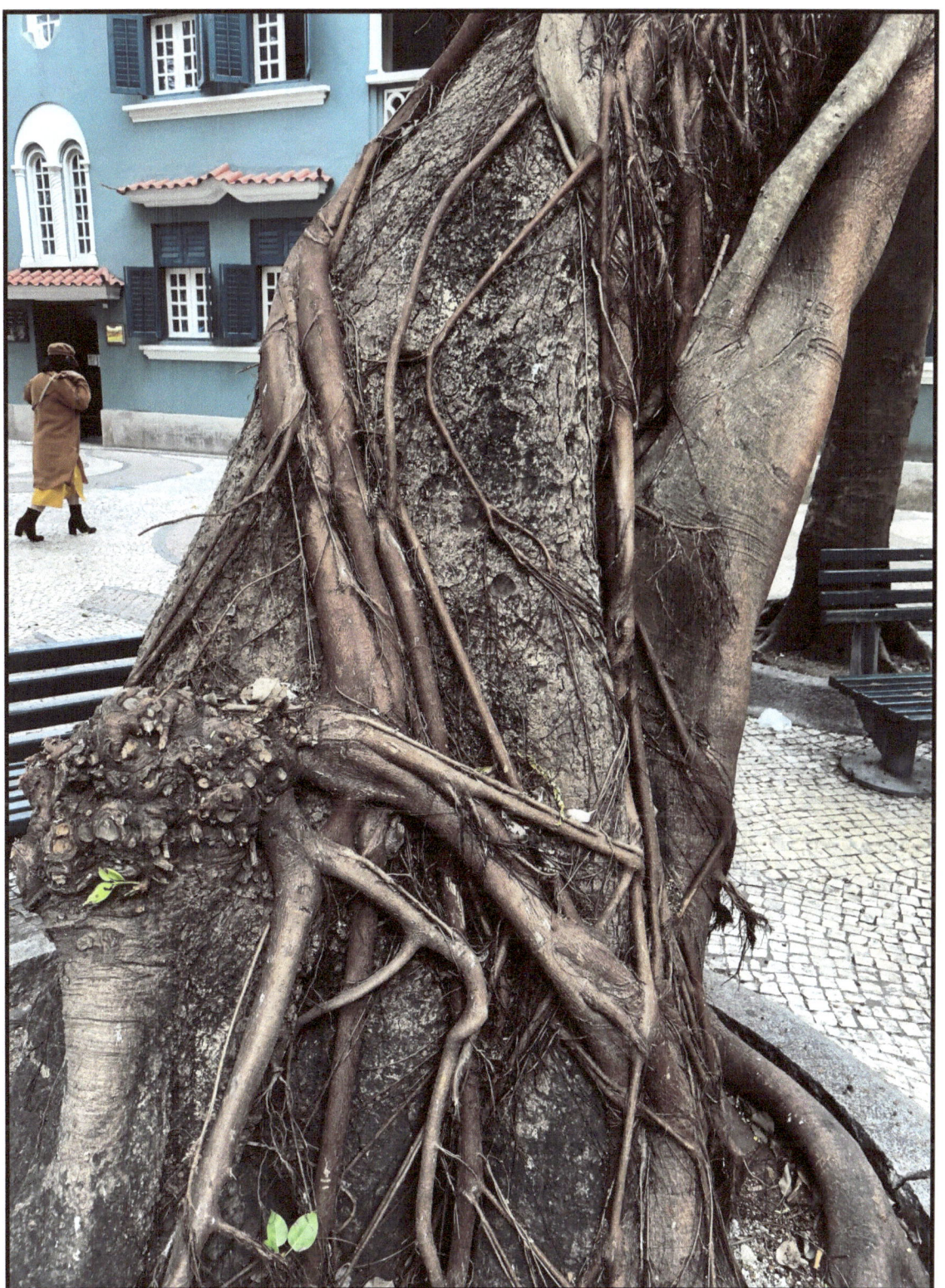

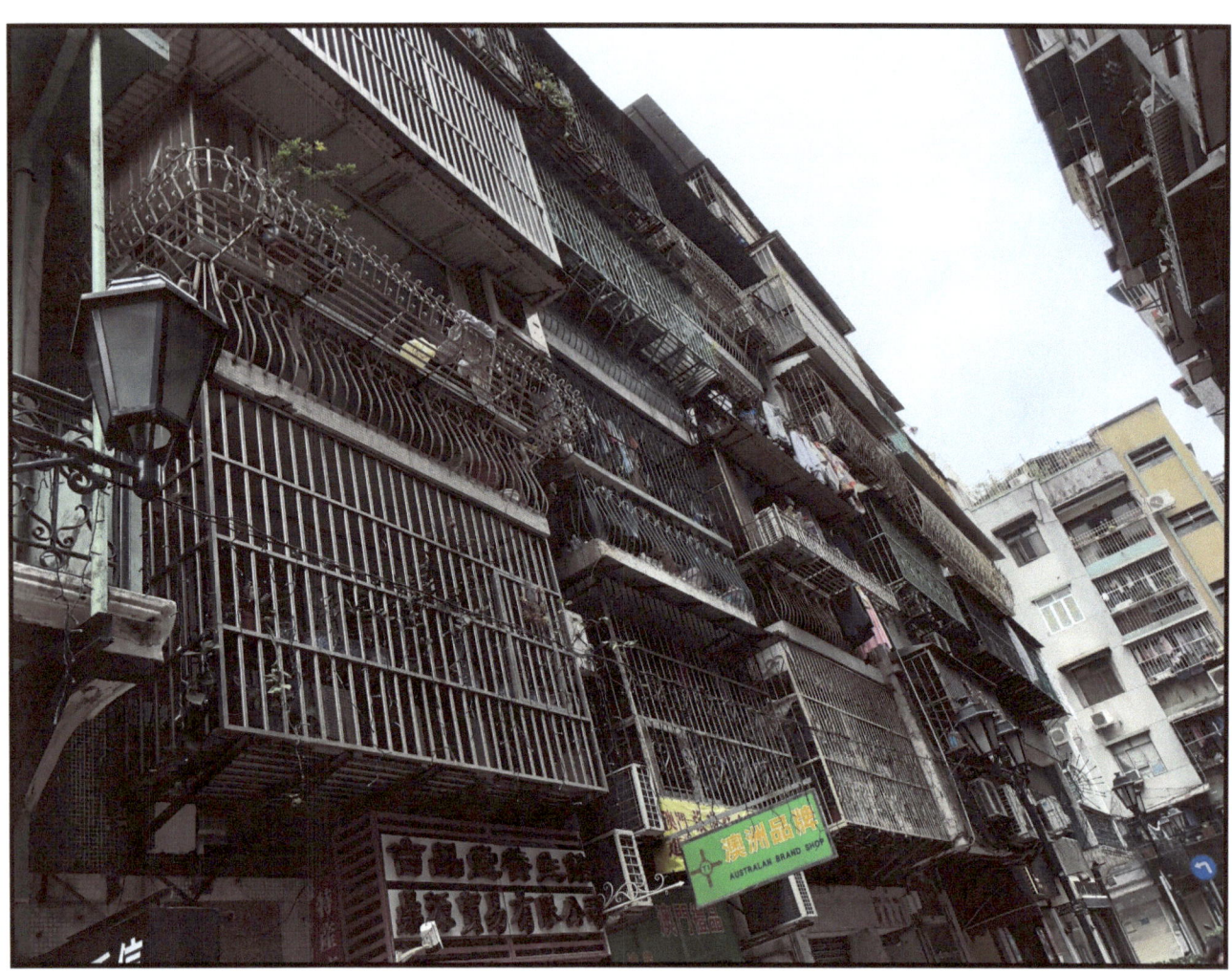

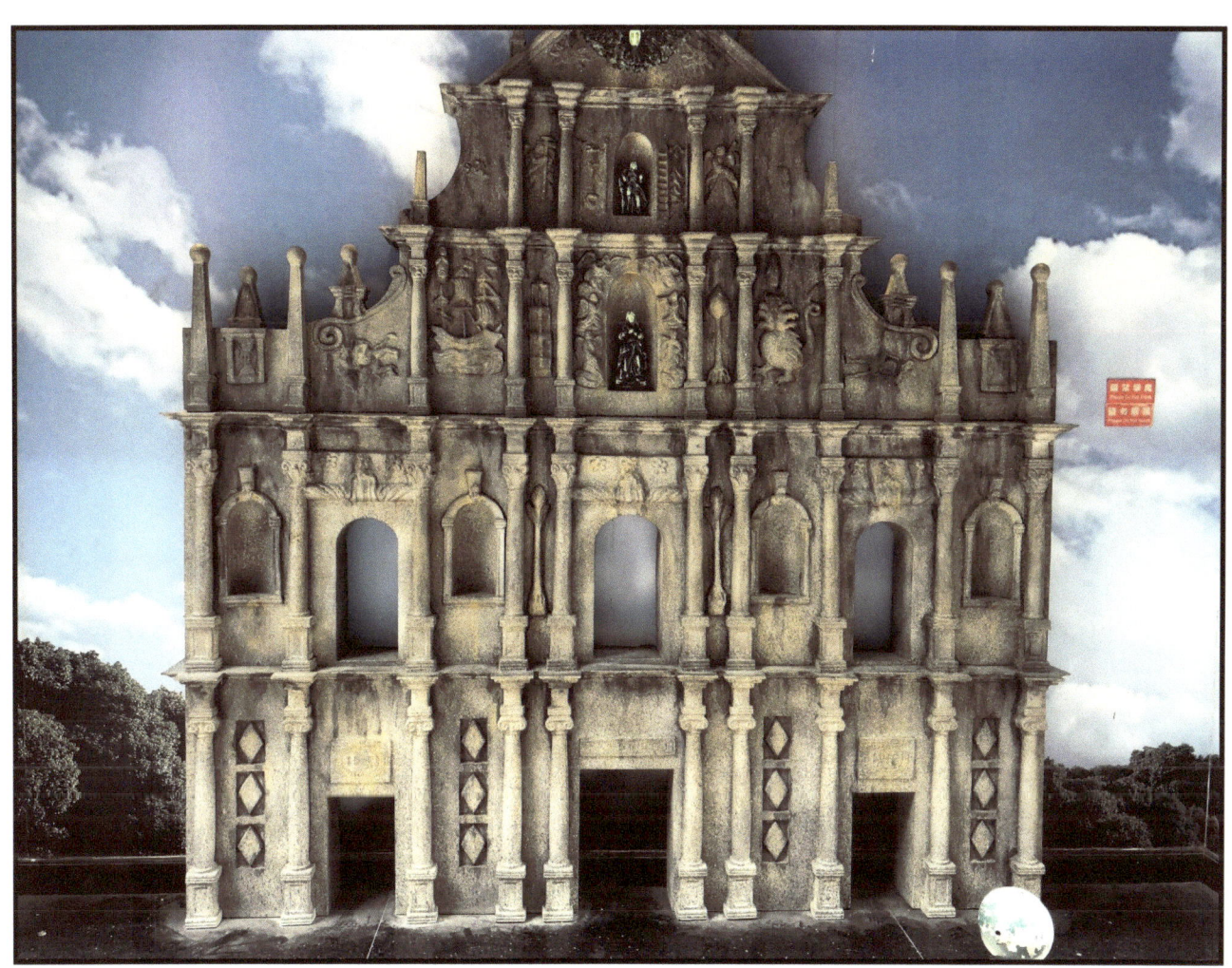

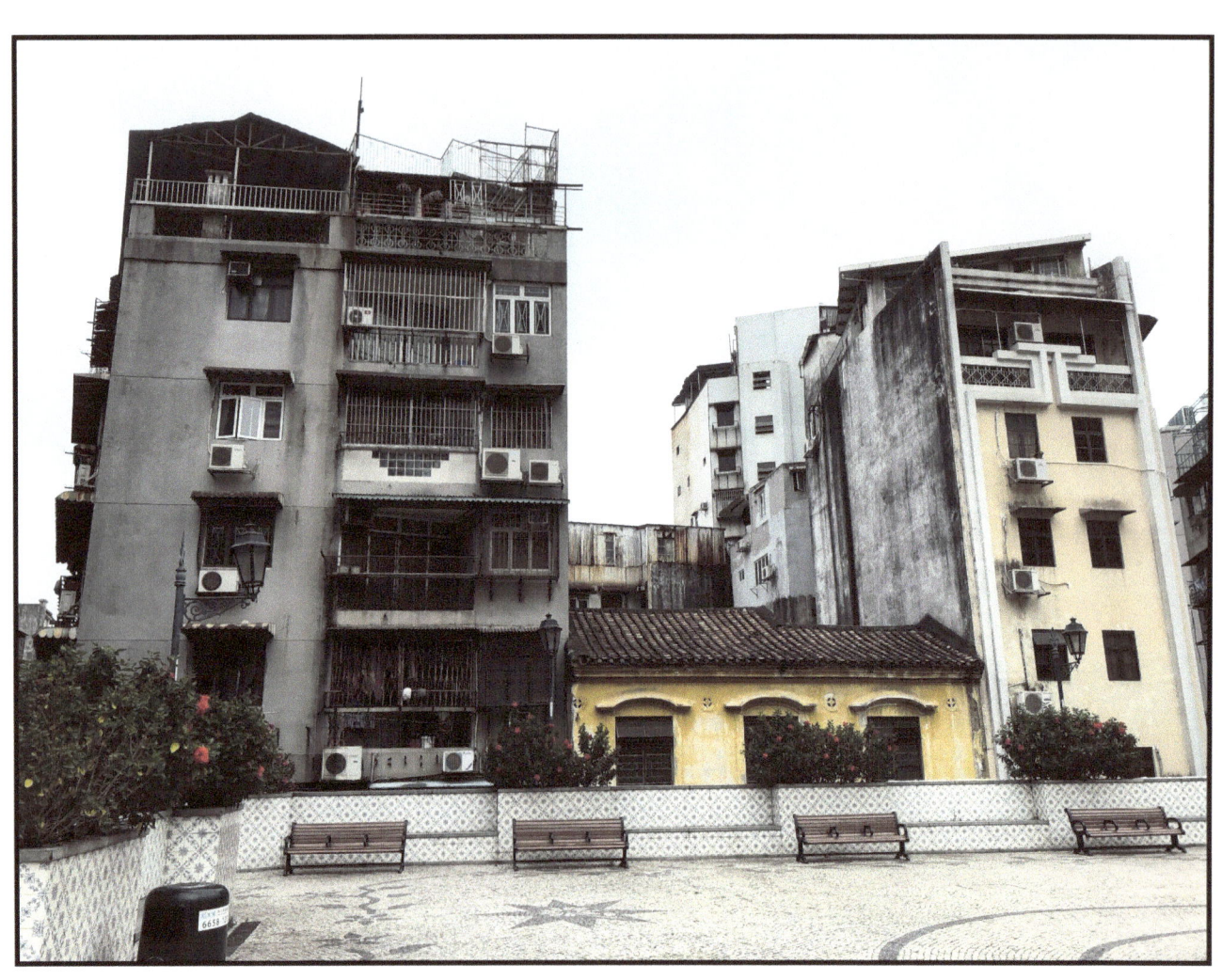

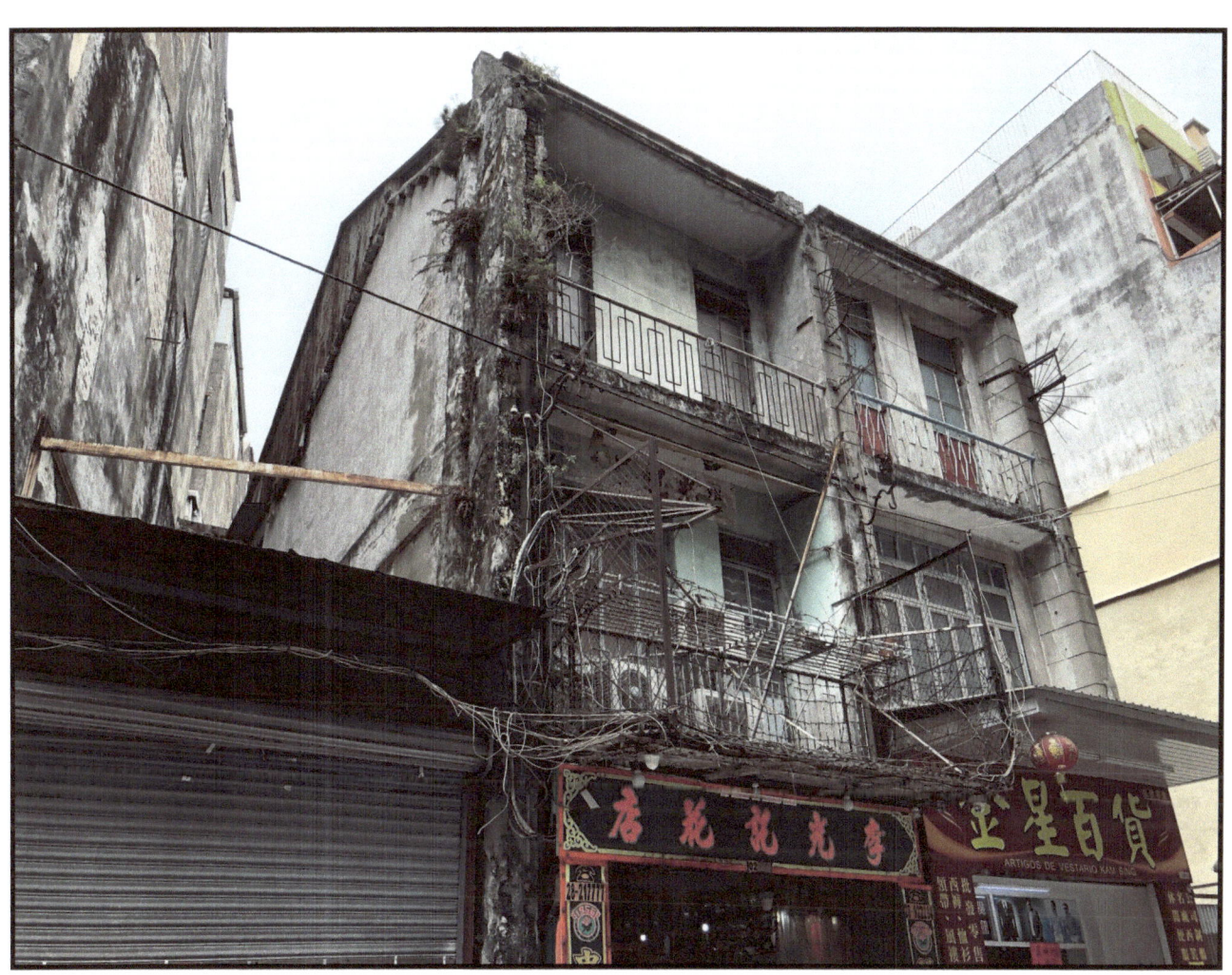

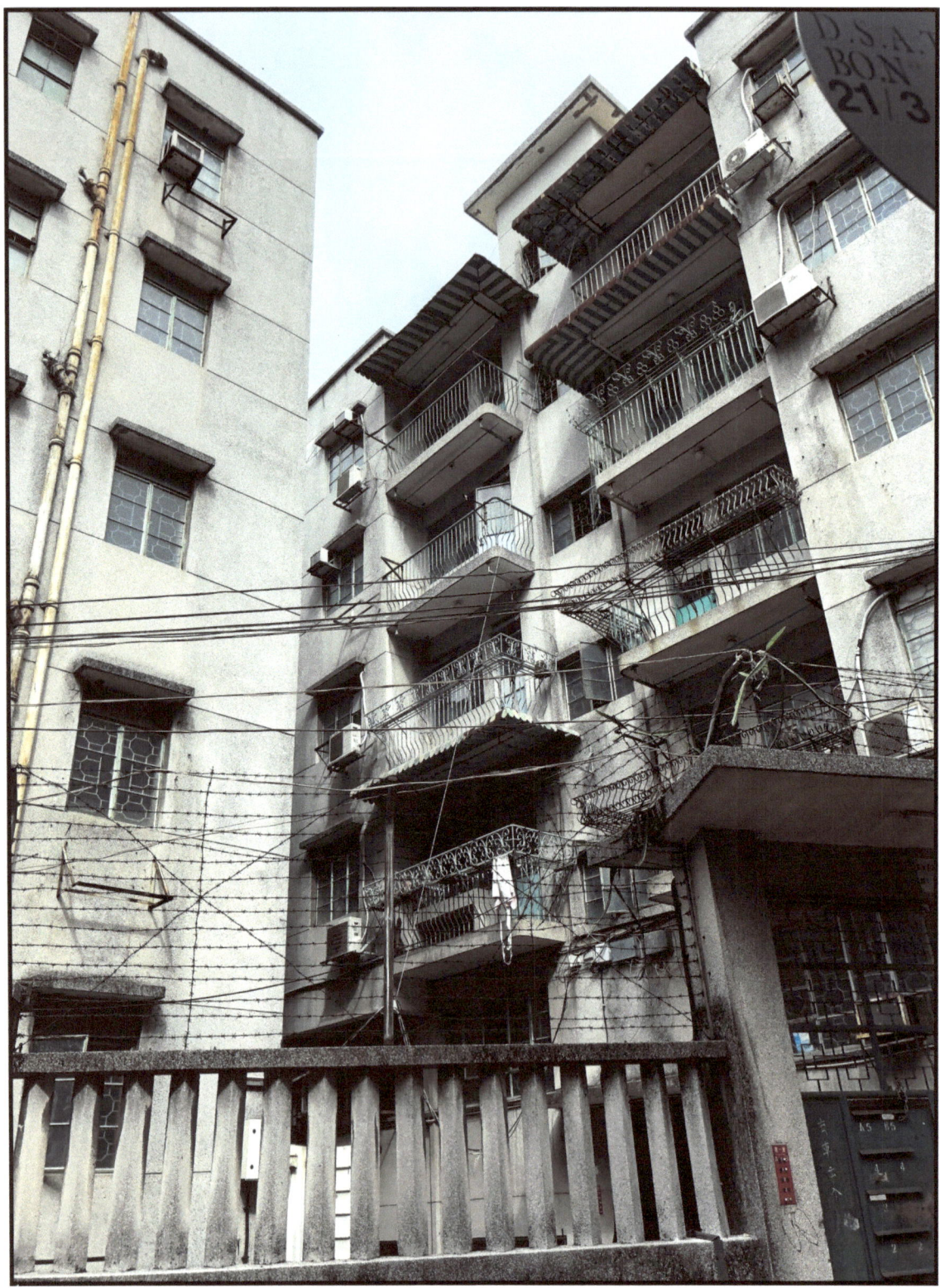

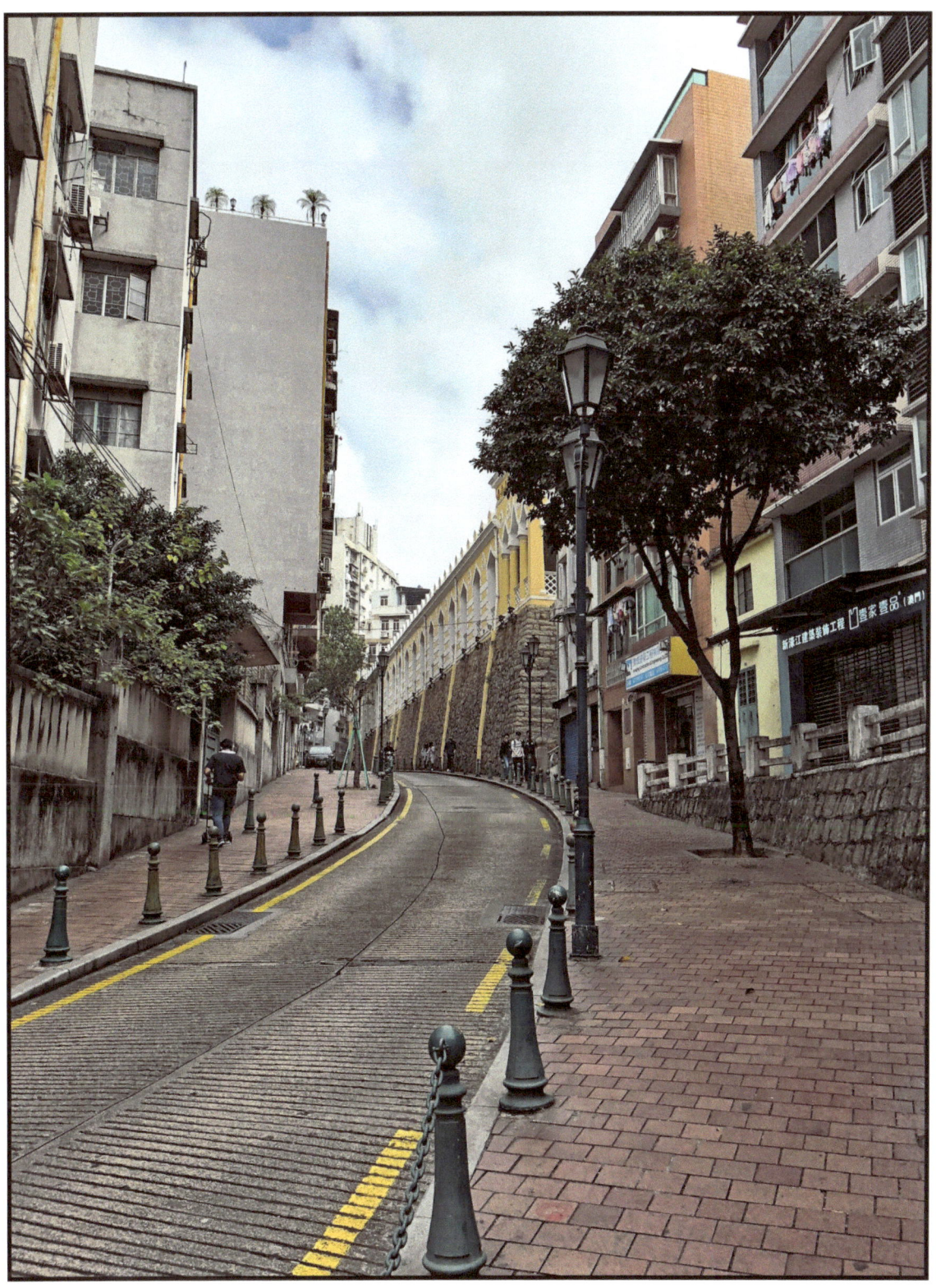

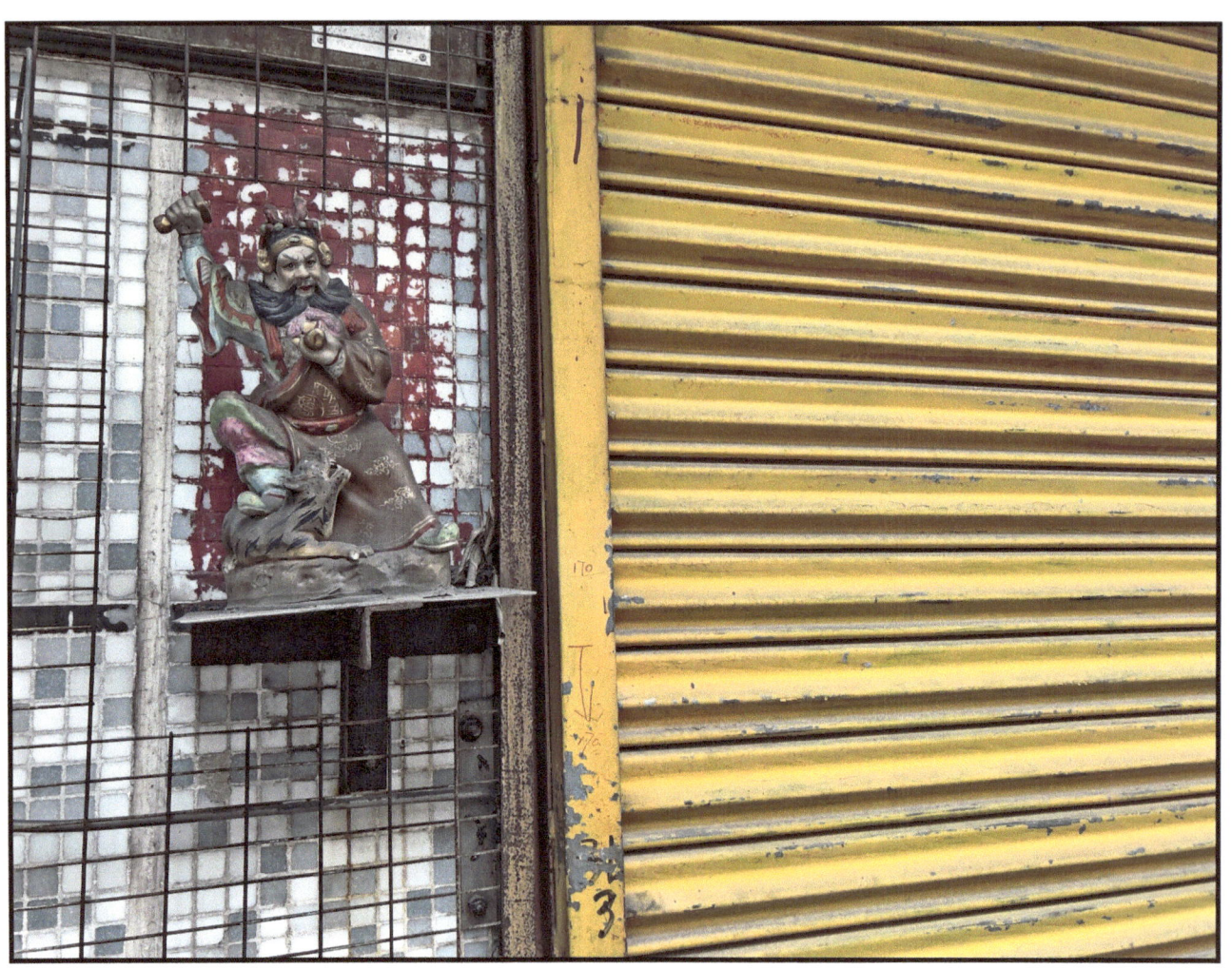

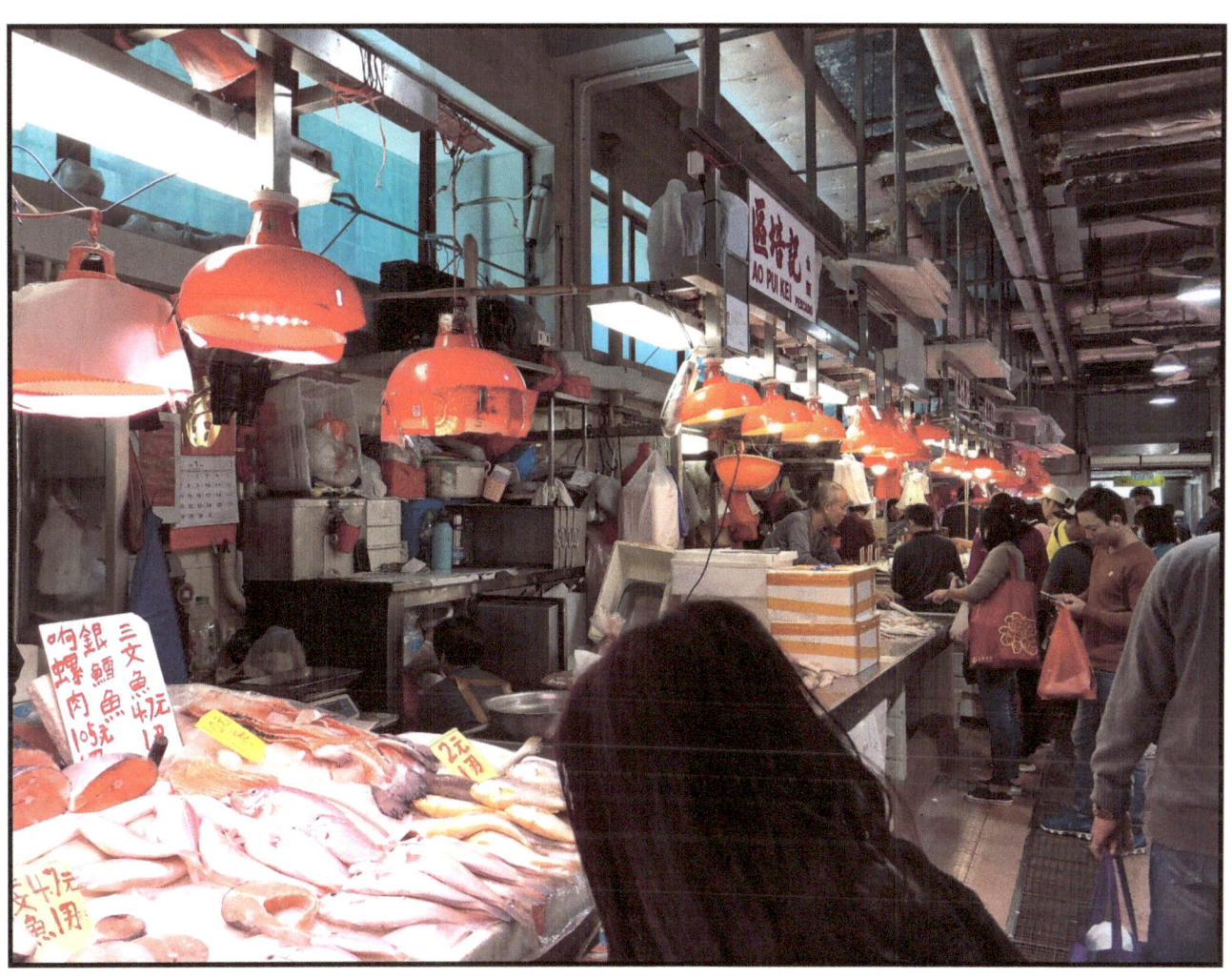

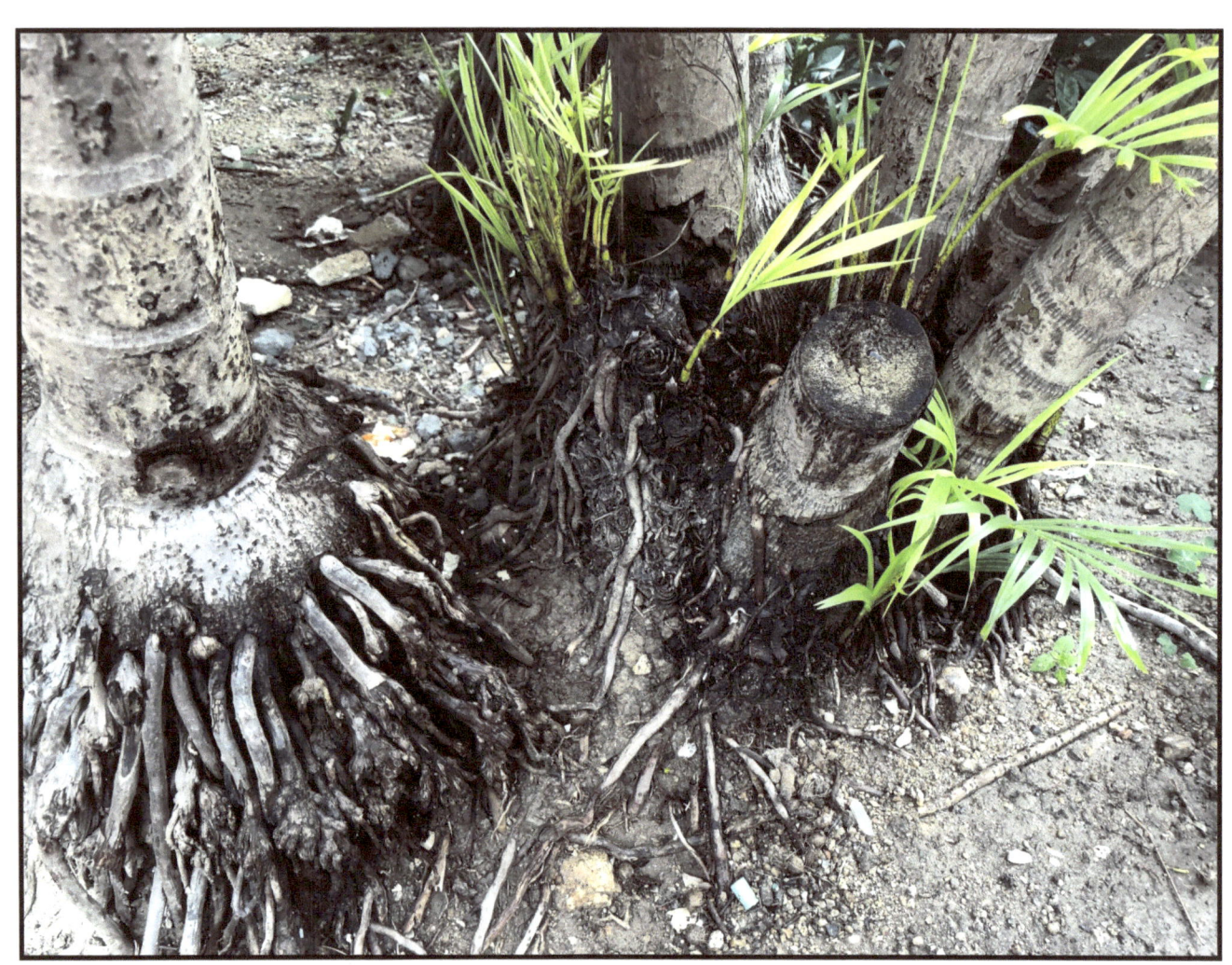

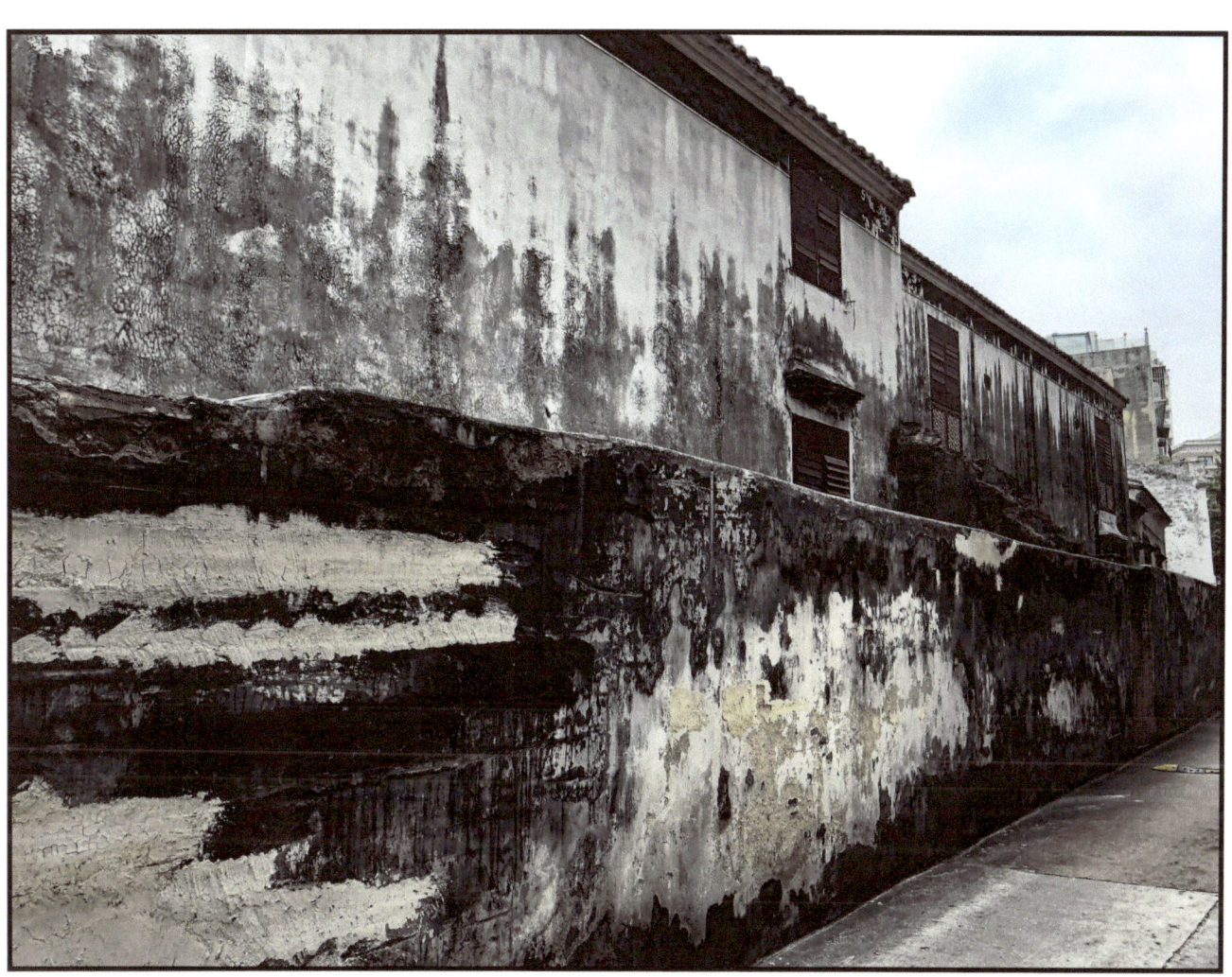

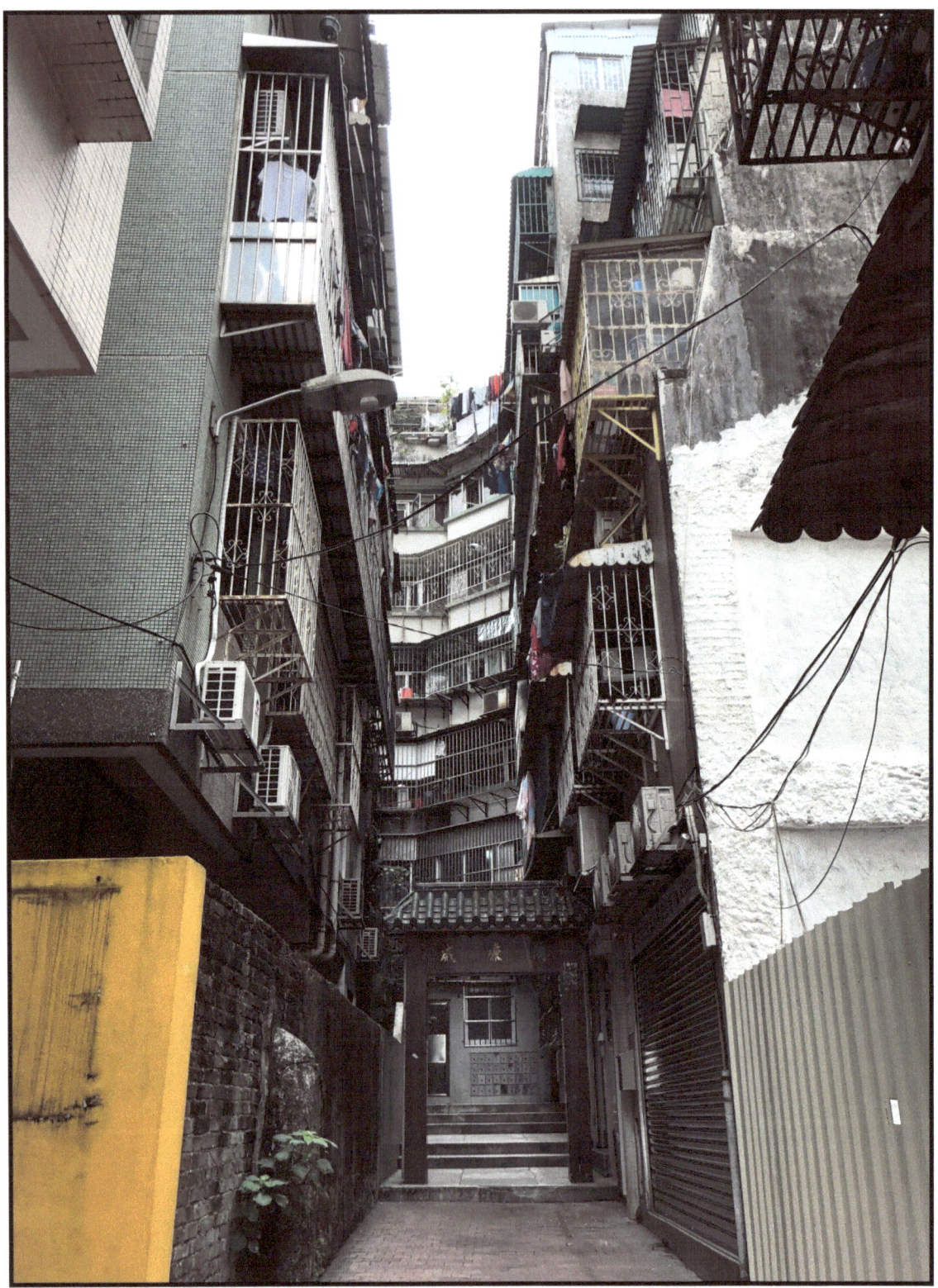

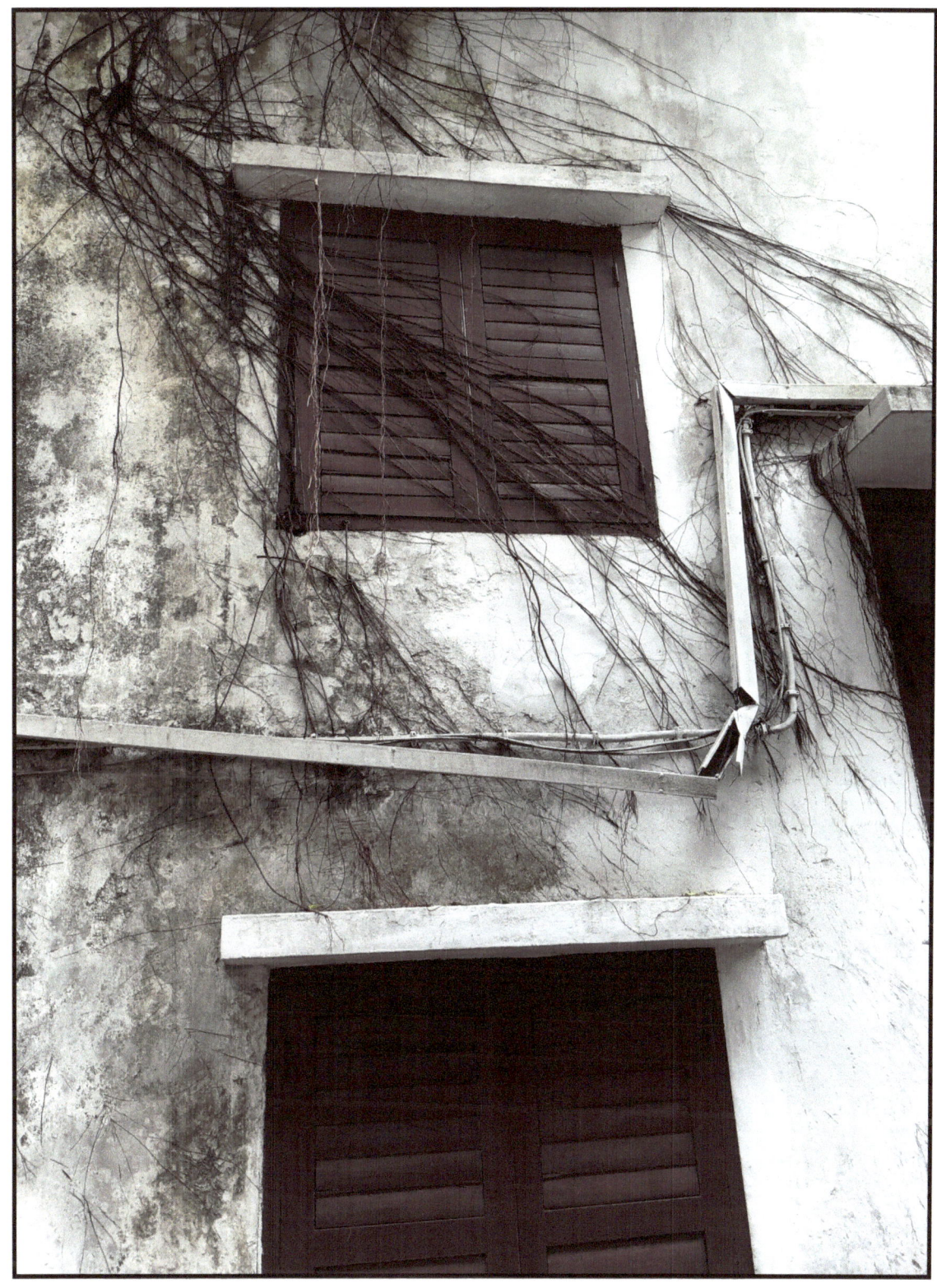

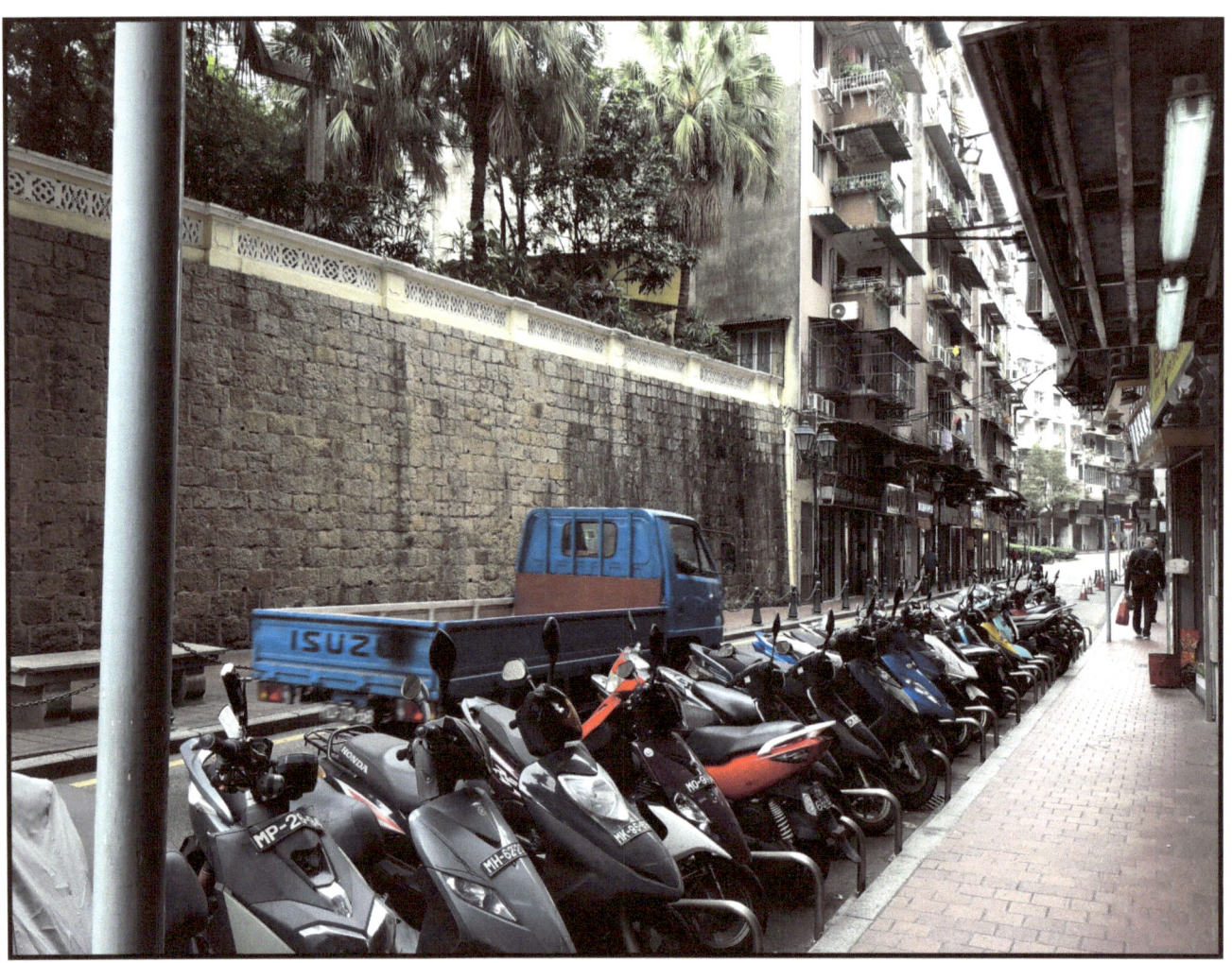

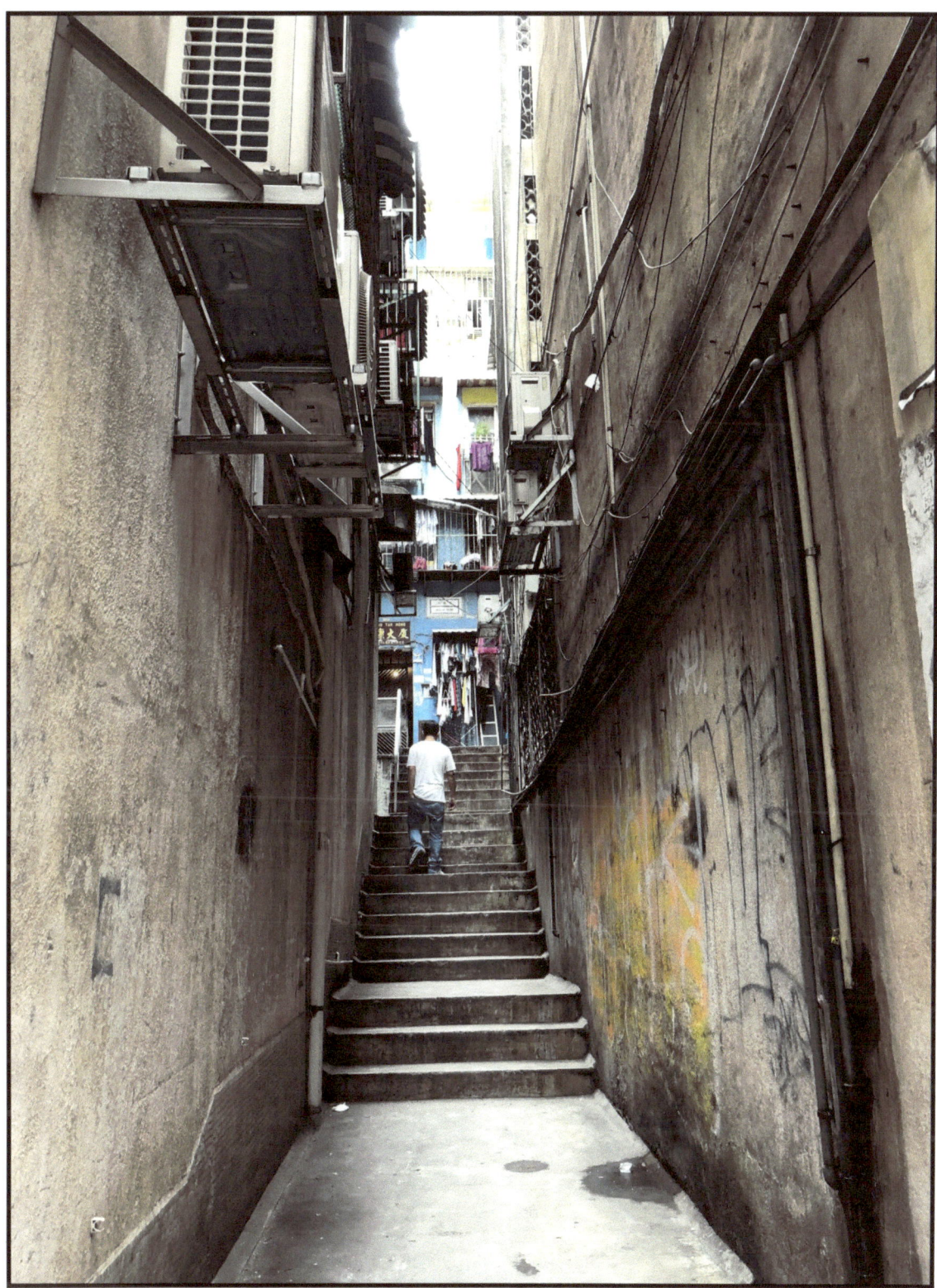

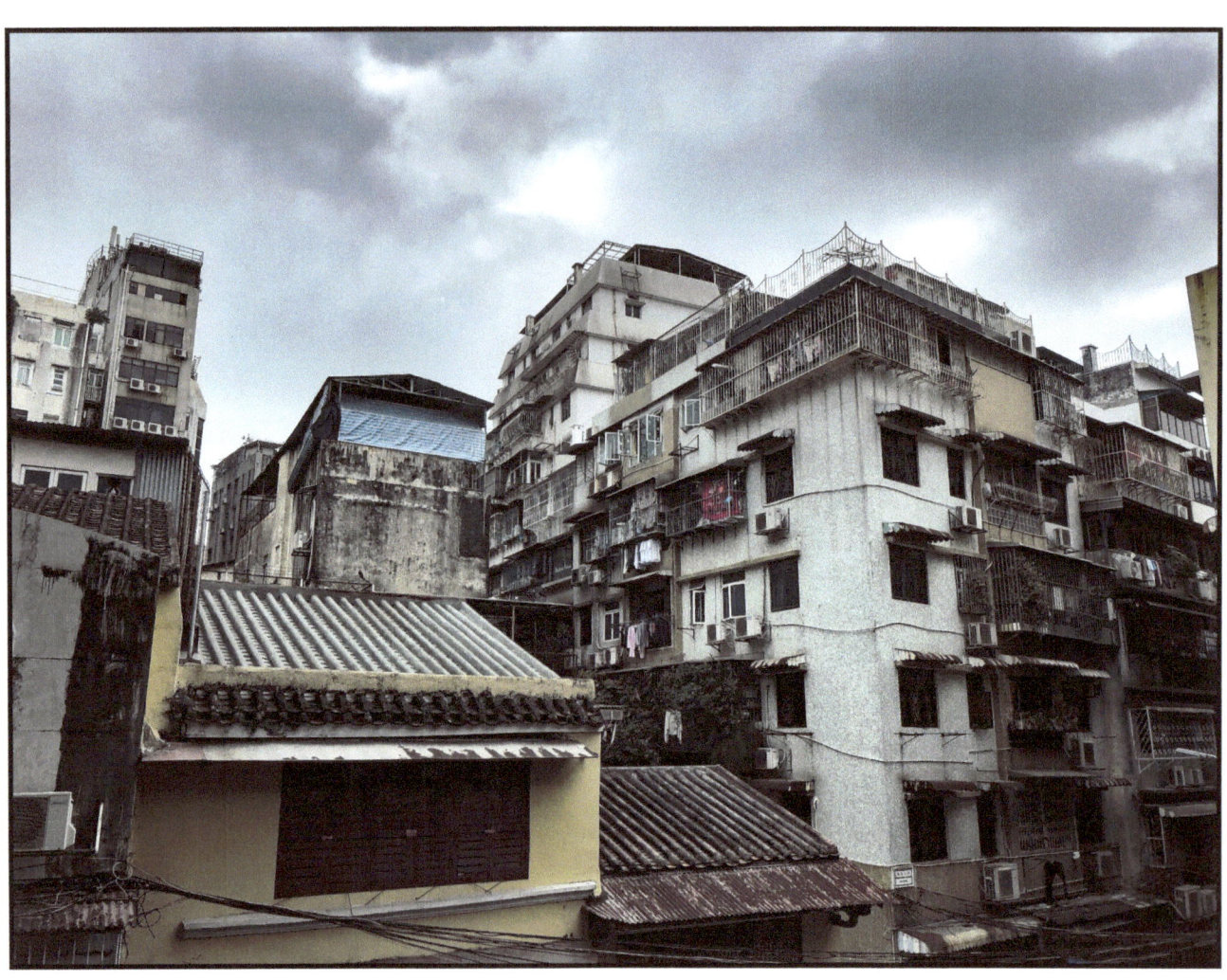

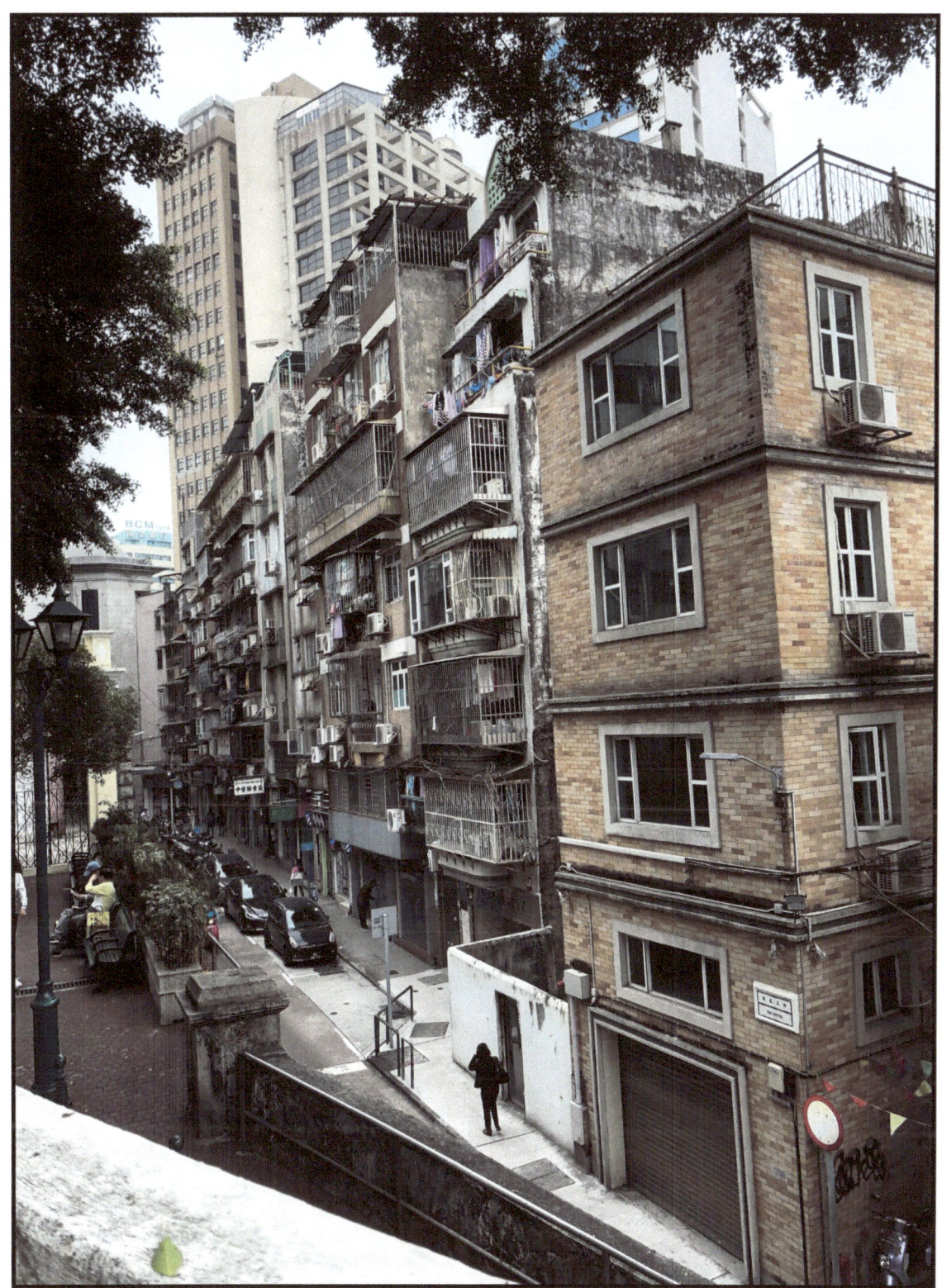

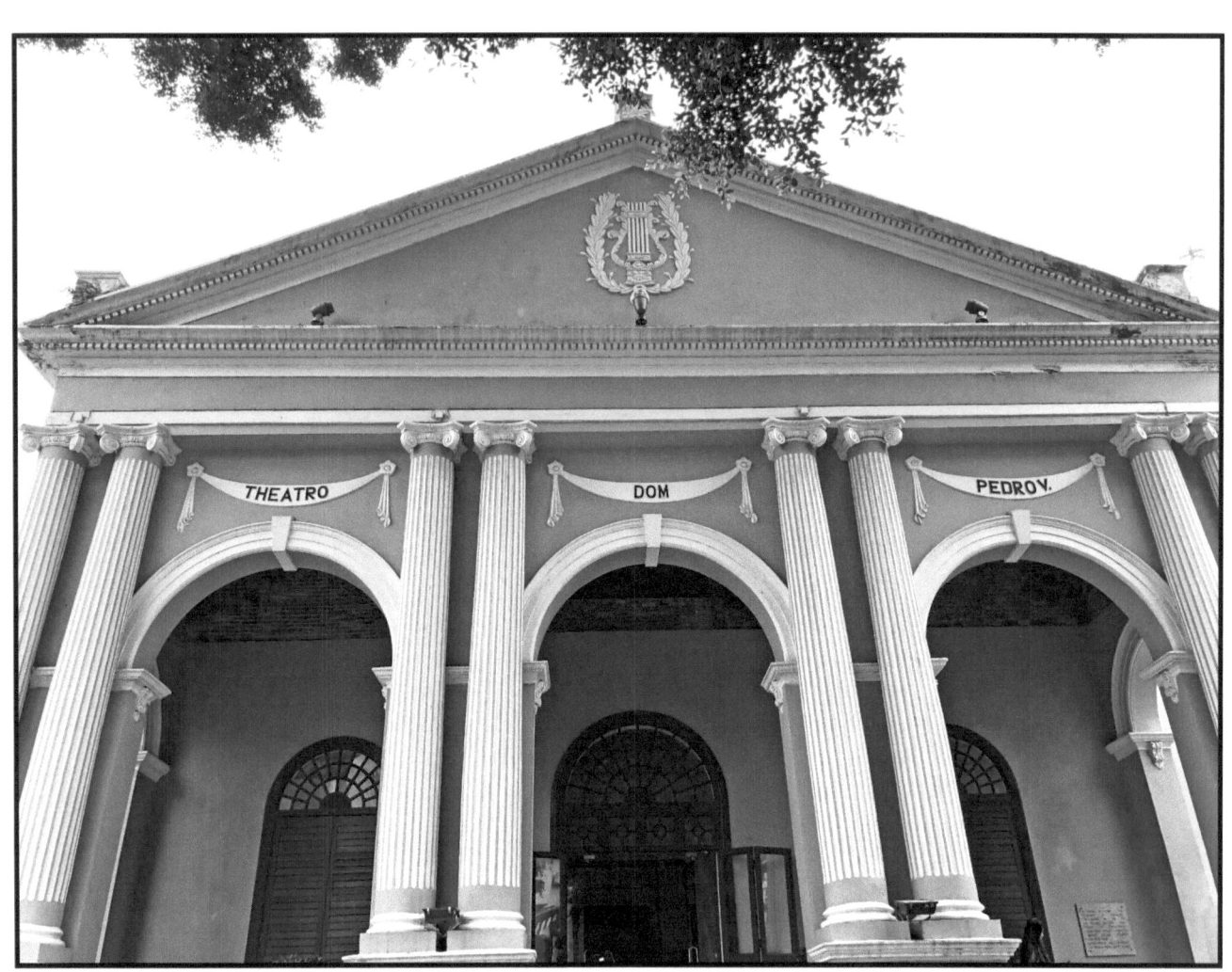

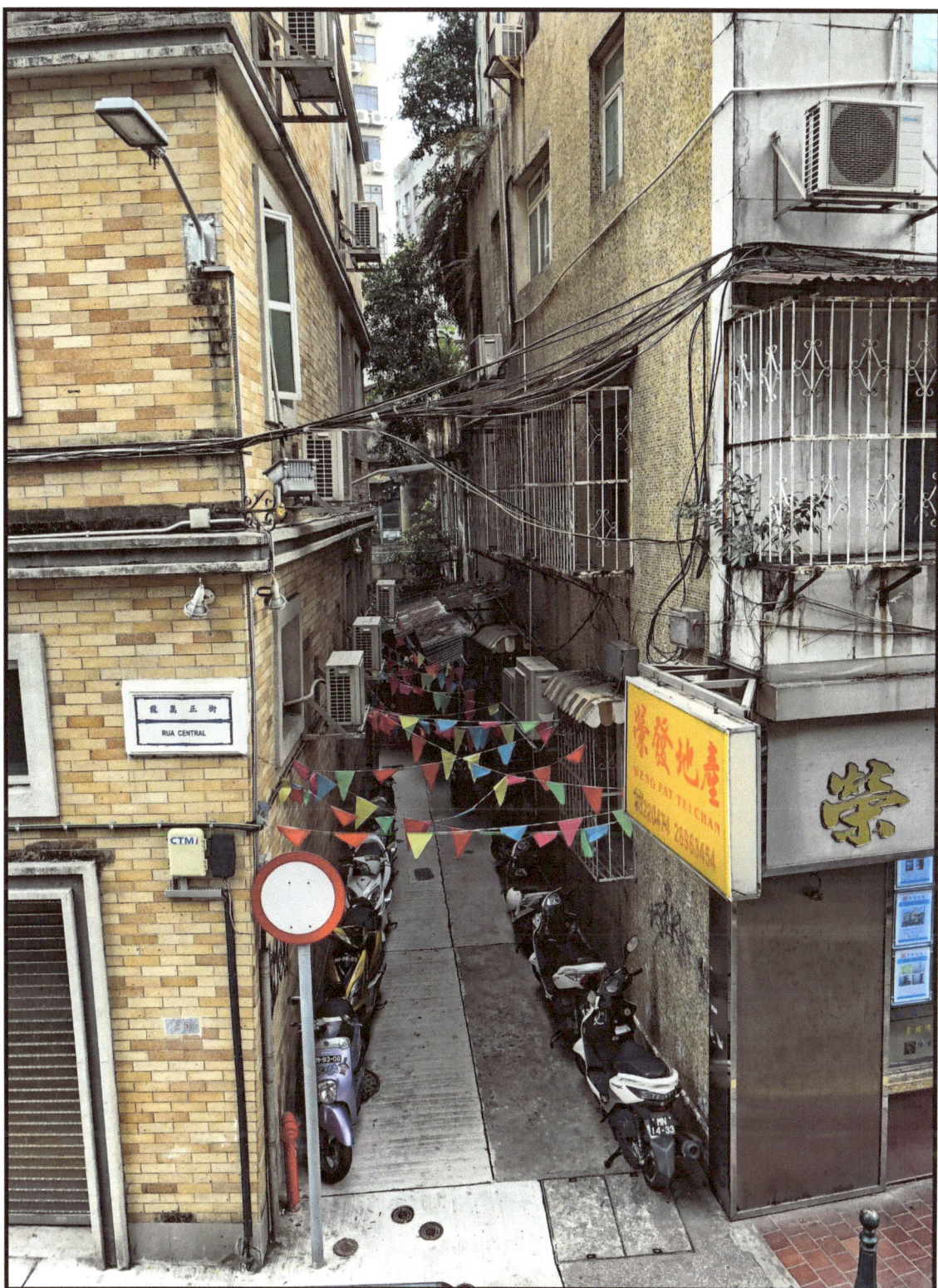

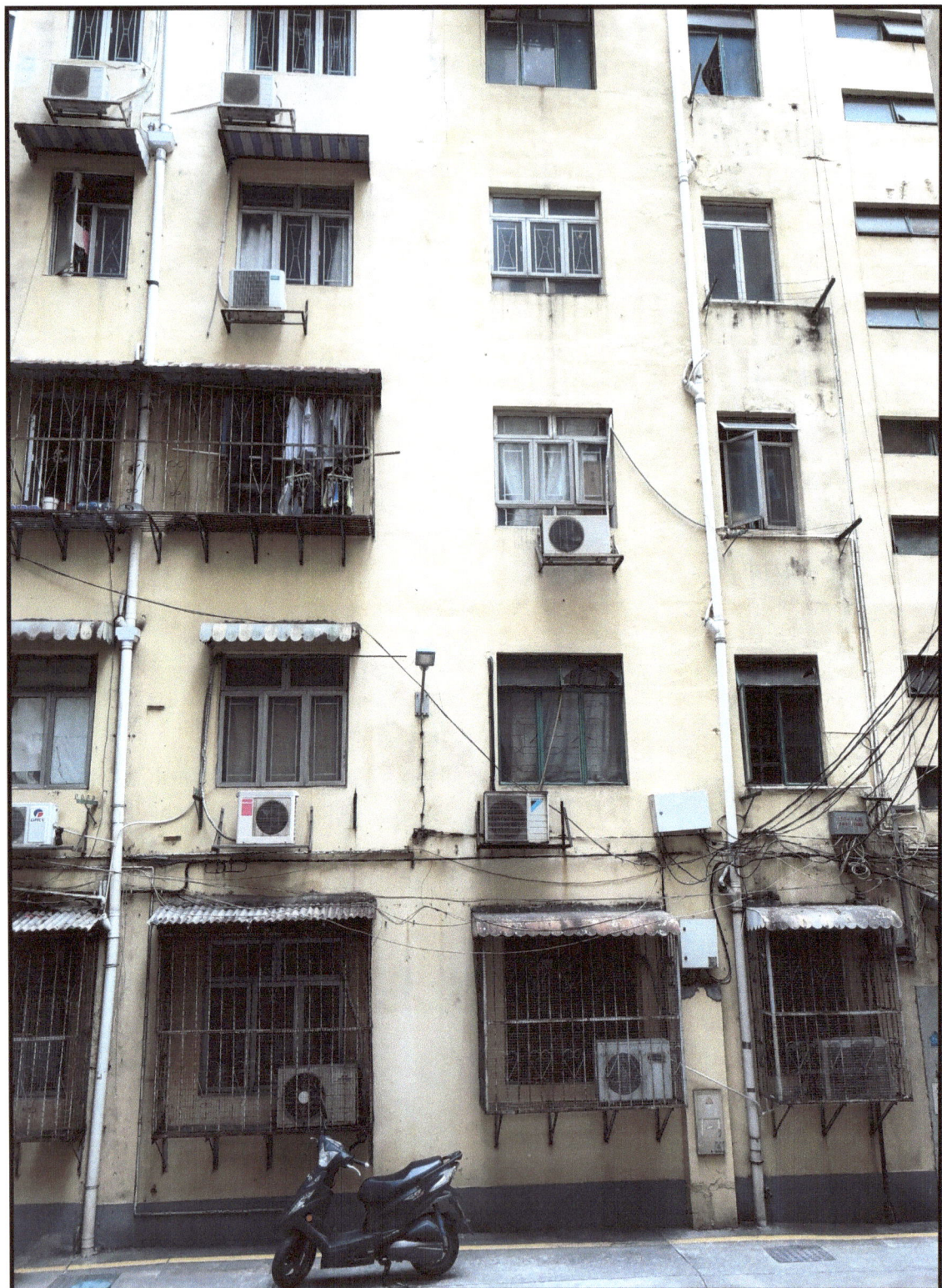

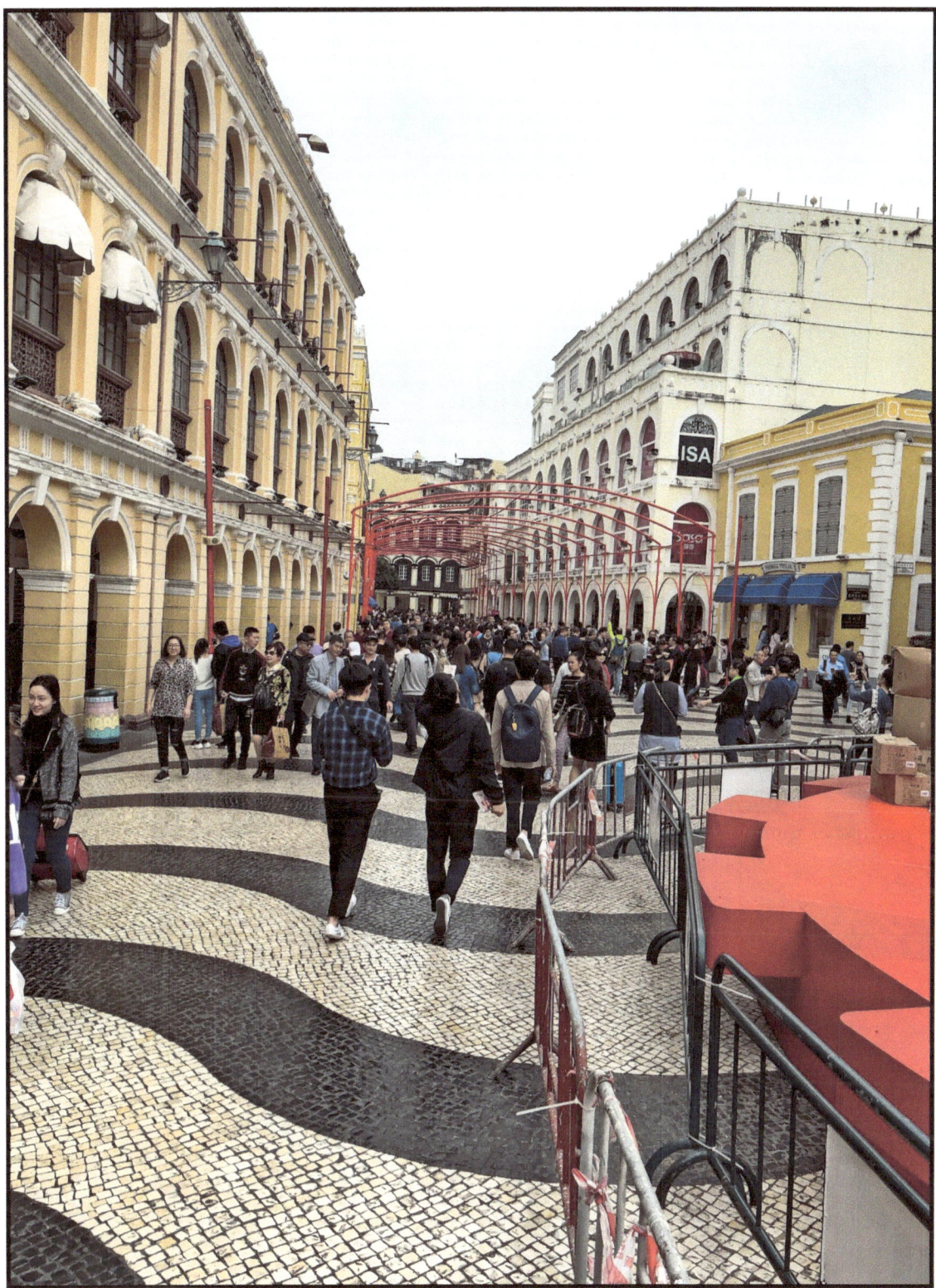

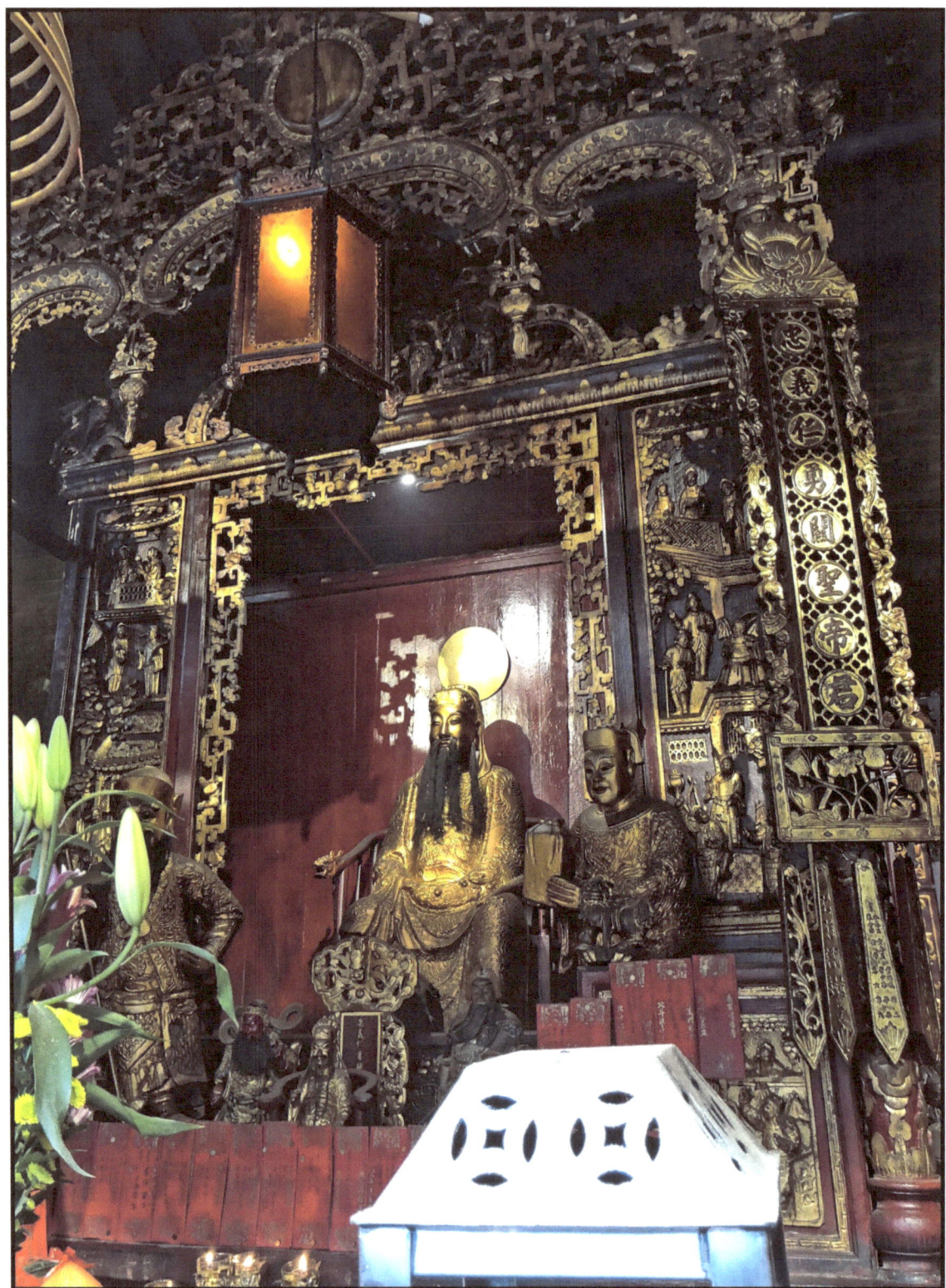

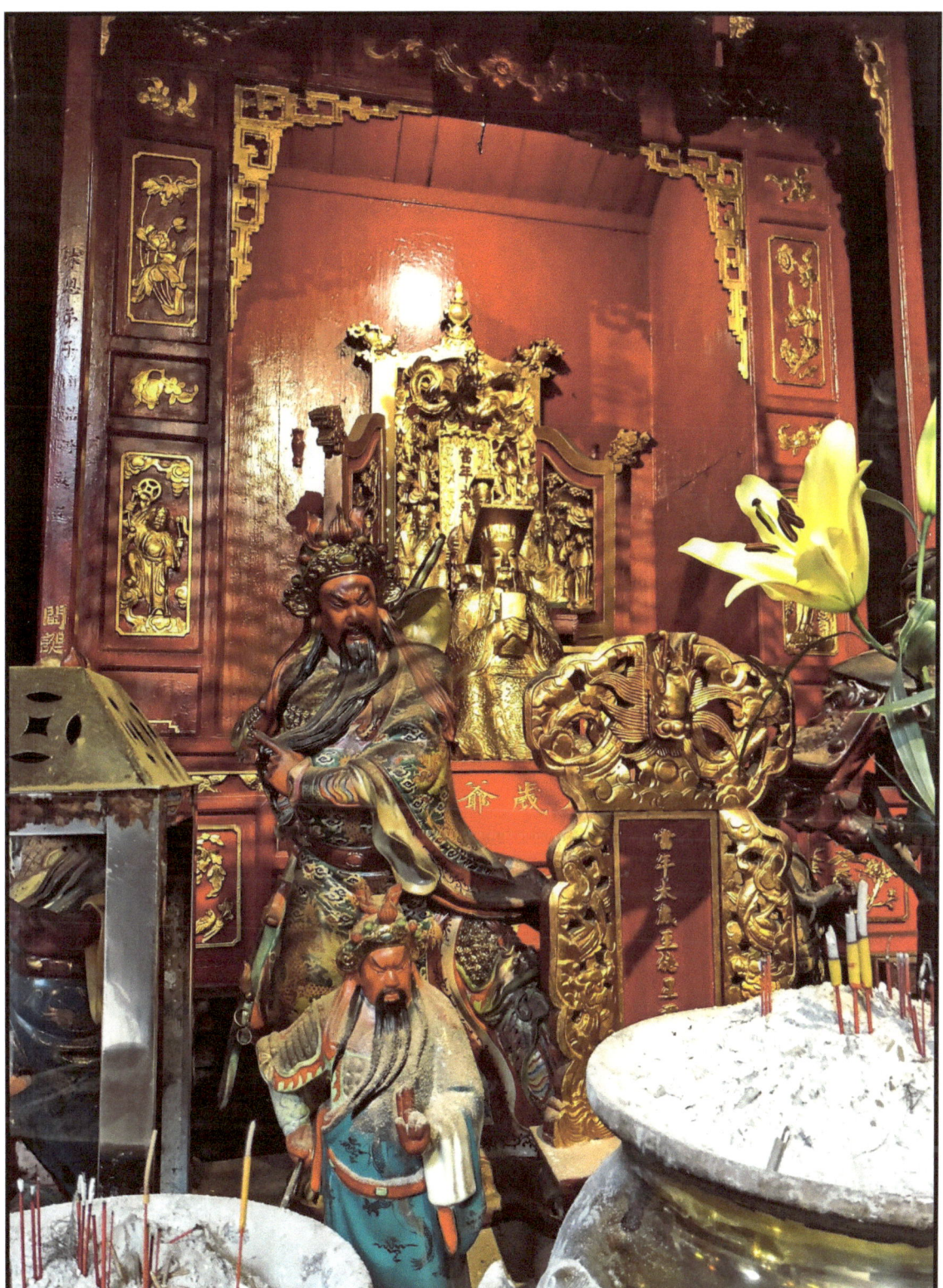

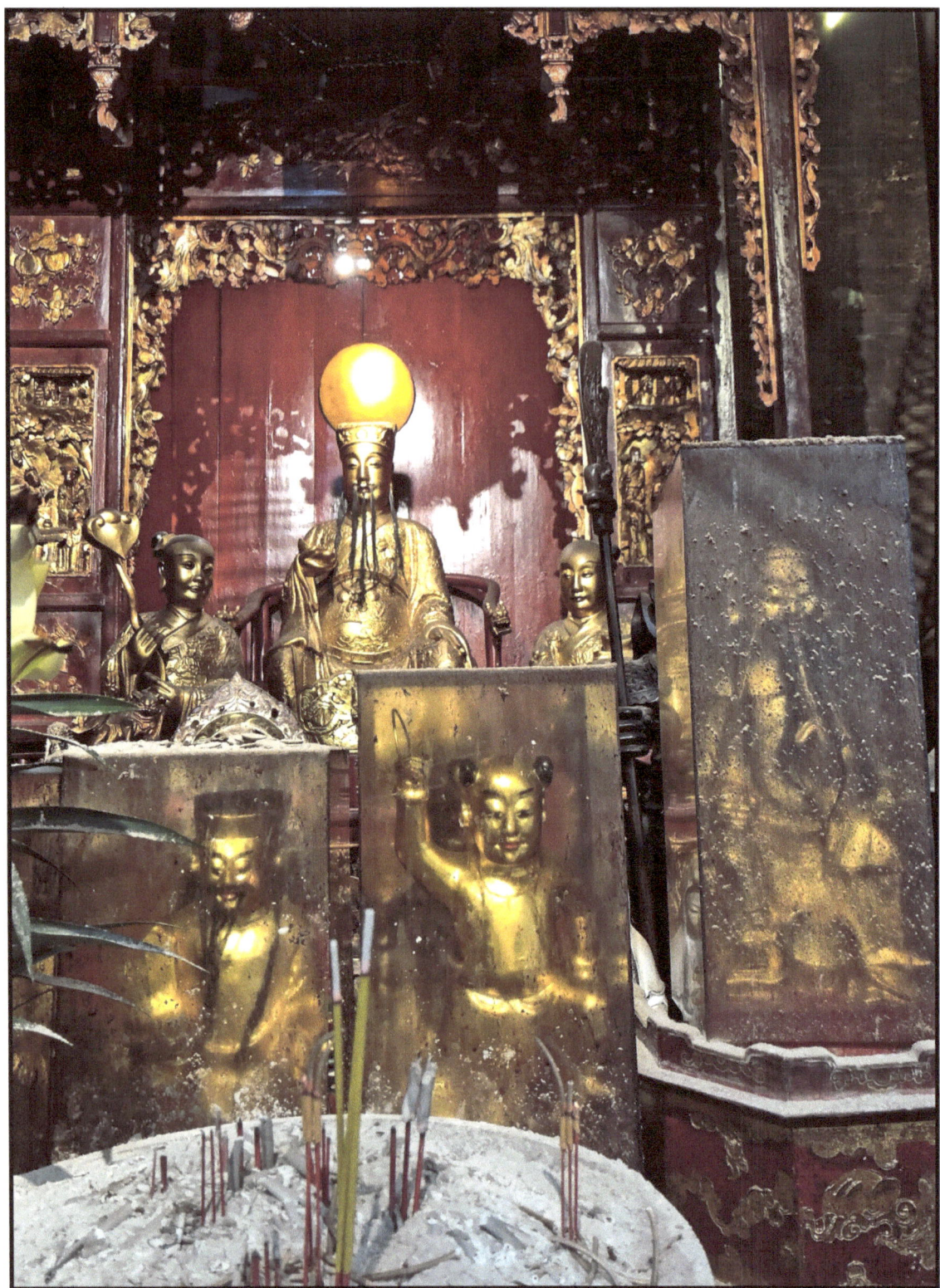

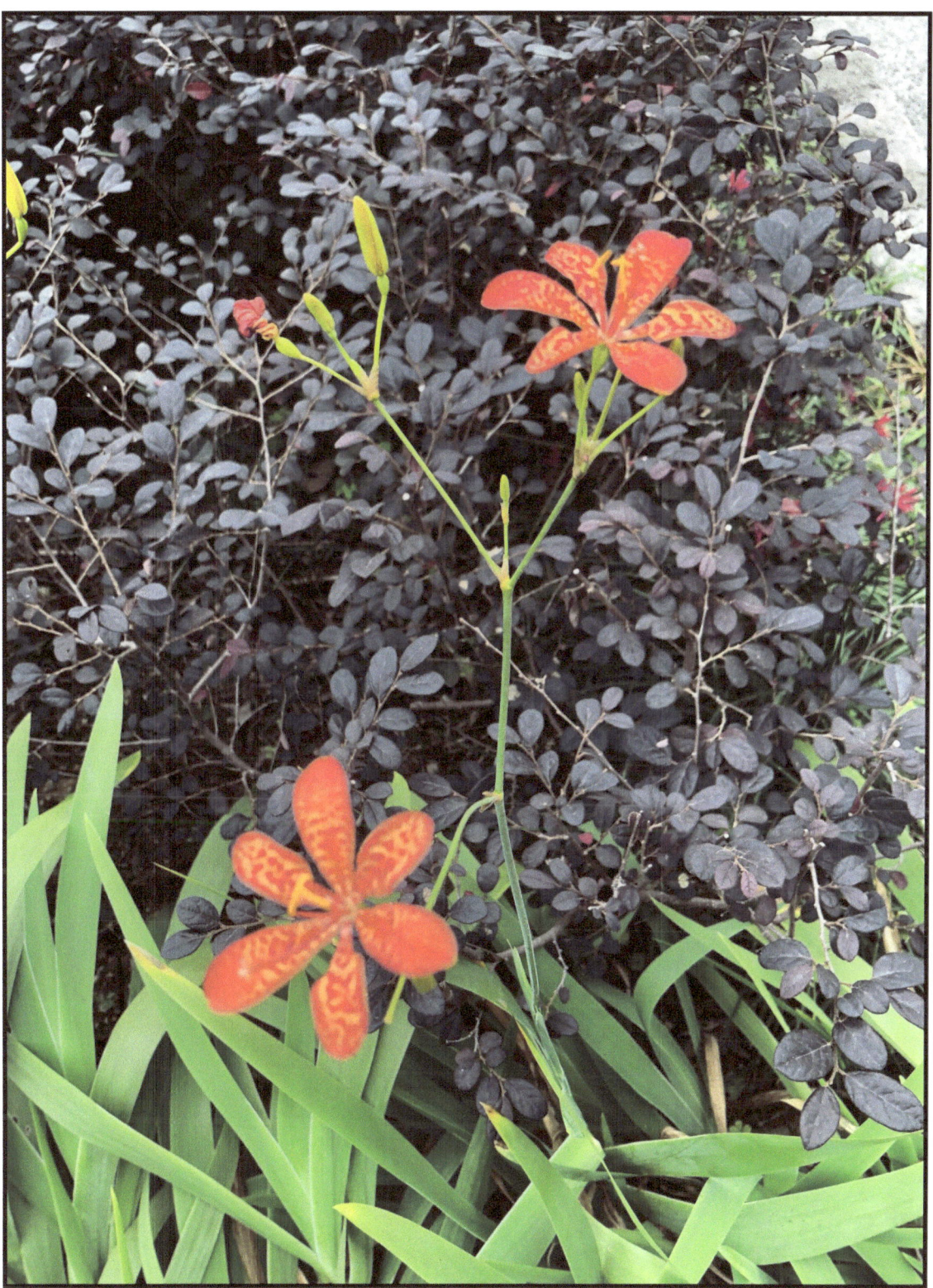

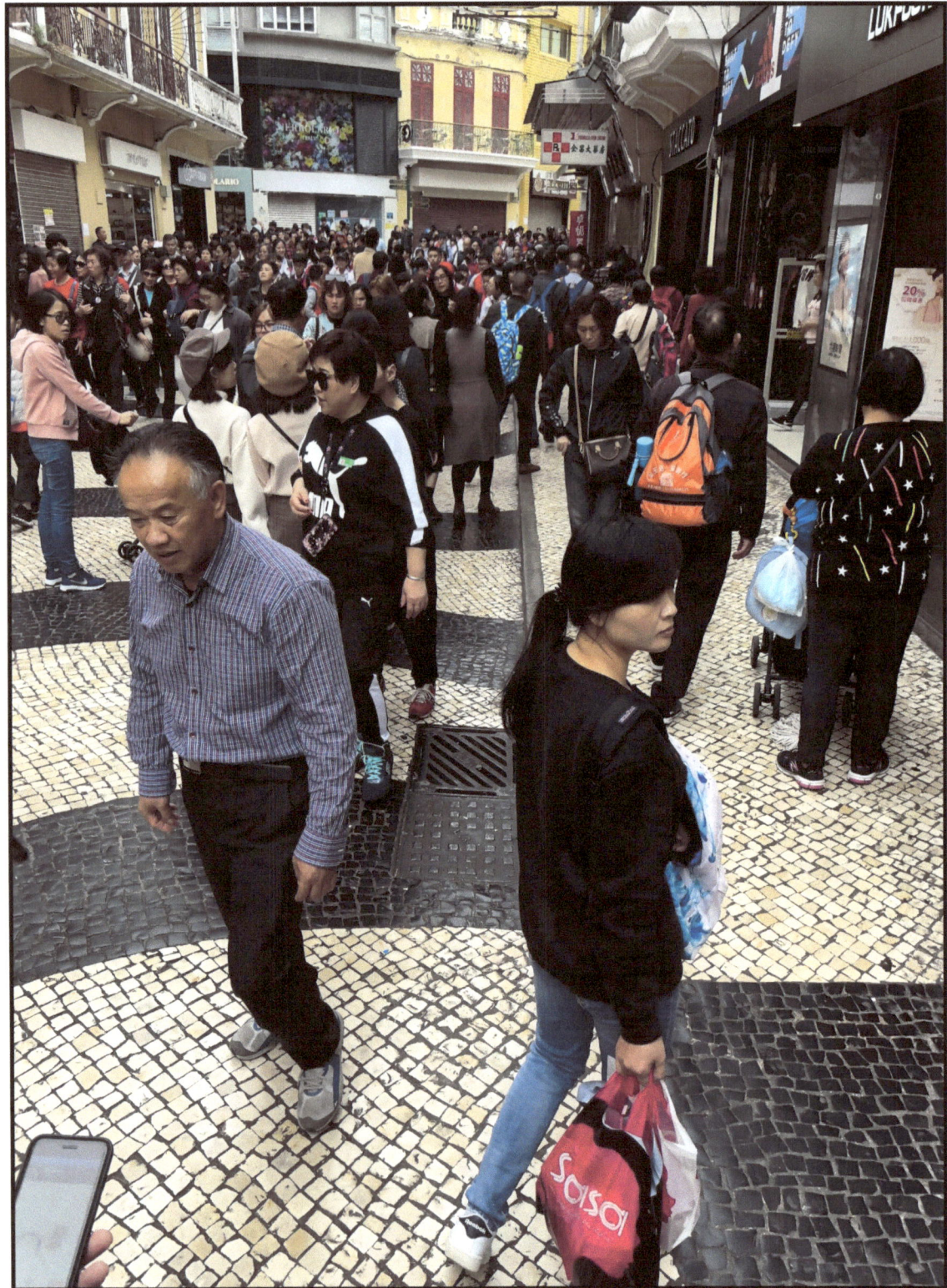

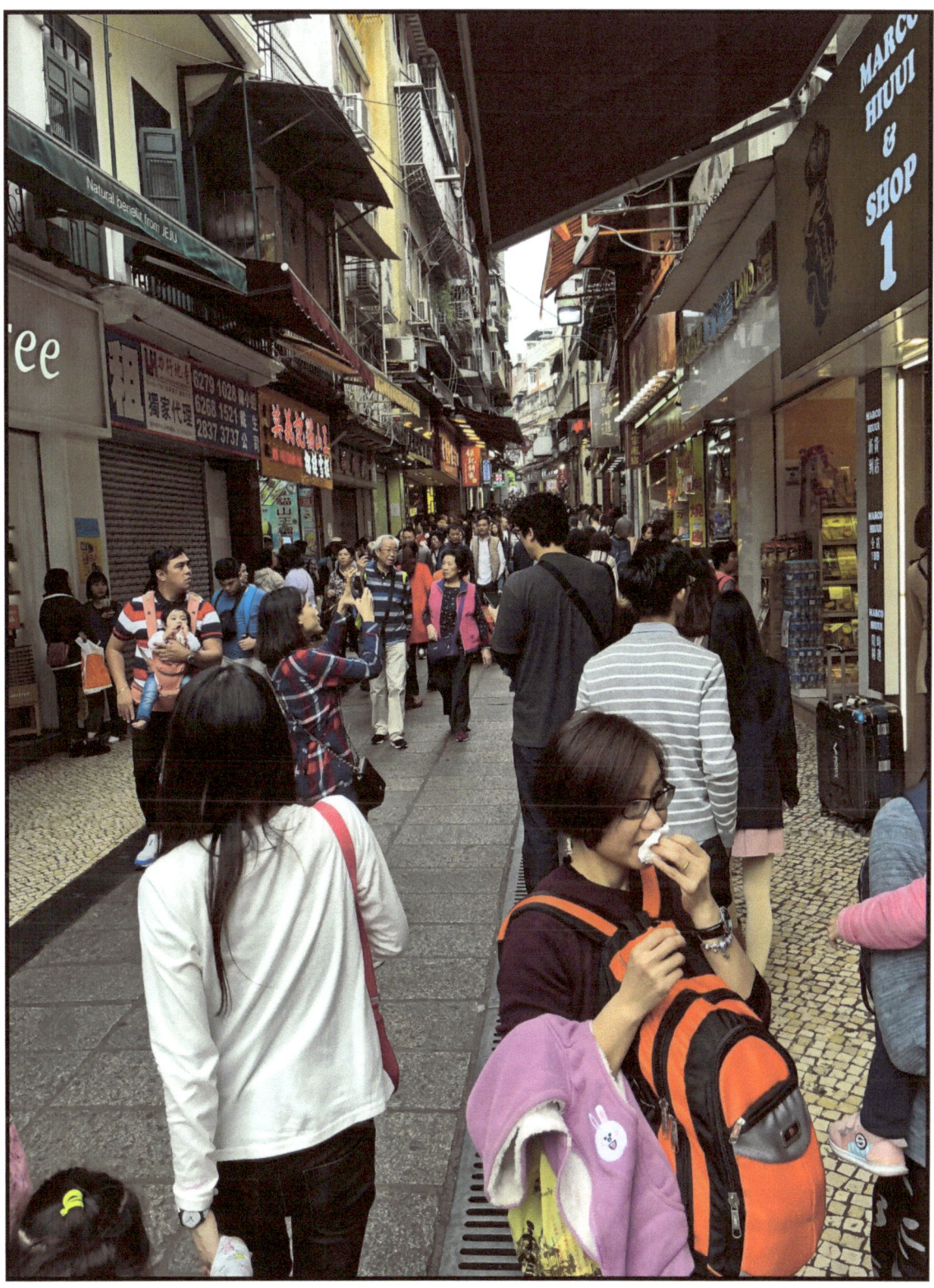

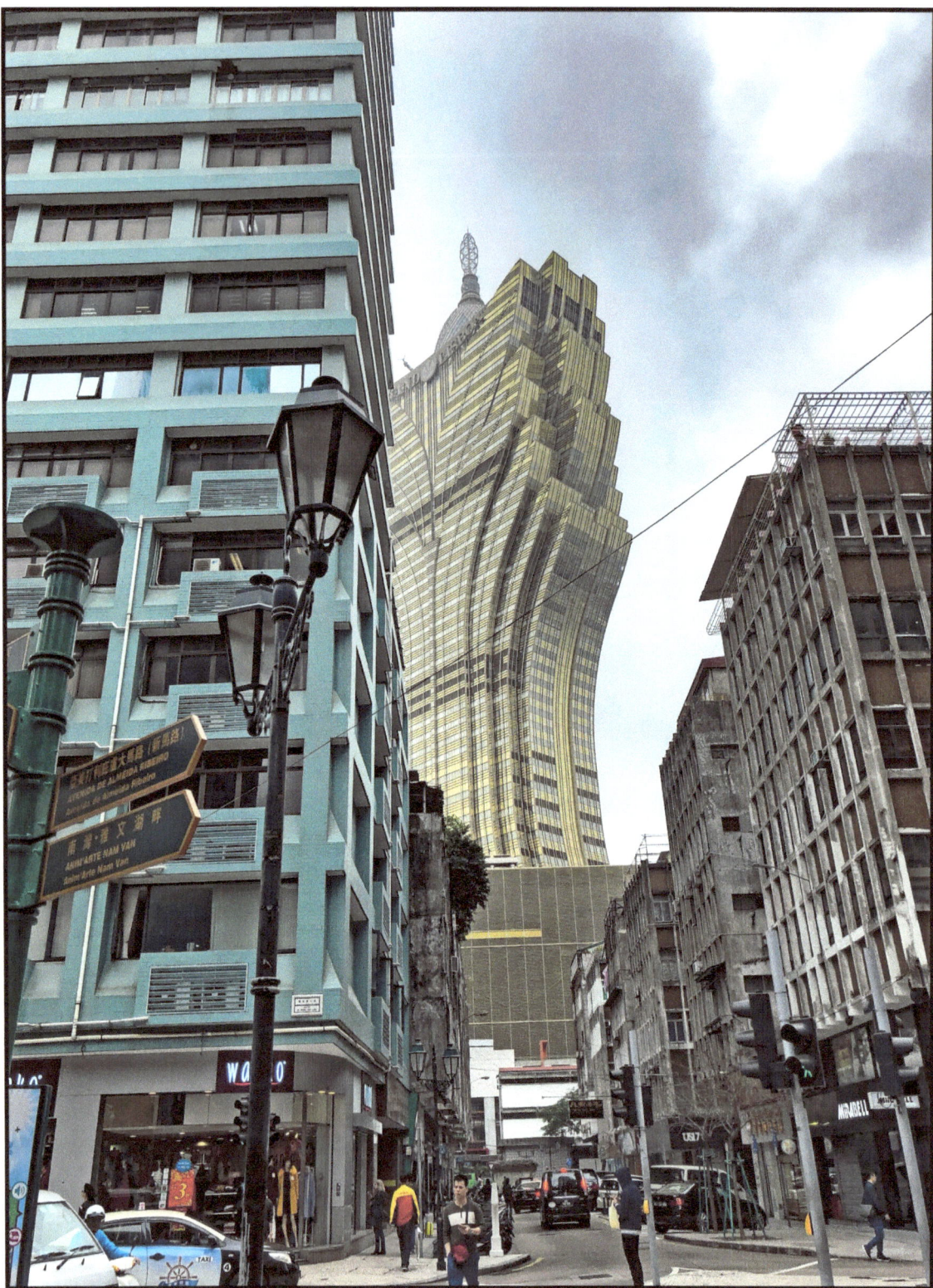

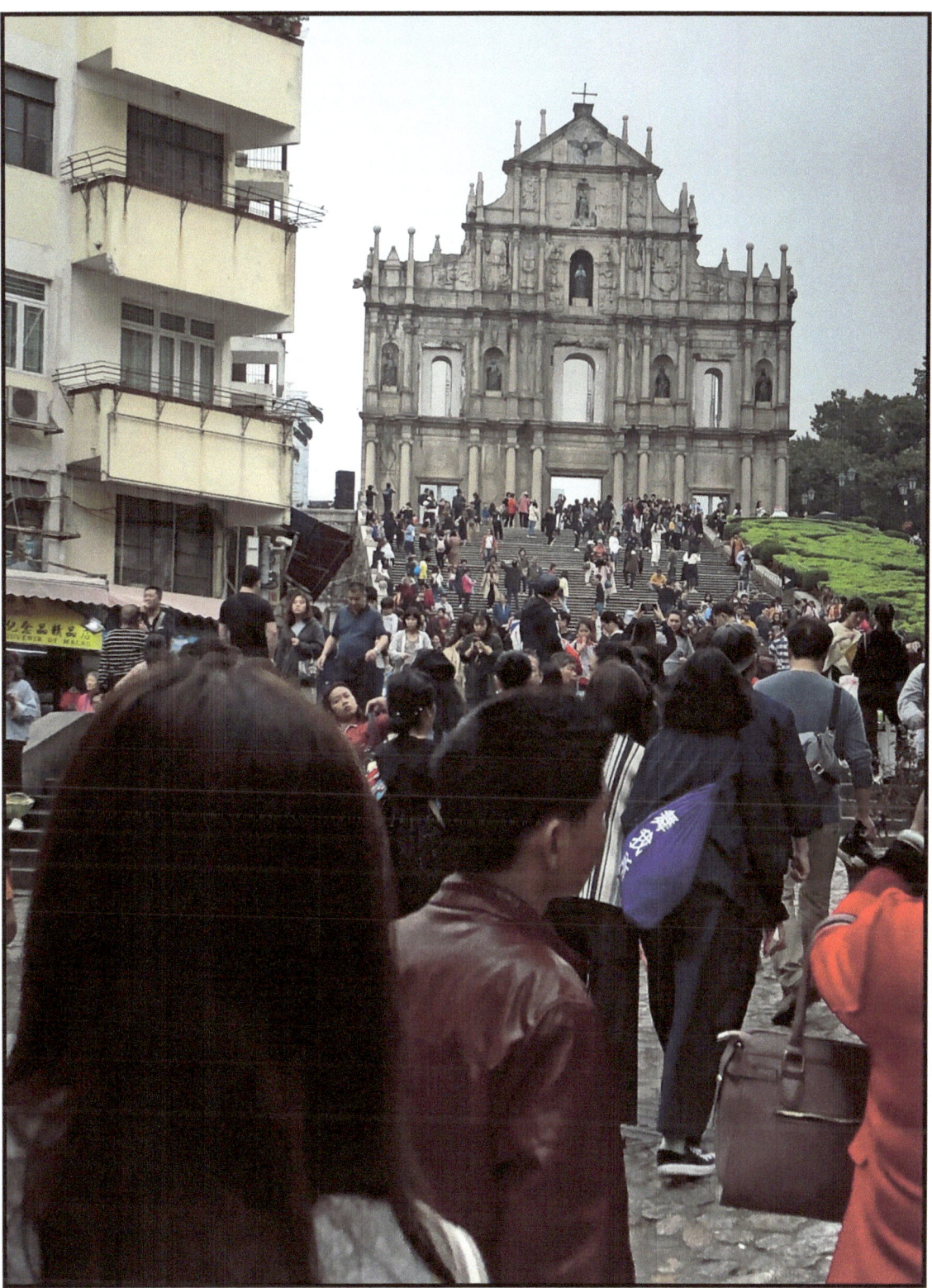

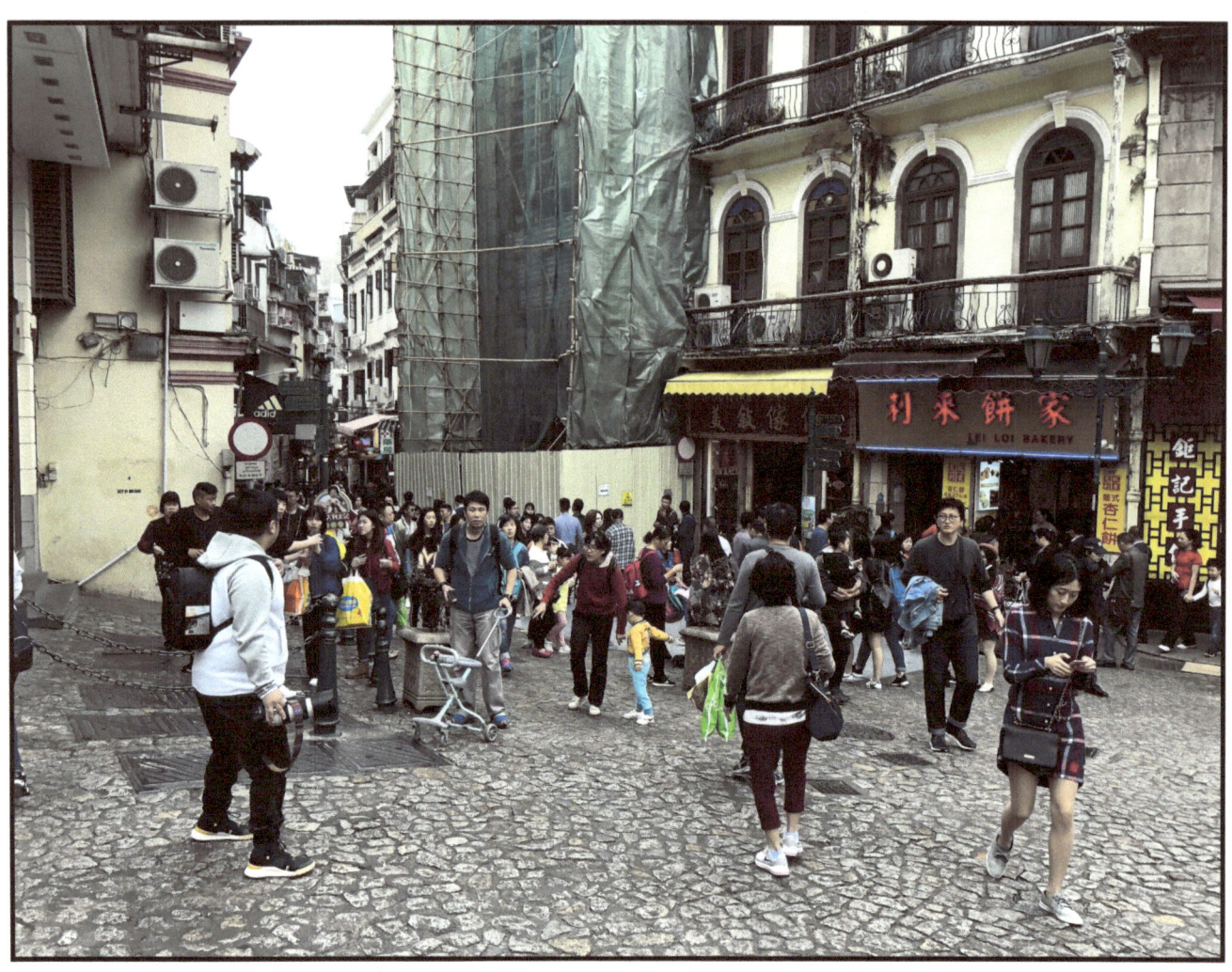

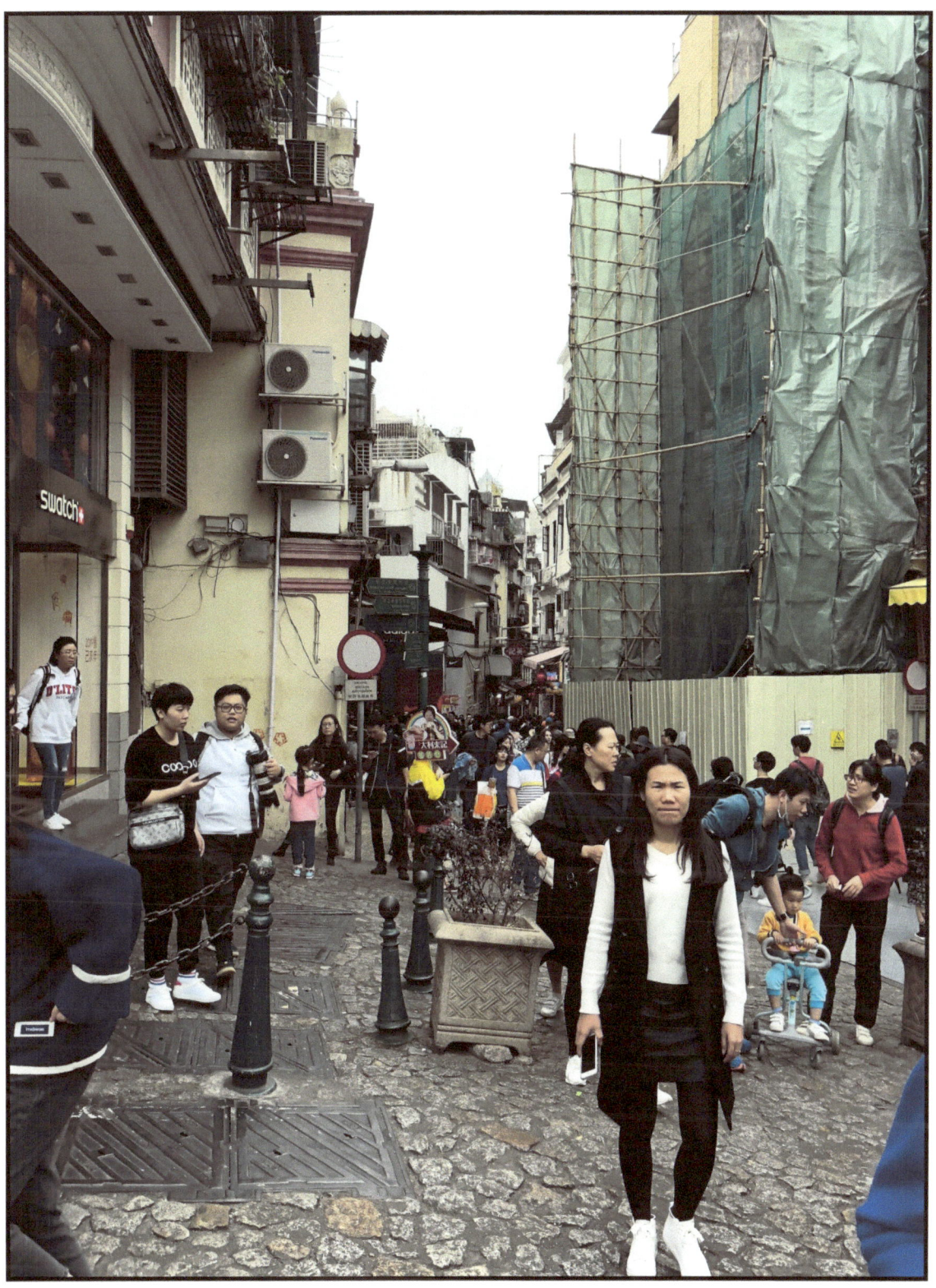

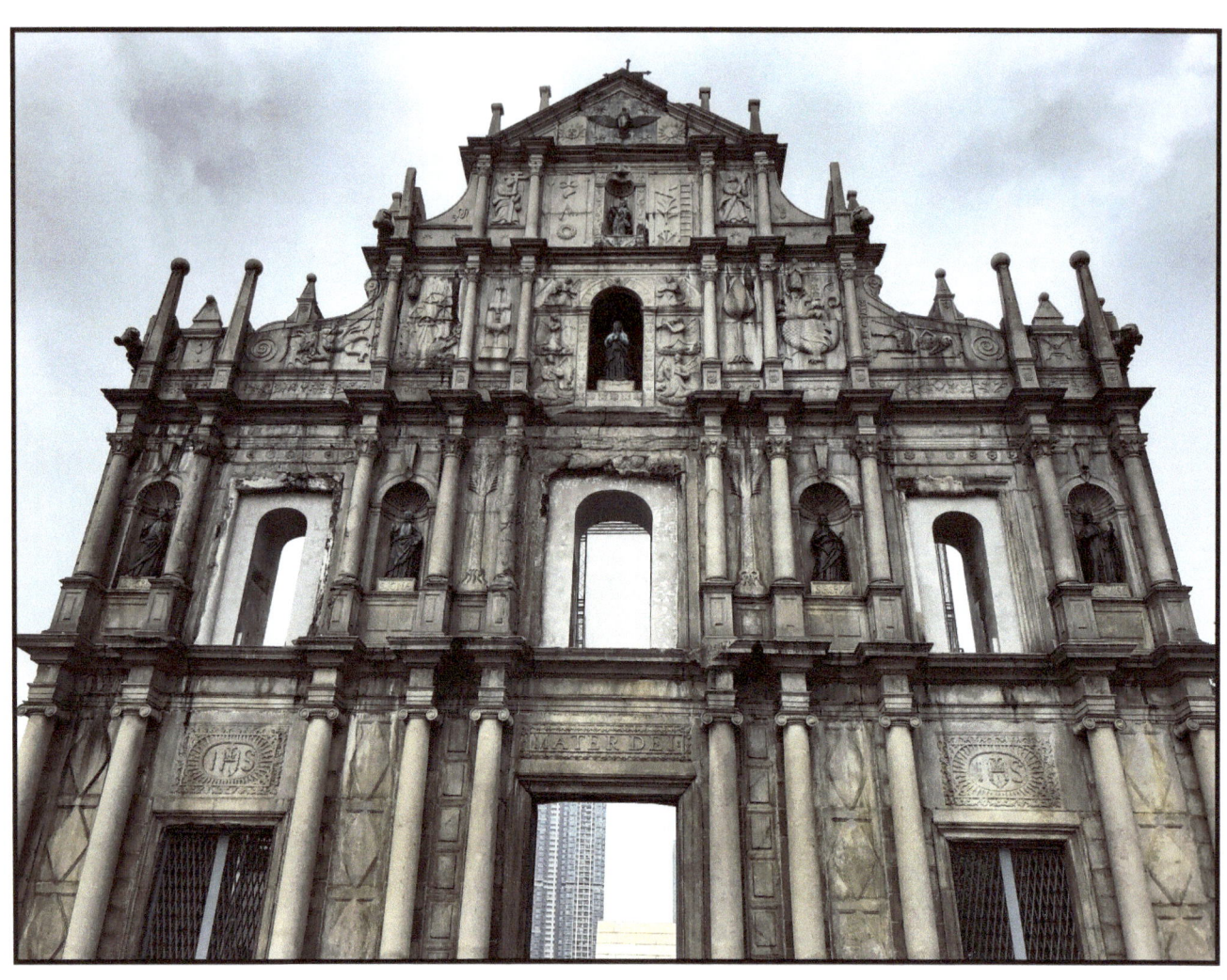

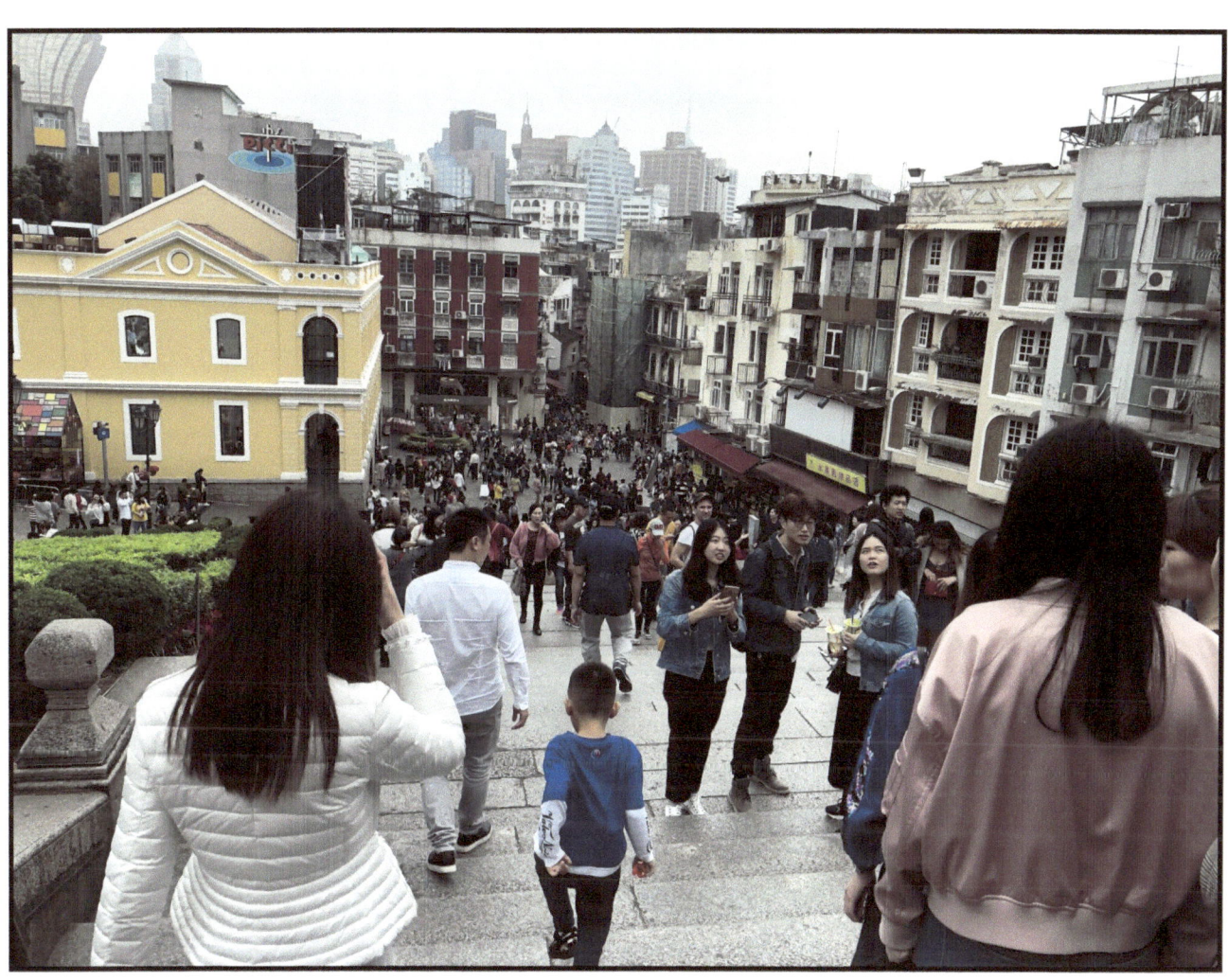

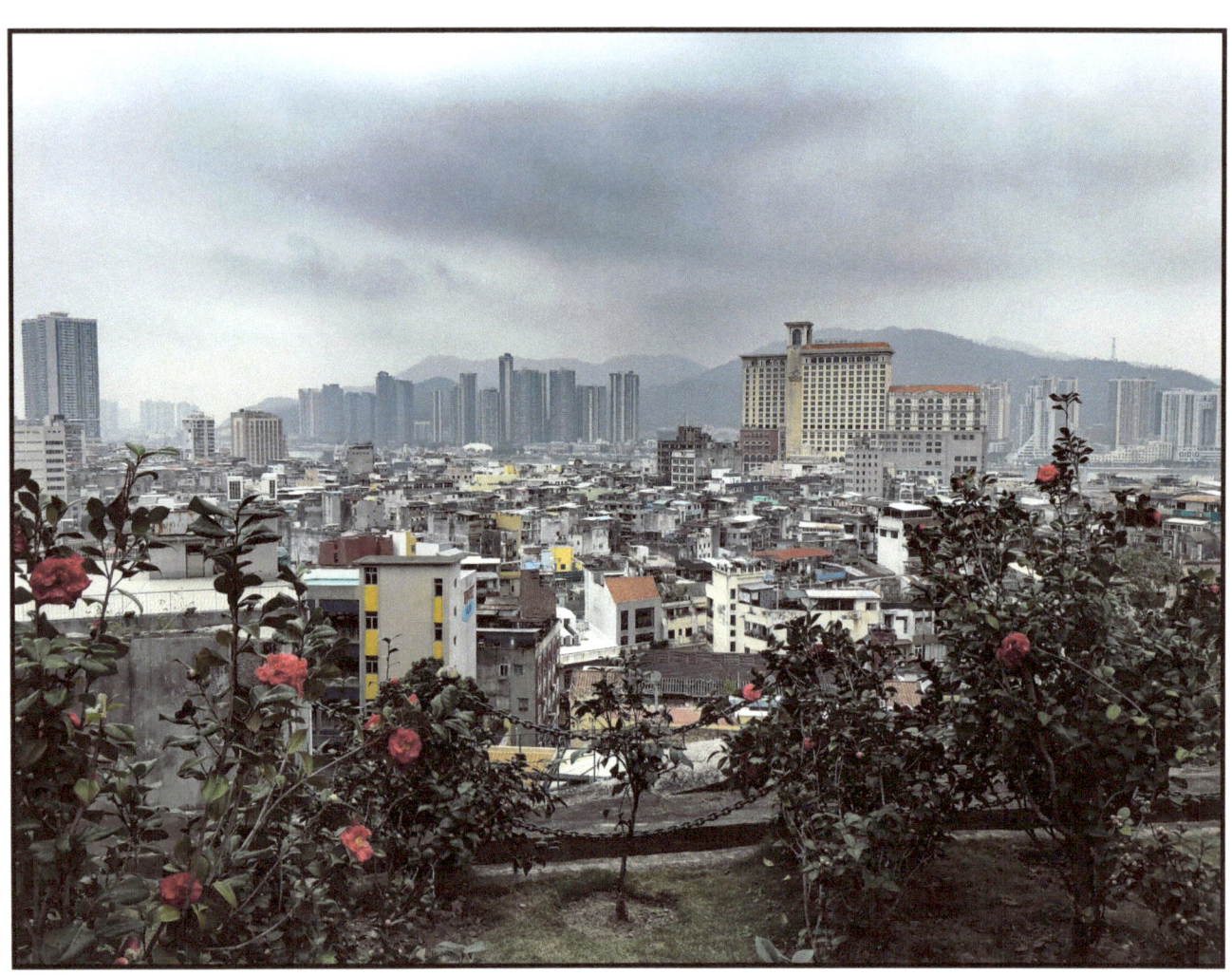

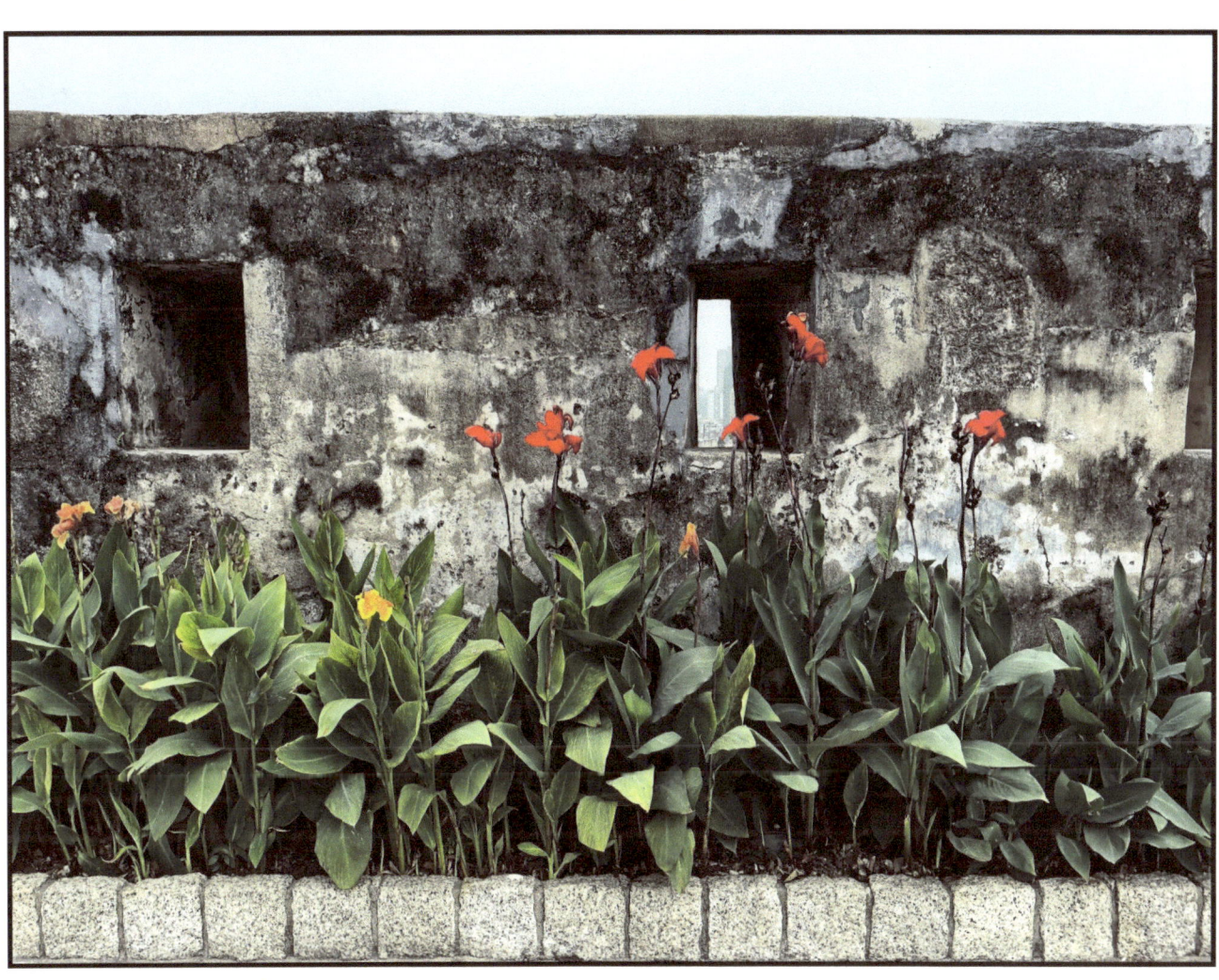

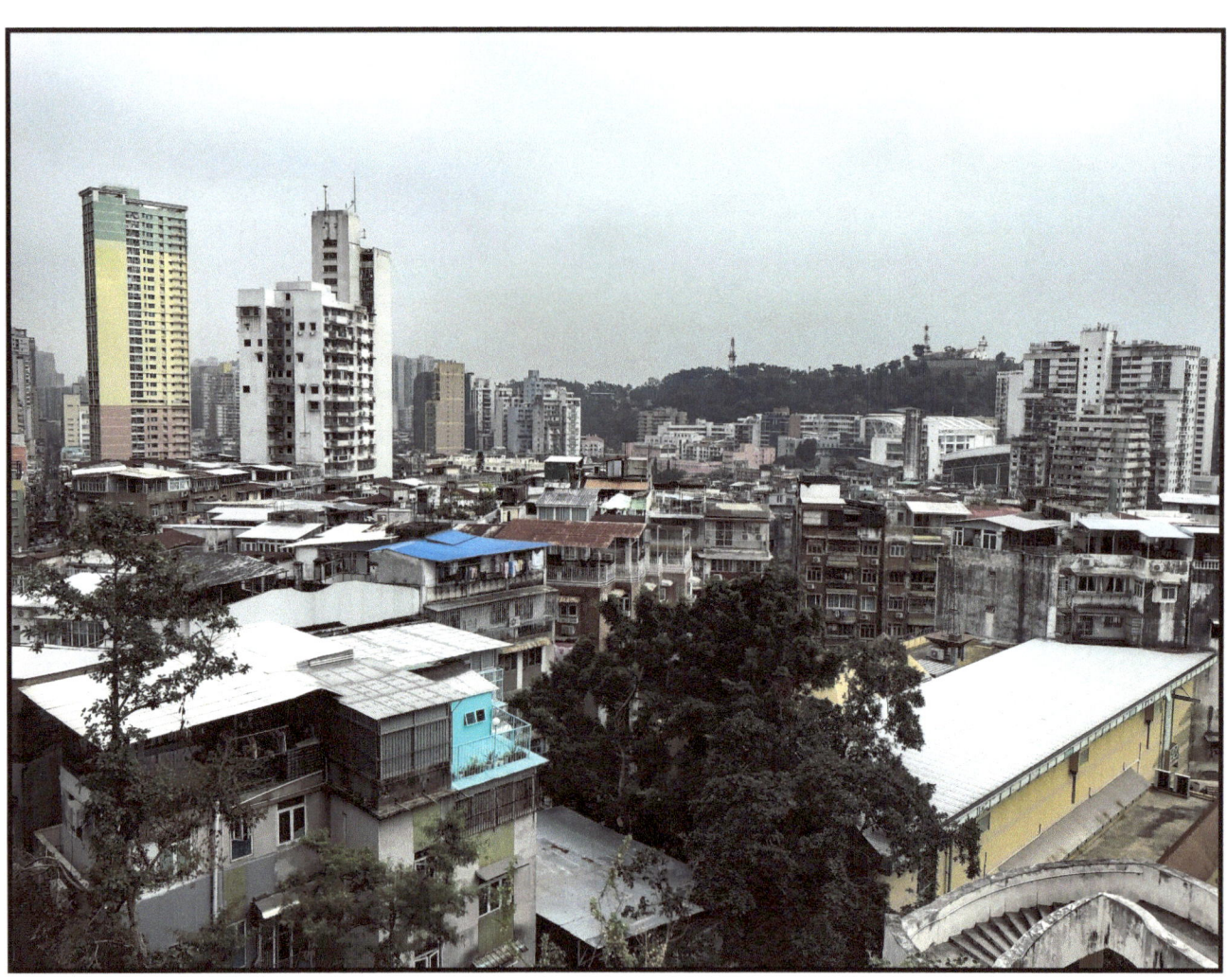

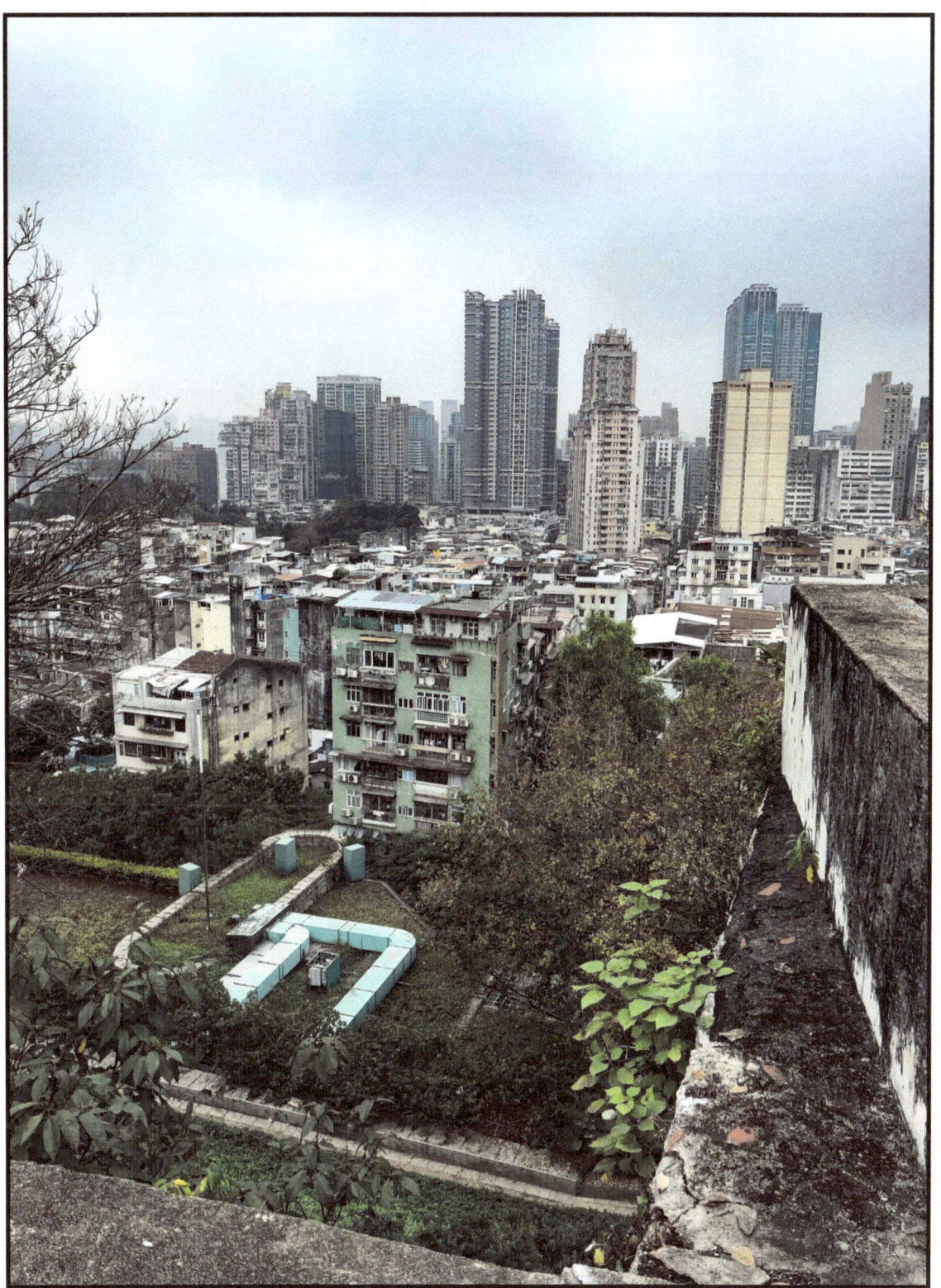

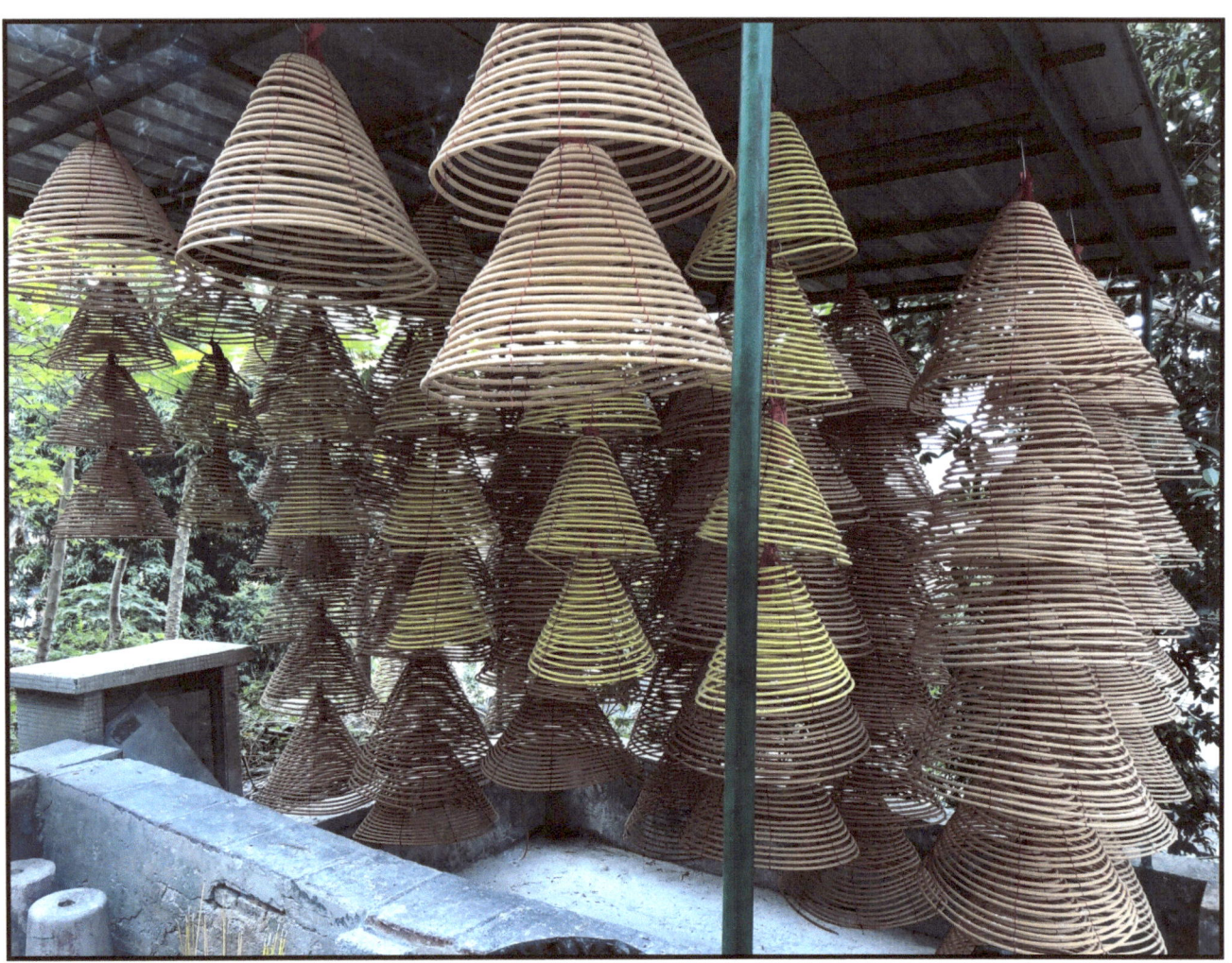

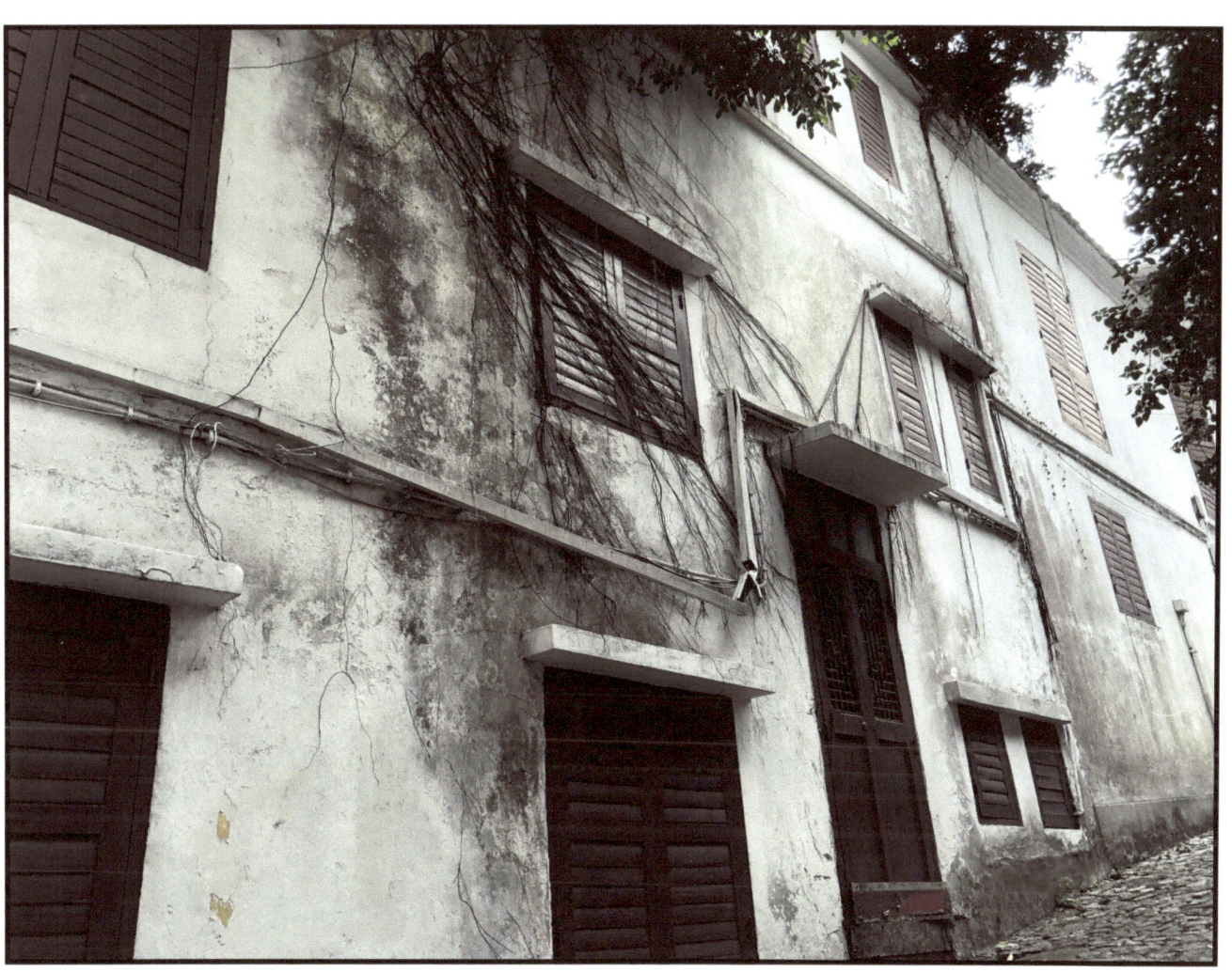

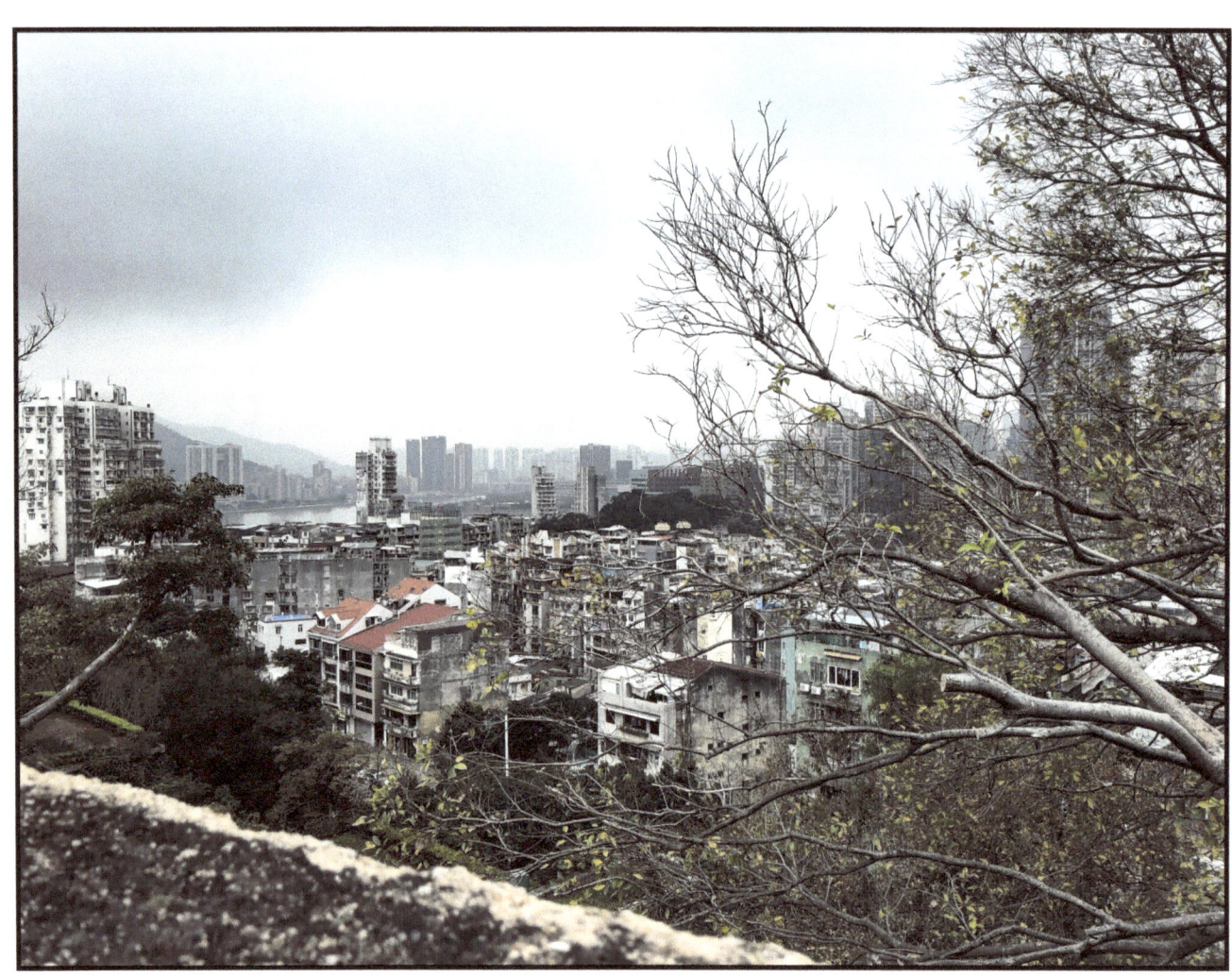

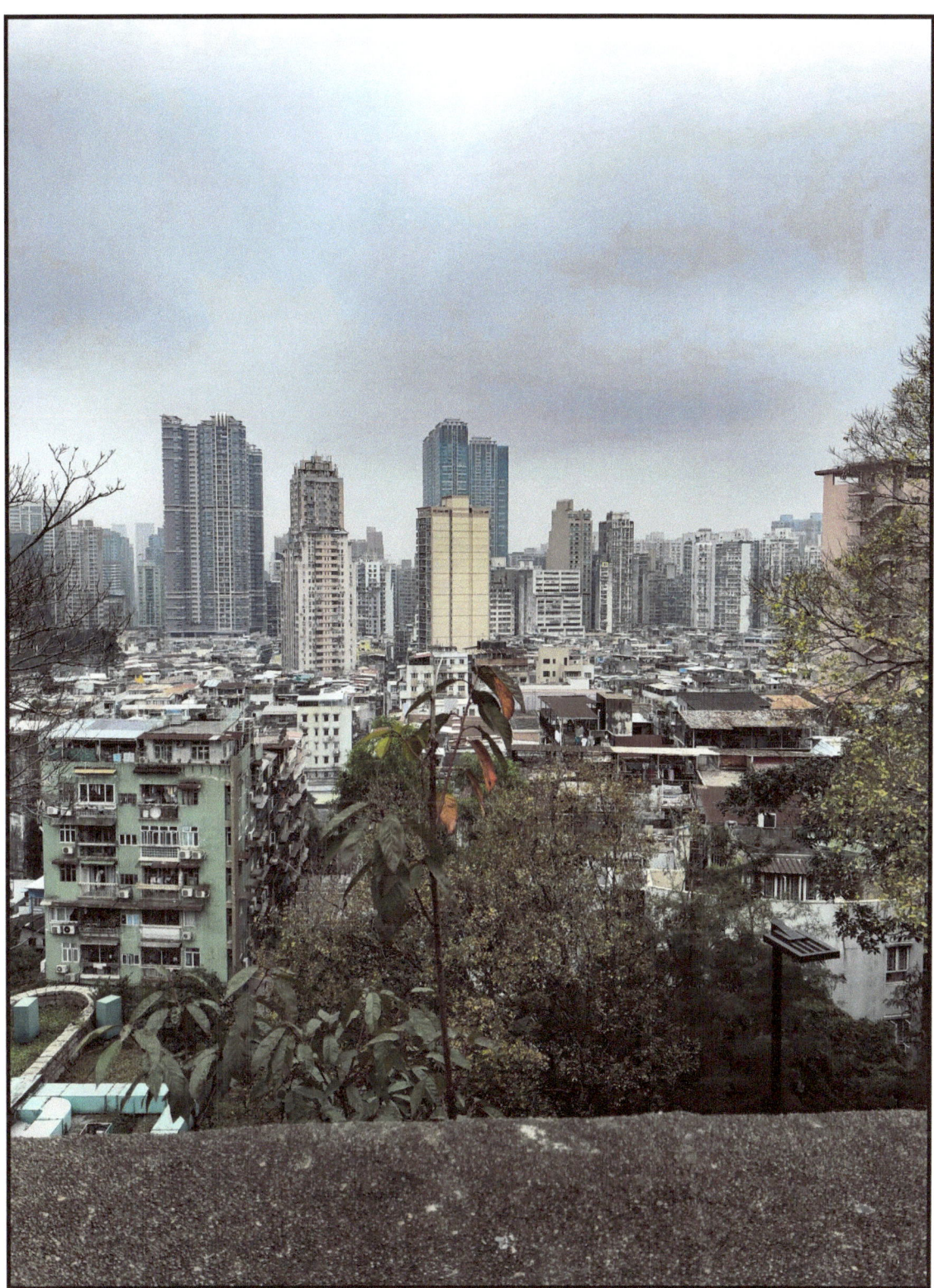

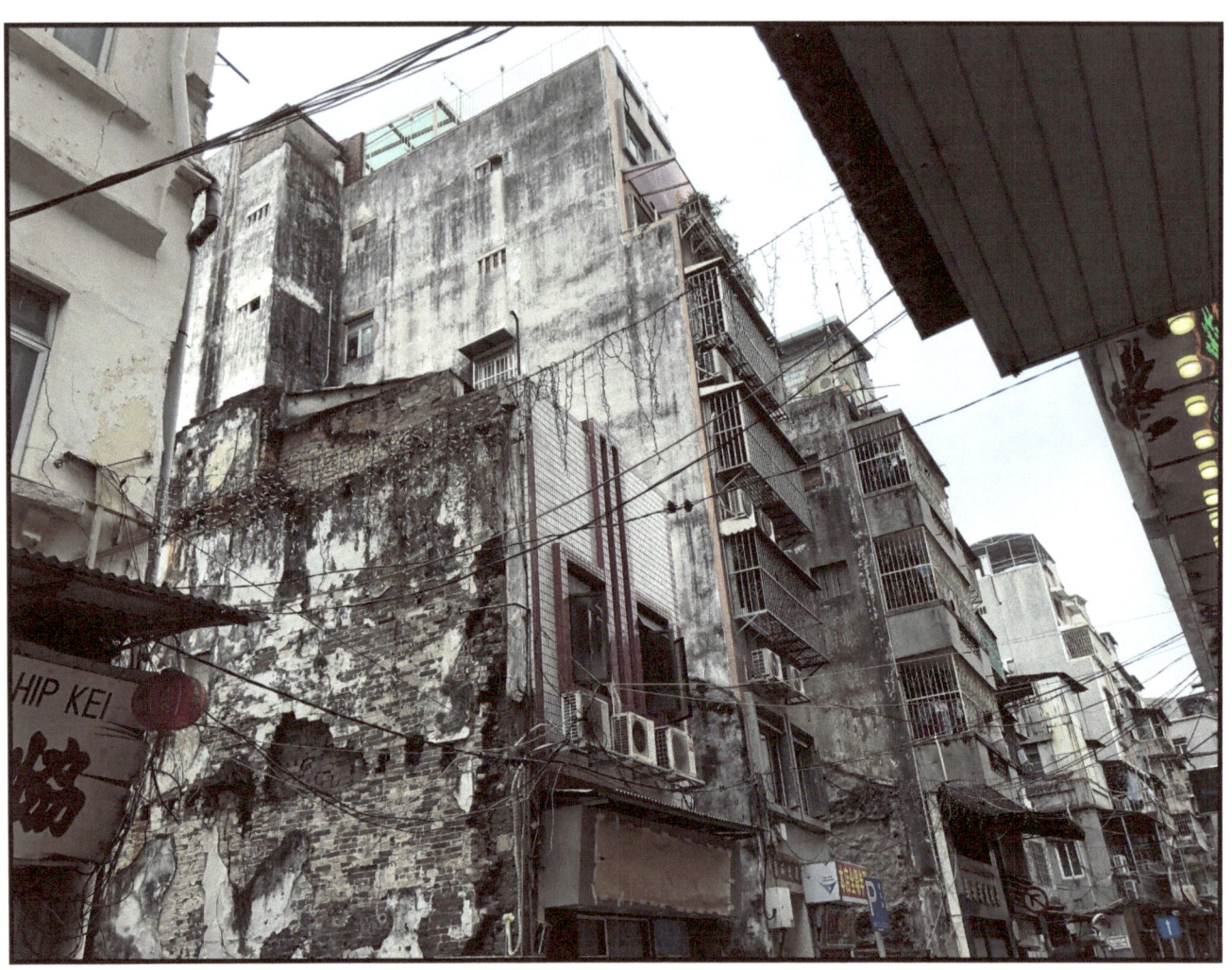

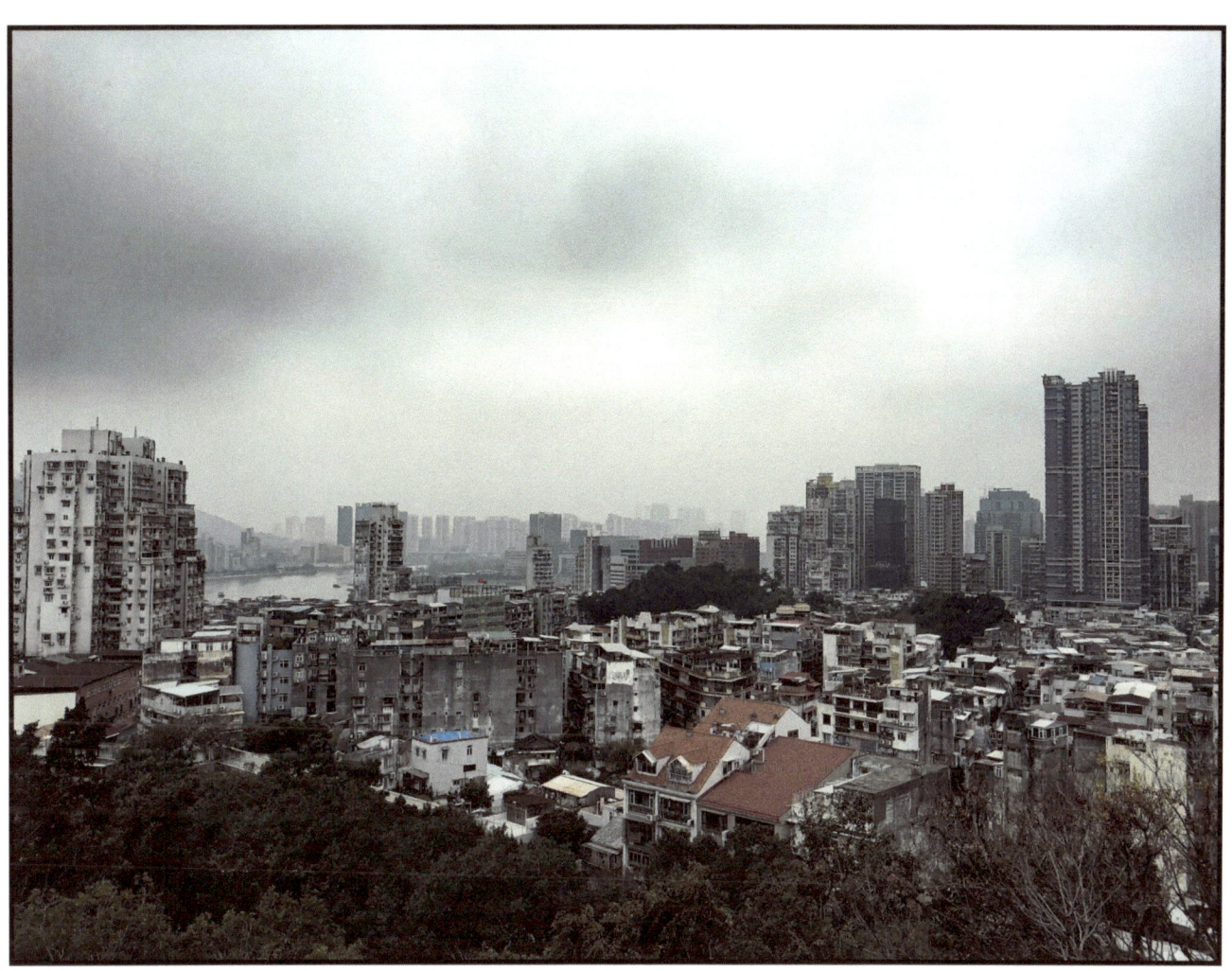

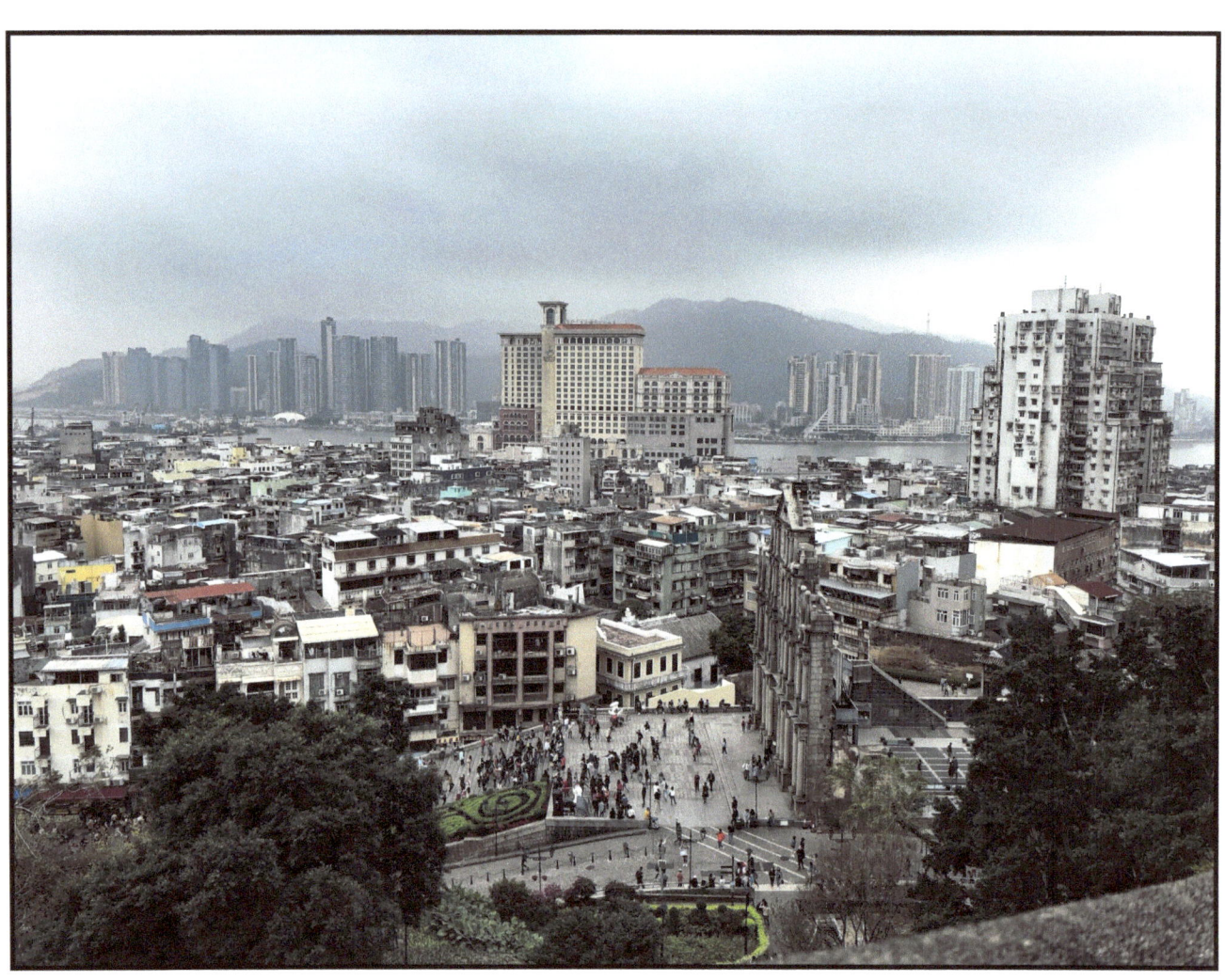

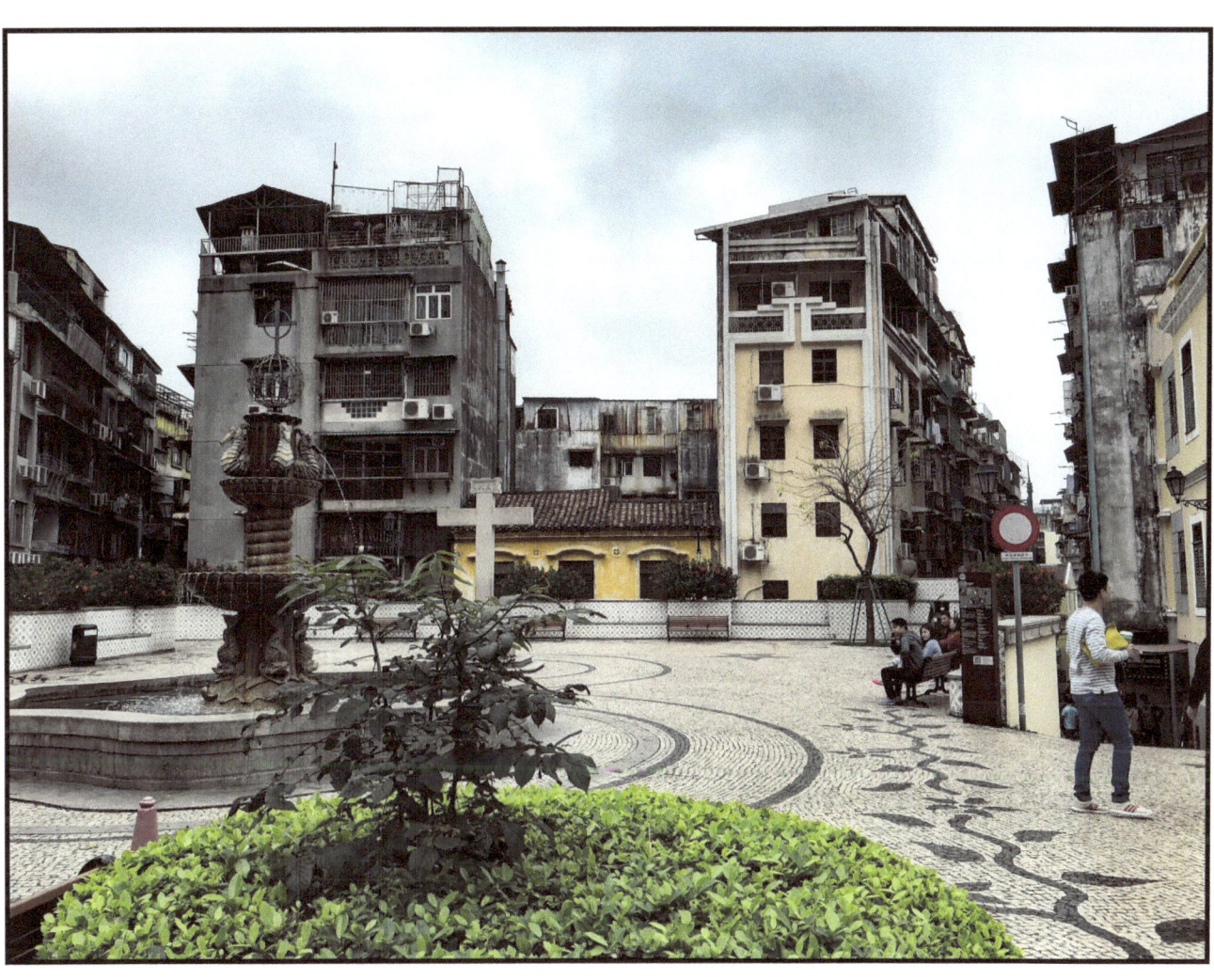

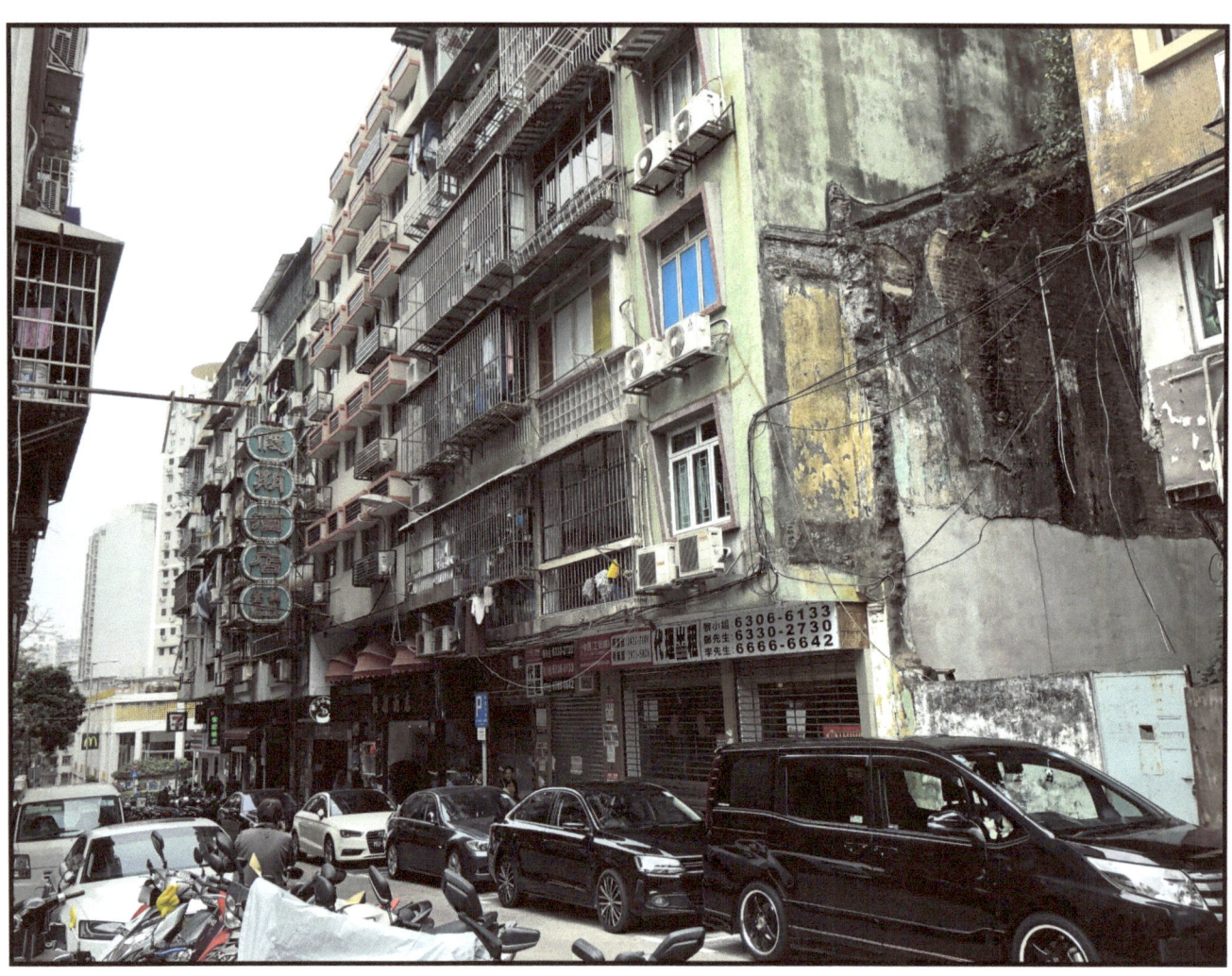

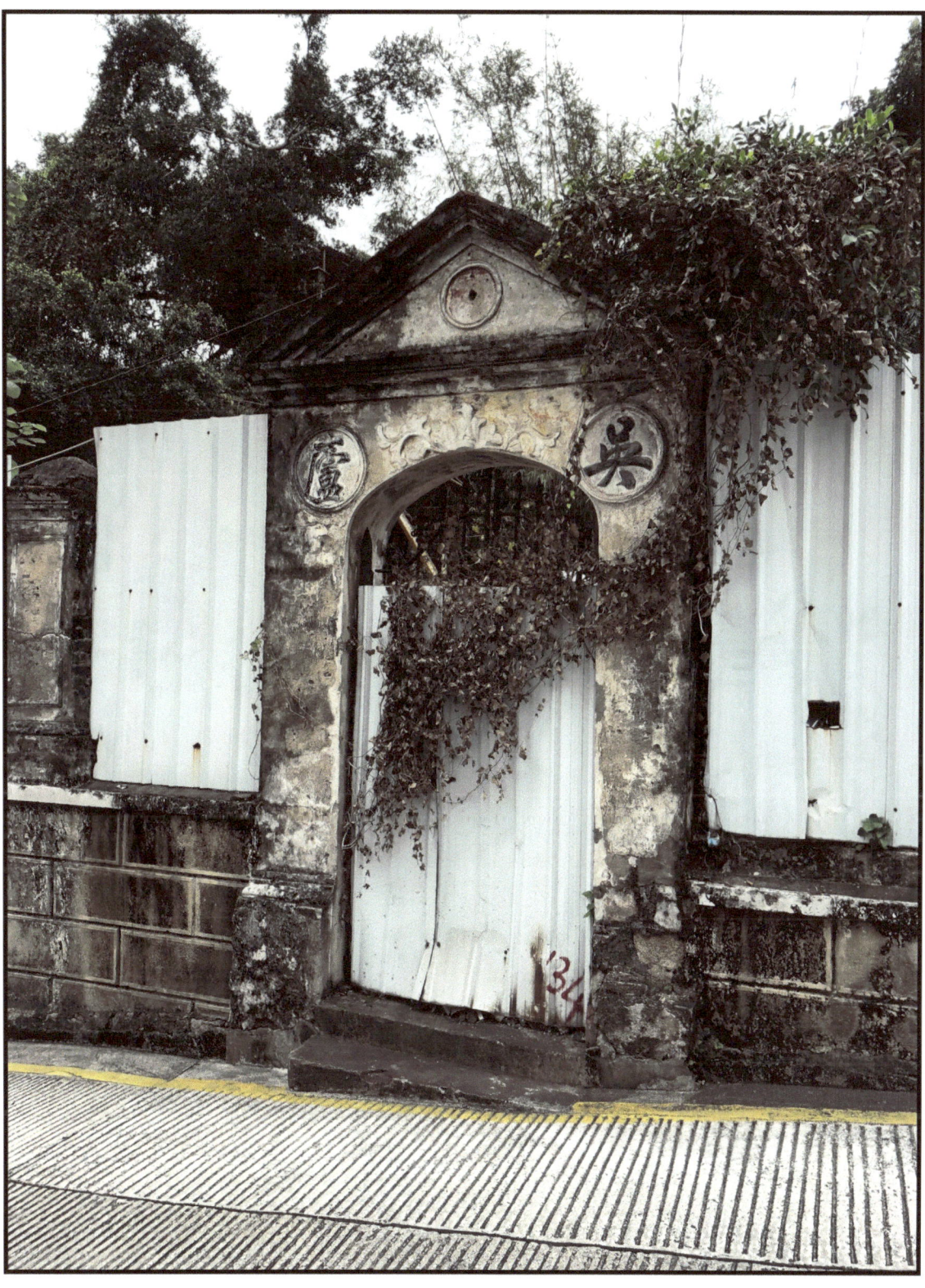

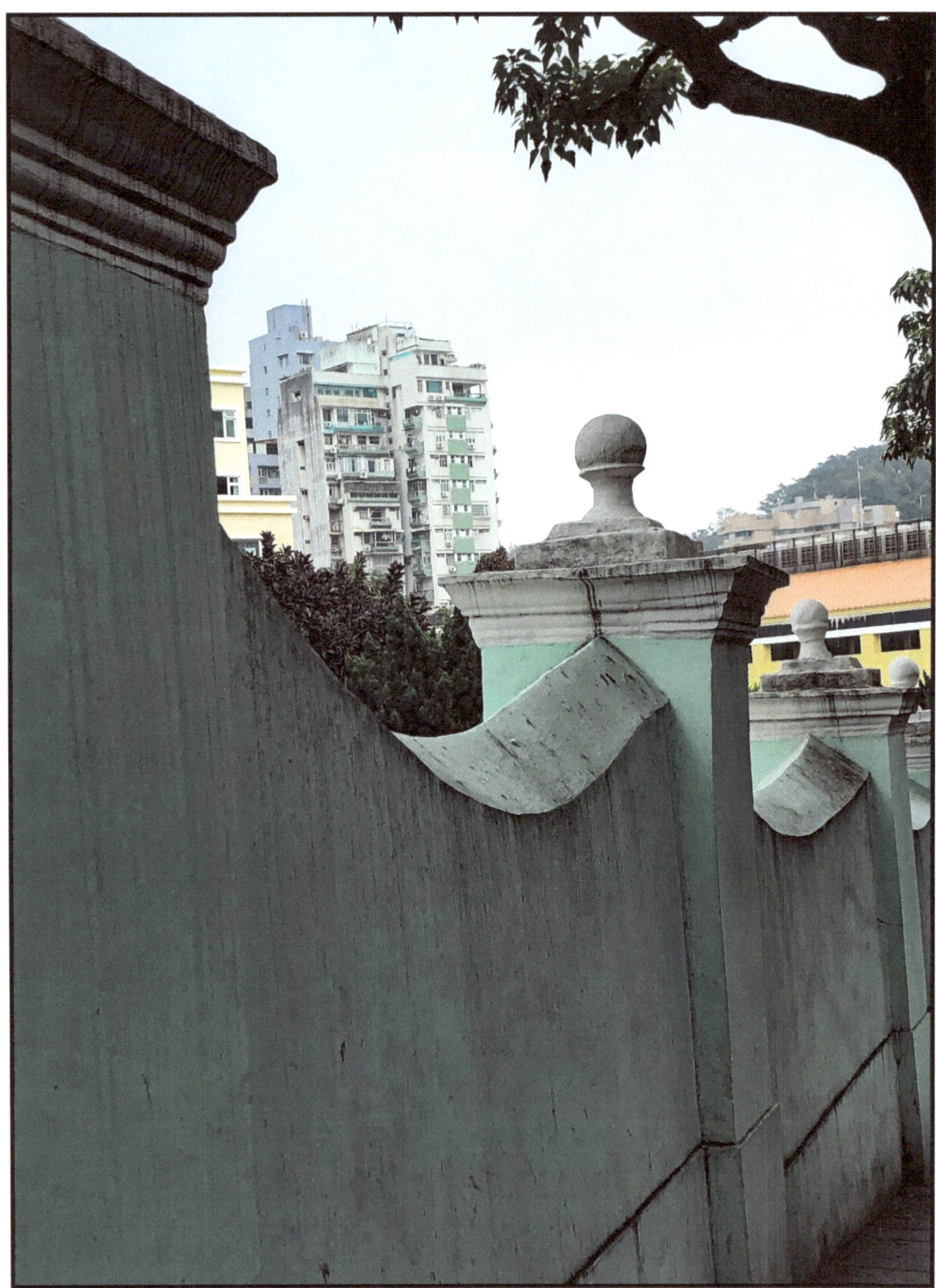

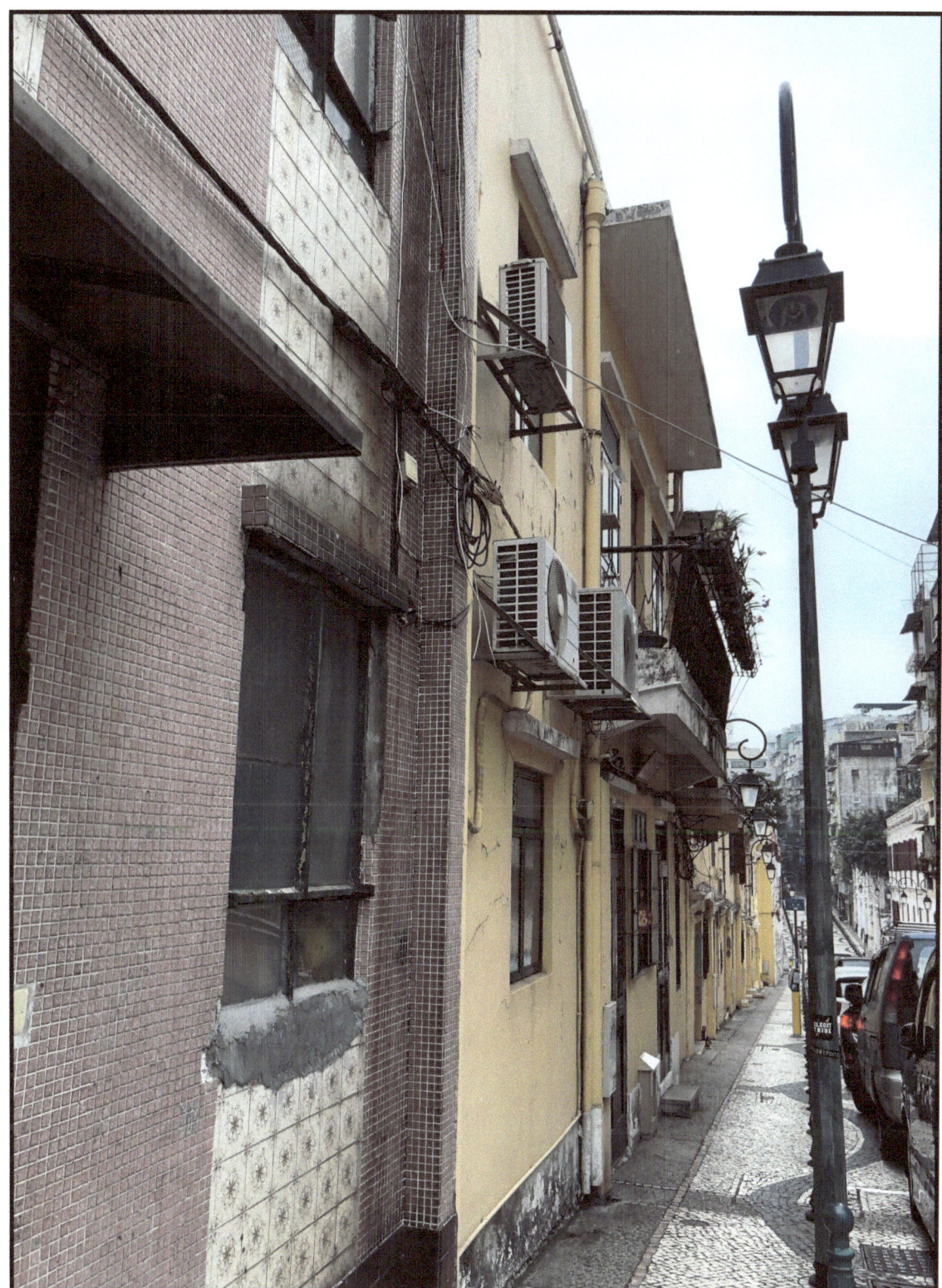

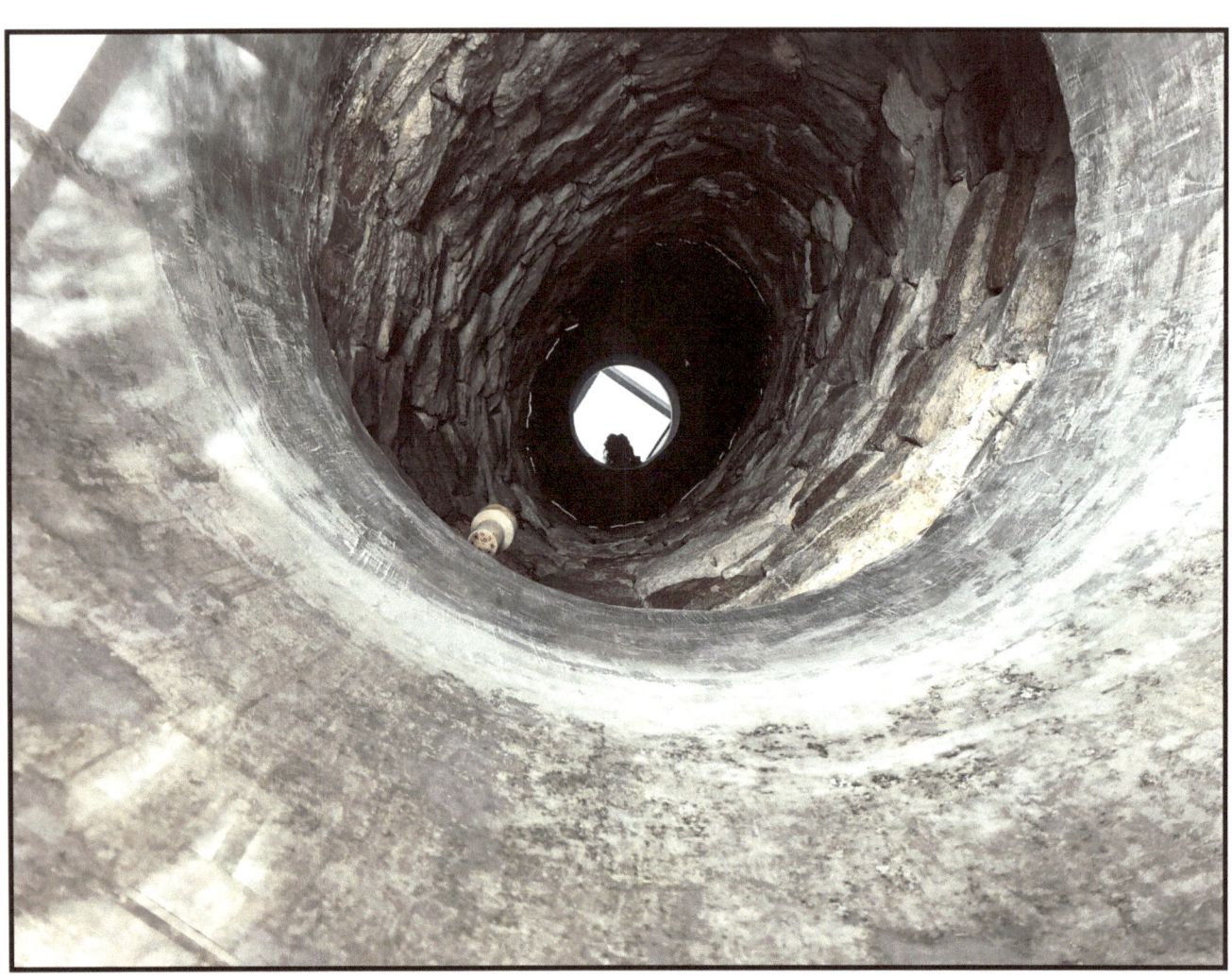

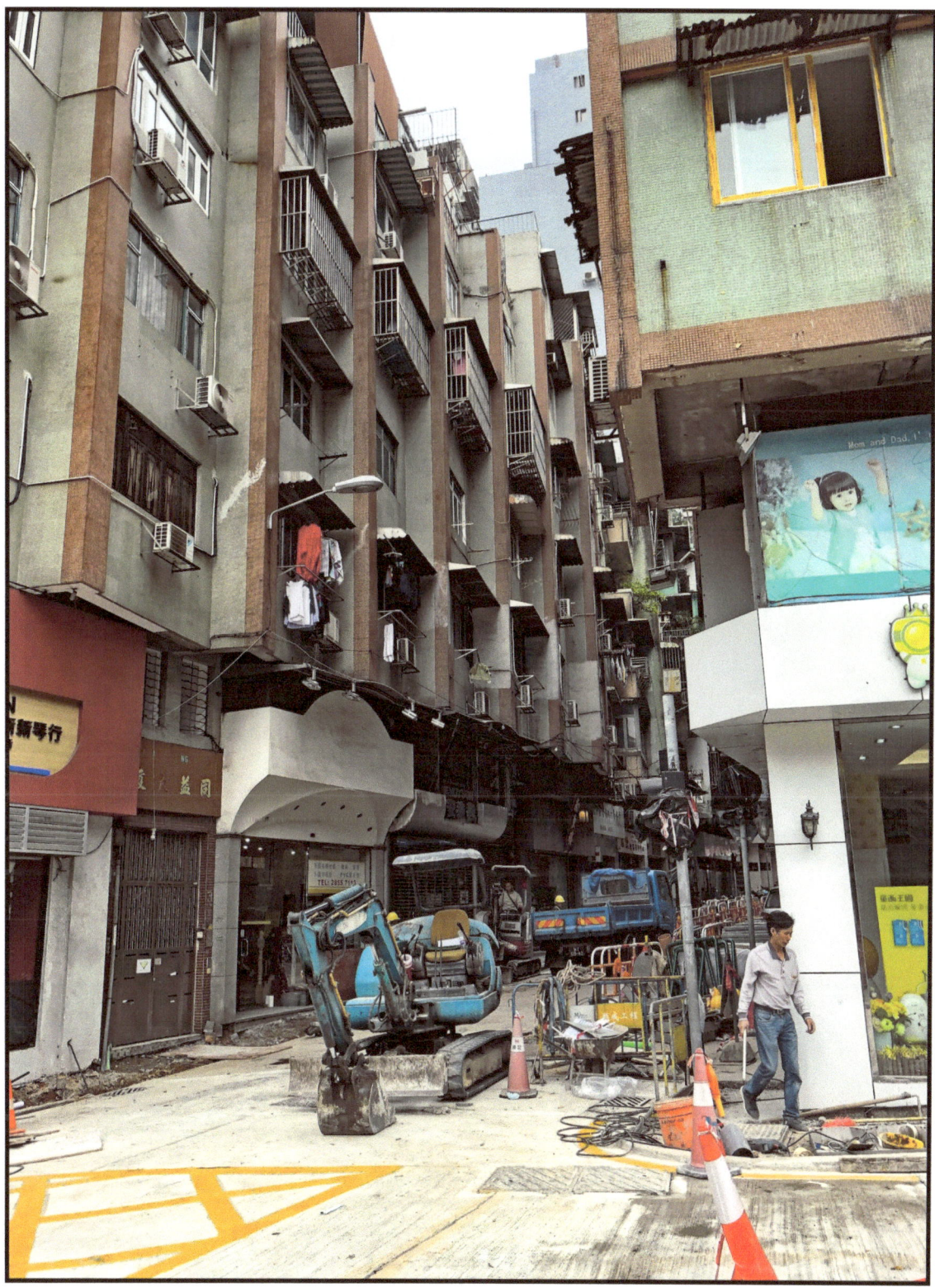

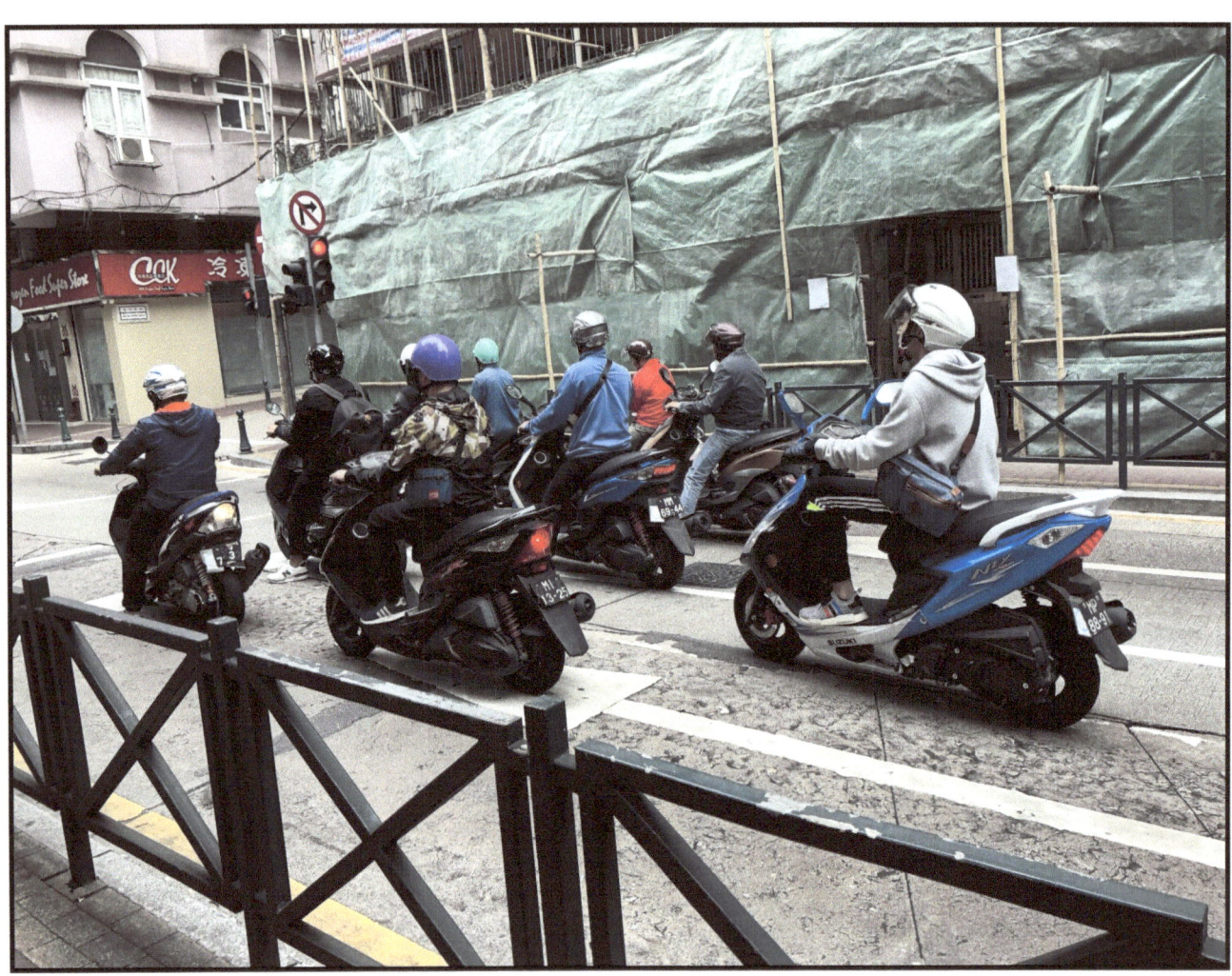

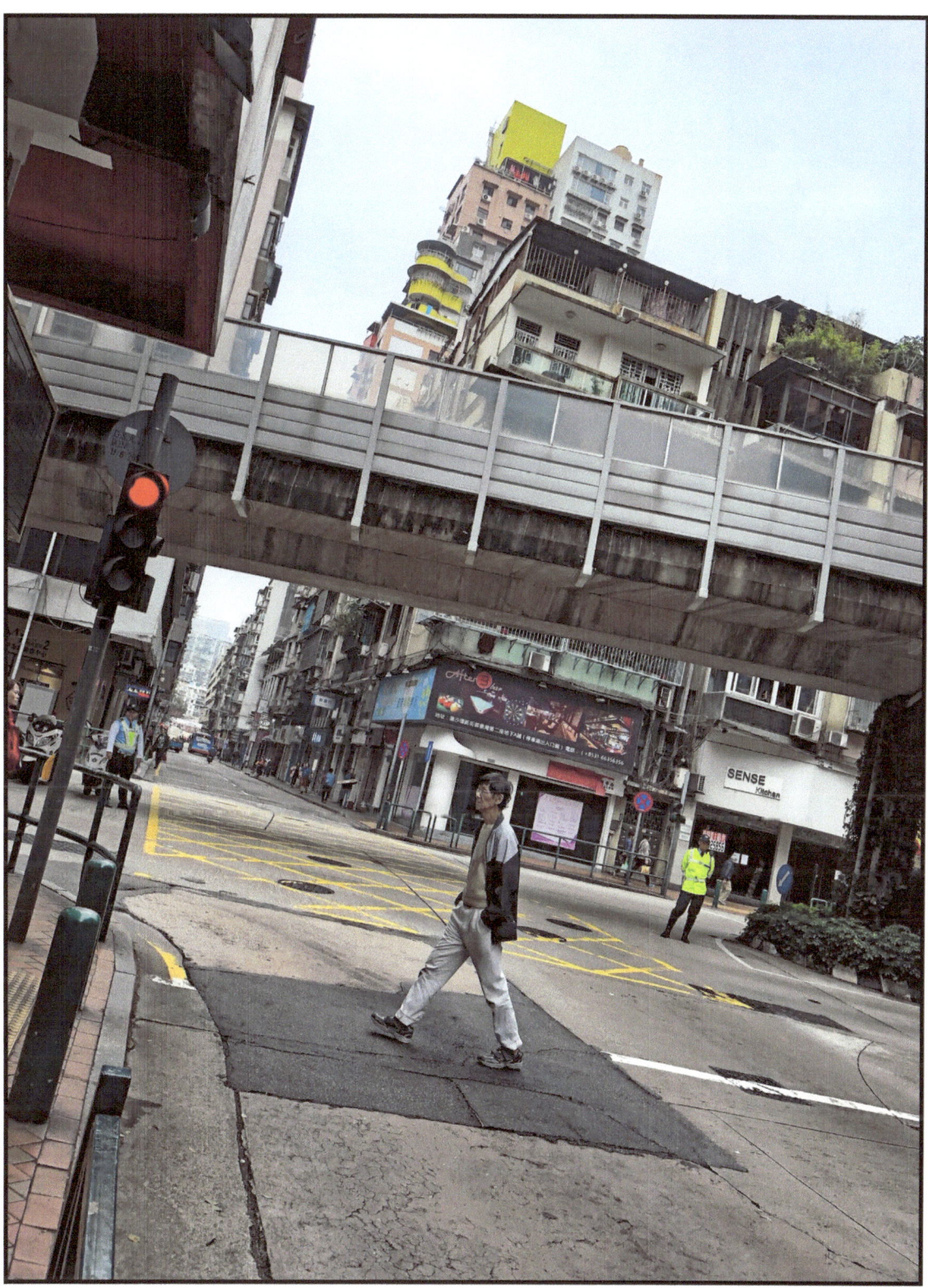

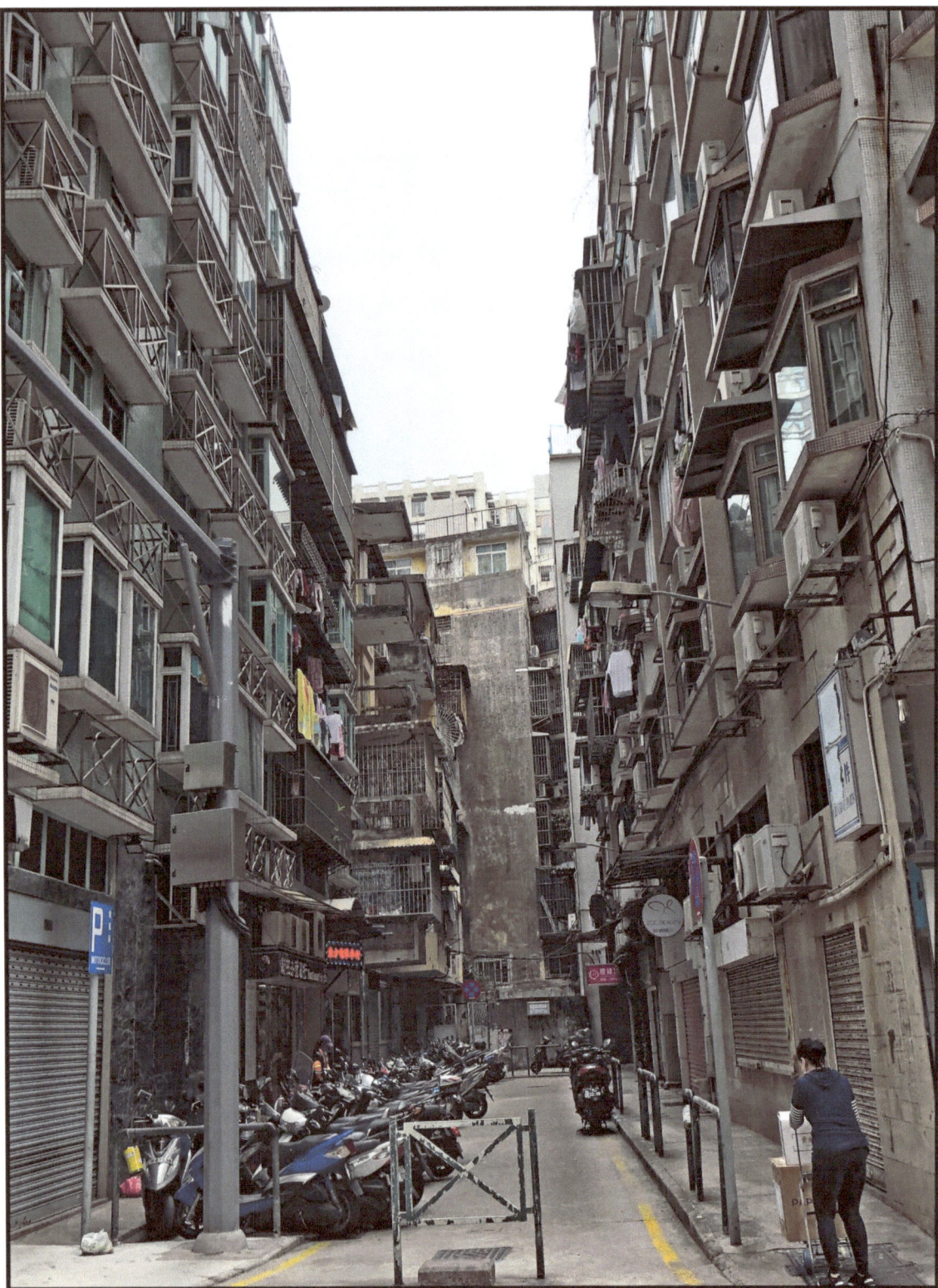

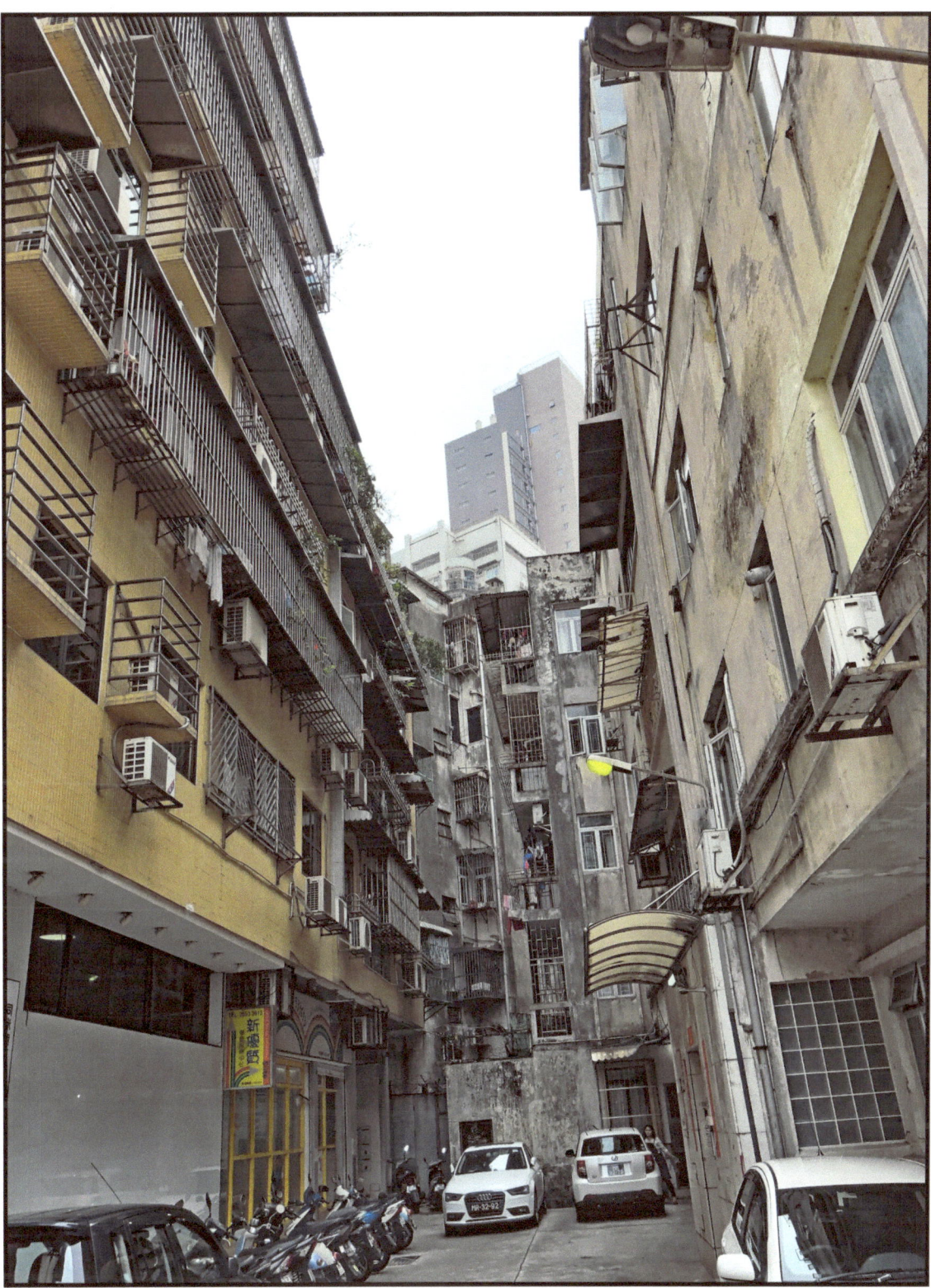

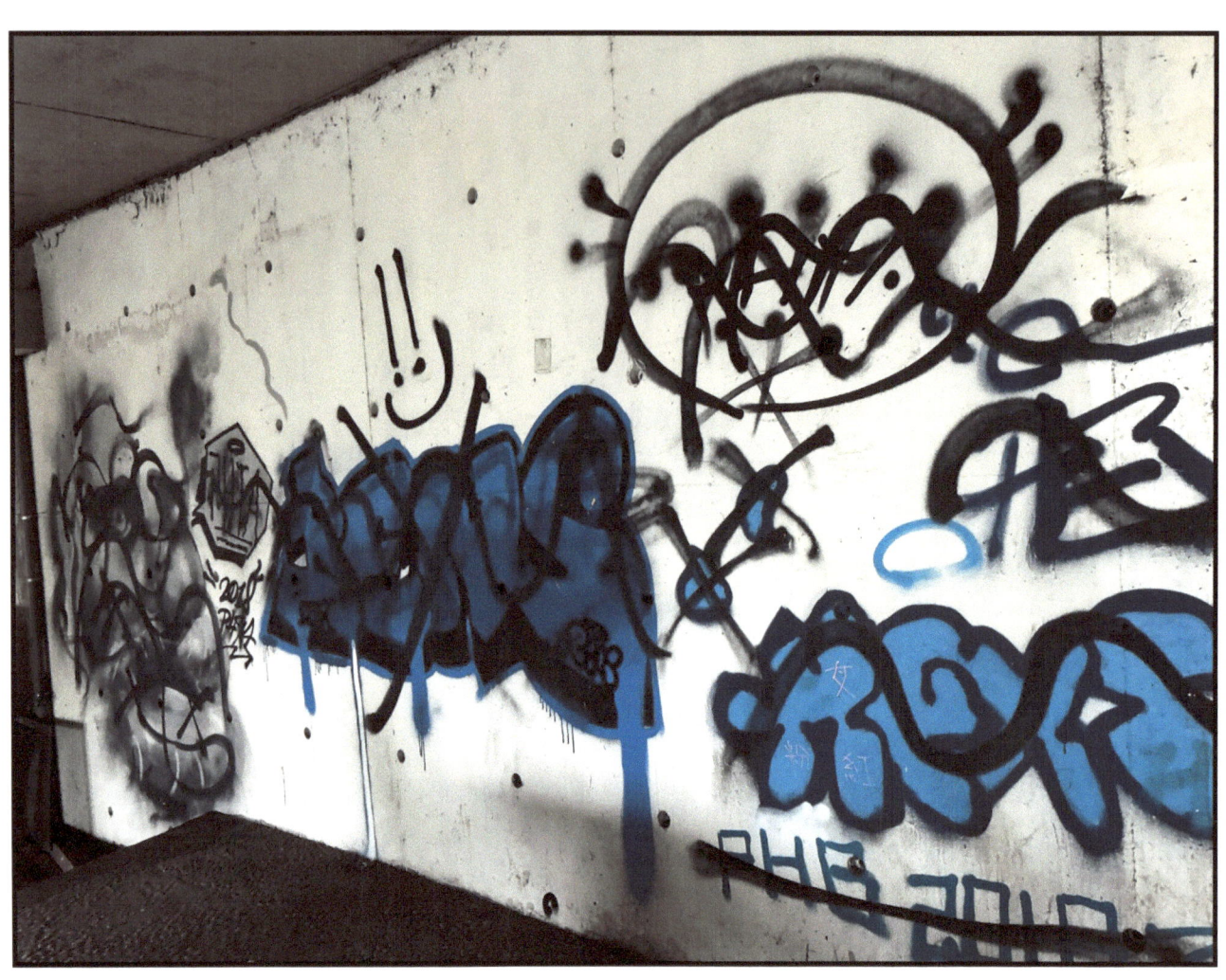

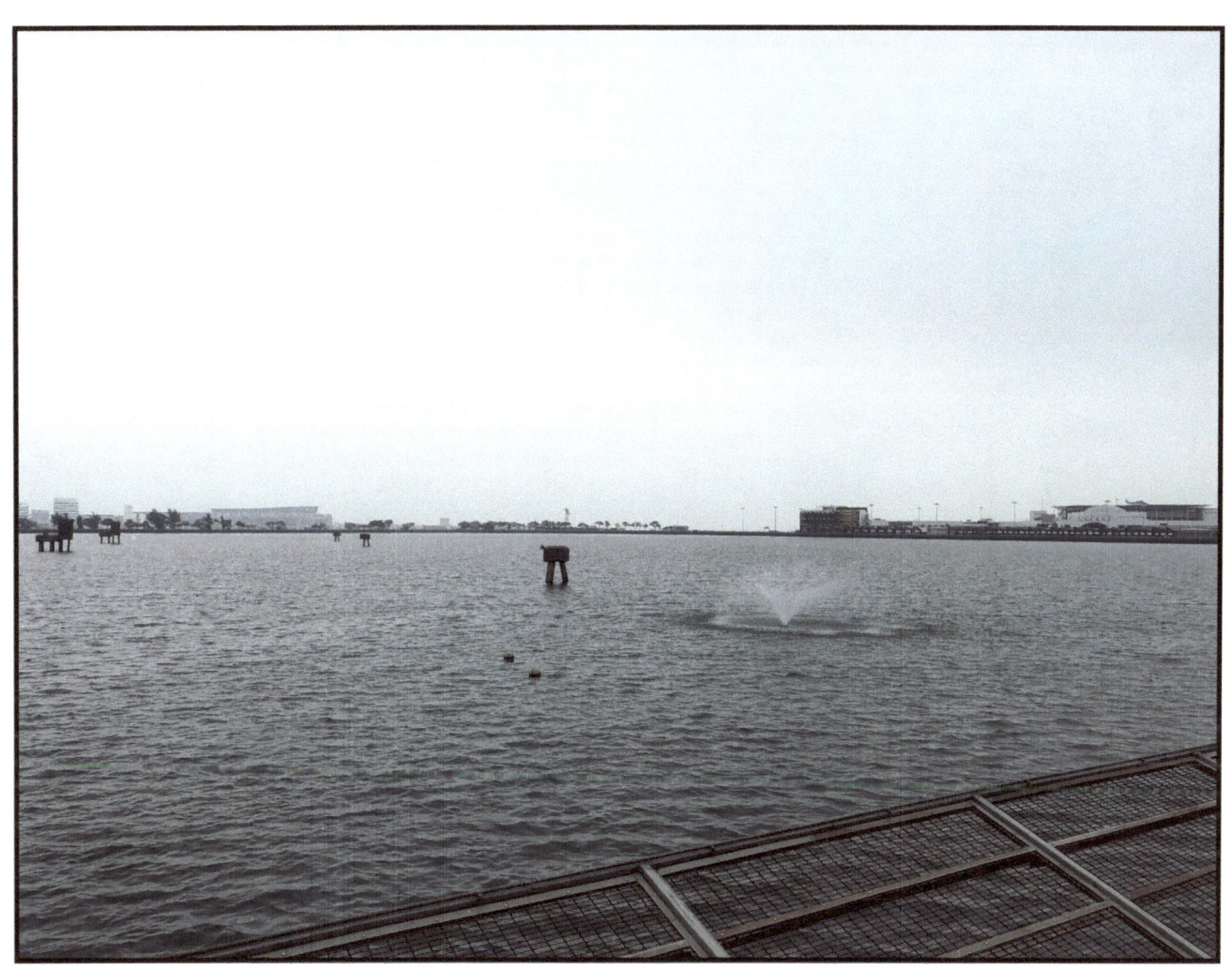

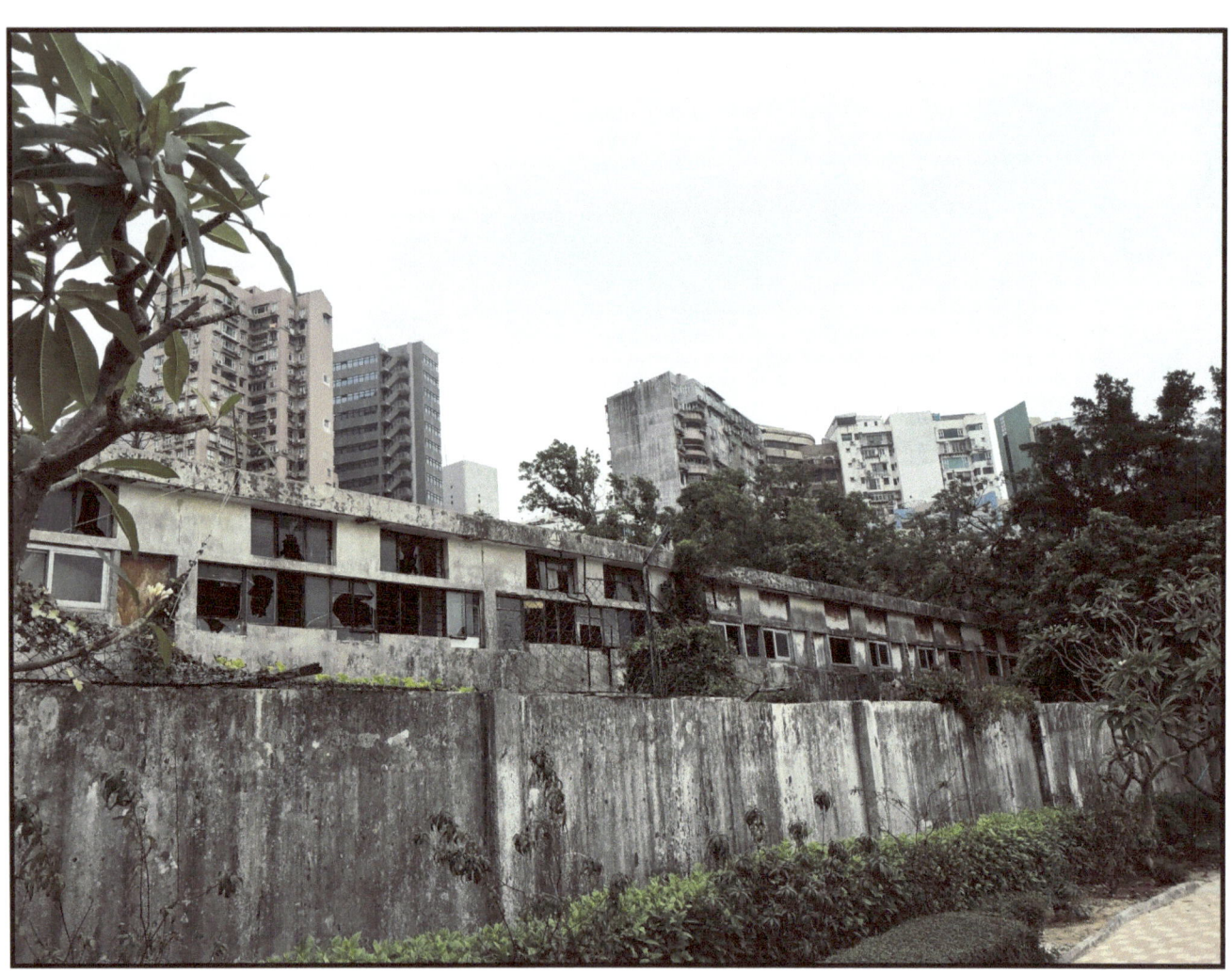

www.ingramcontent.com/pod-product-compliance
Lightning Source LLC
Chambersburg PA
CBHW051153220526
45473CB00003B/755